74 Mr. & Mrs. Ryan

S 31
32 Paul Corbin
33 Pete Smith M
34 Pat Lawford P&u
35 Fernando Perra X
36 Wilt Schaeffler
37 Joe Kraft
38 Rowland Evans M
S 39 Sander Van Ocur'
40 ........... H 753 - 3589 Home
41 Walter Sheridam
42 Swmi von Heintschel H
S 43 Milt Gwirtzman & wife
45 Dick Tuck M
46 Earl Graves M
47 Charles Evers of
S 48 Jesse Unruh and wife
50 Andy Williams and wife of
S 52 George Plimpton and wife
S 54 Chuck Spaulding and wife
56 Mrs. Martin Luther King
   plus three (Earl Graves)

60 Pierre Salinger and wife of
S 62 John Douglas
S 63 Ray O'Connell
64 Tom Johnston and wife M of

S 66 Jiggs Donahue
67 Dr. Watson Pau

# THE

# PROMISE

AND THE

DREAM

# THE UNTOLD STORY

## of

## MARTIN LUTHER KING, JR.,

## and

## ROBERT F. KENNEDY

# DAVID MARGOLICK

Foreword by
## DOUGLAS BRINKLEY

A LAWRENCE SCHILLER BOOK

RosettaBooks®

# AUTHOR'S NOTE

This book is a first for me—the first time I've attempted to write at length about people and events I remember from adolescence. I was sixteen years old in April 1968 when the boy across the hall from me, who awoke to Bob Steele's radio program on WTIC in Hartford every morning, told us the shocking news about Martin Luther King, and then about Robert Kennedy two months later.

Revisiting that time these past months, I realized how little about it I really recalled, in part because it had eluded me to begin with. For different reasons, both Kennedy and King were largely foreign to me.

Like so many others at that time, I considered Kennedy an opportunist—I don't think I'd have used the word "ruthless," though everyone else did—riding on the coattails of both Senator Eugene McCarthy and, almost ghoulishly, John F. Kennedy. As horrifying as Robert Kennedy's death was, it wasn't novel: we'd all been through November 22, 1963, the day that still remains—for reasons I don't quite understand—the saddest of my life. To me, President Bobby was a hopelessly pale imitation of his brother.

And in my privileged place, Martin Luther King was a remote figure. The day after the March on Washington, my mother pointed out to us the coverage in the European edition of the *New York Herald Tribune*, noting that by being out of the country we'd missed something very important. But King had faded some after that, and become more divisive. I remember telling someone very sententiously how much I'd lost respect for him over his opposition to the Vietnam War. Mine were the values of my small, conservative

The unbridled public enthusiasm for RFK's 1968 presidential campaign mirrored that of his brother's eight years earlier.

New England hometown. Of *why* King opposed the war I evidently didn't have a clue.

Studying these two men now only underlined what I have learned about them since — how, in their separate but sometimes overlapping ways, they sought to make our country fairer and more inclusive at home and more intelligent abroad. And how irreplaceable each was, and how catastrophic their deaths were. Congressman John Lewis had it right. "When these two young men were murdered, something died in all of us," he told me. "We were robbed of part of our future."

There is no quick way to master the enormous historical record these two men created, and this book makes no claim of comprehensiveness. It fact, it's a bit eccentric: I have gone where I thought something original was to be found, and said. I've also gone where the material is, and since so much more is available on Robert Kennedy — meticulously (though, in some instances, selectively), the Kennedys assembled vast histories of themselves, while the King papers for most of the years in question here remain less easily accessible — this has unavoidably tilted the book somewhat in Kennedy's direction. Where I felt I had nothing to add, I've gone light or steered clear altogether.

I'm grateful to everyone who helped me try to strip away the myth and the treacle, and illuminate the ways these two remarkable men were and weren't connected. Foremost among them are the extraordinary people who knew them both: Ambassadors Andrew Young and William vanden Heuvel, Harry Belafonte, Representative John Lewis, Clarence Jones, Harris Wofford, Peter and Marian Wright Edelman. I'm greatly indebted to them all. And to Jerome Smith, the Freedom Rider who confronted Robert Kennedy in 1963.

I want to thank Jules Feiffer, the great cartoonist who first bifurcated Robert Kennedy into the "Bobby Twins": "Good Bobby" and "Bad Bobby." Two former Kennedy aides — Adam Walinsky and Jeff Greenfield — are great repositories of RFK history, insight and lore, and put up good-naturedly with my repeated queries. So did James Tolan, Kennedy's longtime advance man. Former attorney general Ramsey Clark reminisced for me from his hospital bed. Victor Navasky, the author of the first great book on Robert Kennedy, was his usual generous self. My thanks as well to historian Douglas Brinkley for writing a characteristically intelligent forward.

Writing history is humbling: you realize how much you don't know, and how dependent you are on folks who do. Authors, like ordinary people, generally fall into three categories: those who can't be bothered to help; those who help, but only to a point; and those who are unstinting. When I've been at the other end of this process, I've probably fallen into the second category. But I aspire to the third, and admire anyone already there.

One person in that hallowed place is the King biographer David Garrow, who repeatedly walked me through the intricate relationship between Martin Luther King and the FBI. Another category of superheroes is those people, authors, and filmmakers who shared from their *forthcoming* works. In this instance, they include Michael Anderson (who is writing on Lorraine Hansberry); Ellen Meacham and Andy Greenspan (now finishing a book and a documentary, respectively, on Kennedy's 1967 visit to the Mississippi delta); and Joan Walsh, who, along with Joy Reid, is making a documentary on the historic week in 1968 when Harry Belafonte hosted *The Tonight Show*, and had both King and Kennedy on as guests.

Writers are thankful for the great extravagance of filmmakers, who put only a small fraction of what they collect on the screen—leaving the rest for us, but only if they are generous enough to do so. That describes Donald Boggs, who shared with me his interviews for *Ripple of Hope*, his very moving documentary about Robert Kennedy's famous speech in Indianapolis.

David Ferriero, the archivist of the United States, helped liberate for me the remarkable, wide-ranging interviews the late Jean Stein did for her book on Robert Kennedy's funeral train. I want to thank Karen Adler Abramson and Abigail Malangone of the John F.

Kennedy Presidential Library—whose collection has remarkable materials on both Kennedy and King—as well as Stacey Chandler, Michael Desmond, and Laurie Austin there.

As always, the master of the *New York Times* morgue, Jeffrey Roth, unearthed treasures for me, including the clippings files he very characteristically rescued from the paper's Washington bureau en route to the Dumpster. (And then, armed with a shpritzer to protect the crumbling newsprint, he even photocopied them for me.) Also, once Eric Fettmann vouched for me, Laura Harris graciously opened up the precious King and Kennedy files of the *New York Post*.

In these files were dozens of articles still outside the reach of ProQuest or newspapers.com and therefore almost impossible to find, by Murray Kempton, Jimmy Breslin, Mary McGrory, James Wechsler, and others. If what follows sometimes seems top-heavy with their words rather than mine, it is largely an homage: I want to honor them, and knew I could not top them. Two other journalists, both former colleagues at the *New York Times*—Jack Rosenthal, who worked for Attorney General Kennedy, and Roy Reed, who covered King's great marches—helped me shortly before they died. I feel blessed to have been in touch with them.

My editor, J. M. Rappaport, was literate and judicious. I also want to thank the various researchers and others who helped jump-start this project when there was little time to spare: Andrew Dunn, Kirk Mcleod, Amanda Millner-Fairbanks, Eboni Boykin, and Elizabeth Spock. Cole Margol and Sean McGowan pitched in later. As did Justin Sayles and the team at North Market Street Graphics—Lainey Wolfe, Vicky Dawes, Ginny Carroll, Stewart Smith, Madeline Brubaker, and Jess Sappenfield. With his conscientious photo research and captions, Matt Maranian gave this book another dimension. With his elegant design, Henry Sanders helped make it beautiful. So did Nina Wiener, in innumerable ways.

Others who helped include Michael Henry Adams, Kathryn Au, Harry Benson, William Bosanko, Taylor Branch, Clay Carson, Kevin Chavous, Xernona Clayton, Gerard Doherty, Parker Donham,

Bill Gigerich, Mary Graff, Earl "Butch" Graves, Jr., Terra Gullings, Martin Halpern, Hon. Thelton Henderson, David and Dick Holler, Jane Klain, Miriam Kleiman, Hank Klibanoff, Hon. Douglas Lavine, Henry Morgenthau III, Ricki Moskowitz, Roger Mudd, Stanley Pottinger, G. Aaron Ramirez, Murray Richtel, Steve Schapiro, Holly Schwartztol, Gary Shapiro, June Shagaloff, Michael Shnayerson, Doratha Smith-Simmons, Jean Snyder, Bruce Stark, George Stevens, Gay Talese, Livael Taveras, Evan Thomas, Clive Webb, Curtis Wilkie, Jules Witcover, and Andrew McCanse Wright. My thanks to them all.

Two more people I should single out. Throughout this process, Amy J. M. Morris has been a source of love, strength, energy, and intelligence to me. I shudder to think what this book would have been like, or whether it would have been at all, without her. Over his long and amazing career, Lawrence Schiller has had an uncanny knack for being wherever things are happening or making things happen himself where they weren't. Larry is a hard man to resist, and—fortunately for me—I couldn't when he offered me this opportunity.

I'm grateful to Jean Kennedy Smith for speaking with me, and to her son, Stephen Kennedy Smith, for his interest and encouragement, and to Robert Kennedy's eldest child, Kathleen Kennedy Townsend as well, who graciously agreed to see me.

When we met at the Mayflower Hotel she told me this book was a bad idea. "Just because two people live at the same time, and are engaged in two different worlds, and talk to each other ten times during the course of their lives or twenty times, does not make a book," she said. She said it very politely, and allowed that maybe I'd prove her wrong.

I hope I have. But I thank her, too.

—David Margolick
New York City, 2018

# FOREWORD
## DOUGLAS BRINKLEY

In a sense, the Sixties—with all of its promise, turbulence, and tragedy—began with a pair of telephone calls from Jack and Bobby Kennedy two weeks before the 1960 presidential election. The civil rights leader Dr. Martin Luther King, Jr., had been arrested in Georgia on a trumped-up traffic violation, and a judge had sentenced him to four months of hard labor alongside hardened white criminals, putting his life in danger. From a Chicago hotel room, Jack, the Democratic presidential nominee, dialed King's wife, Coretta, to offer sympathy and comfort. Almost simultaneously, the tenacious Bobby called the Georgia judge from a pay phone in Long Island, urging him to release King on bail. Within hours, King was free.

Throughout white America, the bold telephone calls were low-bar news. But in the African-American community the word spread like heat lightning: the Kennedy brothers had aligned with King in a showdown with the segregated South, and had sprung the reverend free. By contrast, the sitting vice president and Republican nominee, Richard Nixon, had remained silent as King was arrested, sentenced, and jailed.

Hoping to capitalize on the intervention, Kennedy's campaign arranged for two million copies of a pamphlet titled "The Case of Martin Luther King: 'No Comment' Nixon Versus a Candidate with a Heart, Senator Kennedy" to be distributed to black churches the Sunday before the election. Printed on pale blue

The King-Kennedy consociation largely took shape posthumously in the public imagination. The two men met in person only a dozen or so times and only once were they photographed standing alongside one another, at the White House Rose Garden on June 22, 1963.

paper, the pamphlet came to be known as the "Blue Bomb" for its timely effect. In 1956, President Dwight Eisenhower had won 39 percent of the black vote. Now, in 1960, Nixon captured only 32 percent—a decline that helped Jack Kennedy prevail in Illinois, New Jersey, Michigan, South Carolina, and Delaware. Had Nixon chosen to defend King, he very well could have bagged those seventy-four electoral votes, and with them the election. Instead, as the reeling Sixties began, the Kennedy brothers and King began their march to the mountaintop, linked forever as the animating spirits of the burgeoning civil rights movement.

Looking back five decades later, it is easy to see the parallels with that fractured decade, and to understand why half a century hasn't dimmed Dr. King's relevance. Then as now, racial, cultural, and political fault lines were etched in fire. The Vietnam War was ripping the country into two camps, hawks versus doves, and giving birth to a massive, youth-led protest movement. Against this backdrop, the hippie movement, the sexual revolution, the nascent environmental movement, and the struggle for women's rights tore daily at the fabric of conventional American life, even as the Cold War with the Soviet Union threatened to turn hot, risking nuclear annihilation. At a time of intractable division, the ongoing space program—itself a product of Cold War rivalry, but with the sheen of ennobling human destiny—seemed like the only thing that gave Americans a sense of shared purpose.

Through it all, with piety and bravery, Dr. King marched toward a more just future, and challenged all Americans to follow. Armed with unwavering moral clarity and dedication to nonviolent resistance—"a courageous confrontation of evil by the power of love"—King went to battle against the segregation laws and institutionalized racism that had replaced slavery as African Americans' daily lived experience. Over the thirteen years of his short life that he devoted to the cause, King walked a fine line, maintaining his laser focus on civil rights even as he was emboldened to speak out against the Vietnam War and raise his voice to demand jobs, fair wages, and educational opportunities for the nation's poor.

It was on this playing field, fighting for American equality, that King's story met that of Robert F. Kennedy, a hard-nosed lawyer and prosecutor who, over the course of the tumultuous 1960s, opened his heart and soul fully to the plight of Americans oppressed by poverty and discrimination. Just four years older than King, Bobby Kennedy came from one of America's wealthiest families and had enjoyed the ultimate insider experience, helping his older brother rise to the Senate, serving as a Senate counsel, then managing his brother's winning campaign for the White House. Appointed attorney general in the new administration, he underwent a rapid education in the realities of segregated America, quickly turning his deeply held sense of moral justice to the fight for equality. Despite their sometimes tense relationship, King himself sensed Bobby's potential as an ally, telling confidants soon after the Kennedys entered office, "Somewhere in this man sits good. Our task is to find his moral center and win him to our cause." Over the next seven years, as King staged the campaigns that would move the civil rights struggle to the center of the national consciousness, Bobby Kennedy staged his own, parallel crusade — not just for a change in America's discriminatory racial laws, but for a wholesale redemption of the nation's soul.

For Bobby Kennedy, the causes of racial equality and social justice became the concerns that propelled his public life, both as attorney general and then, after his brother's assassination, as a senator and 1968 presidential candidate. Scathingly criticized by fellow Democrats for his relatively low-key opposition to the Vietnam War (against which he eventually took a strong stand), he was best known during these years for speaking out on behalf of those unable to participate fully in American life. His full-tilt travels into the underbelly of the American Dream exposed him to the impoverished, desolate lives of grape pickers and day-laborers, seasonal workers and the down-and-out.

Just as Martin was spiritually motivated by Gandhi and Christ, Bobby took inspiration from Saint Francis of Assisi, the Catholic saint who venerated nature and preached compassion for the vulnerable, the poor, and the downtrodden.

As a senator and presidential candidate, Bobby took the side of those seeking safe low-income housing, of rural Americans who were starving in the "richest country on earth," of African Americans struggling for basic rights and equal opportunities, of Hispanic Americans who often lived as an invisible underclass, and of others who simply lived on the wrong side of the tracks or out of the mainstream.

Both Bobby and Dr. King, each from his own direction, were completely dedicated to smashing Jim Crow, showing a strength of purpose that made them the most relentless civil rights leaders of the freedom decade. Americans sensed that both men were grappling with a question at the core of the nation's sensibility, if not its soul: for whom does America exist? Is it for everyone, or only for those privileged by race, religion, ethnicity, or some other artificial signifier? That the cause of equality has progressed in the half-century since their deaths would no doubt please Dr. King and Senator Kennedy. But at the same time, neither would be surprised that race and equality remain uniquely divisive issues in twenty-first-century America, nor that rising income inequality has created a yawning chasm between the haves and have-nots.

Coming to prominence at a time of rapid transformation in the media landscape, King and Kennedy were adept at exploiting both word and image. King was one of the greatest orators in American history, speaking tirelessly, perspiration aplenty, before audiences large and small. Bobby Kennedy too, though sometimes awkward before a microphone, was able to summon transcendence when history demanded. But beyond their words, both men excelled at creating vivid, frozen imagery that burned itself into the retinas of a newly TV-centered nation. Think of King's protest marches and mass rallies, historic events that not only captured public attention but were also powerfully symbolic. The sight of Dr. King leading a march in the Heart of Dixie or speaking before a quarter-million people at Washington's National Mall was impossible to misunderstand. Full of self-assuredness, a true Christian believer, his voice and countenance seemed to encompass the entire earth.

Bobby's affect was less dramatic but no less powerful, following a model set by first lady Eleanor Roosevelt in the 1930s and early 1940s. Constrained from overt advocacy by White House politics, Roosevelt learned to cast an entirely new means of influence by simply showing up. By visiting D.C. slums and destitute West Virginia mining towns with the humble goal of learning about the people who lived there, she showed the nation sights it couldn't ignore.

When Bobby Kennedy toured the Pine Ridge Indian Reservation in South Dakota in 1968, evening news programs carried extended reports showing him walking with the Oglala Lakotas who lived there, asking questions about the deplorable conditions he encountered. The image is well-remembered today, in part because in that era other presidential candidates shied away from the needy, eager instead to keep the pictures from their campaigns upbeat and pleasant. In contrast, Kennedy visited hungry children along the Mississippi and people living in rat-infested Harlem tenements, giving the nation images from which it could not turn away. It is these kinds of pictures, illuminating an uncompromising dedication to securing equality and opportunity for all, that keep both Dr. King and Bobby Kennedy ever-fresh in the national consciousness to this day.

On April 4, 1968, the day Dr. King was shot in Memphis, Kennedy was flying to Indianapolis, where he was scheduled to give a speech in anticipation of the upcoming state primary. Typically, he had planned the speech for an African-American neighborhood, an open-air event on a corner where anyone could come and see him. As soon as his plane landed, he was informed that Dr. King had died. The news had yet to be broadcast, but it was expected to ignite rioting, so advisers urged Kennedy to cancel his speech. He refused.

When he arrived at the site, Kennedy found a crowd later estimated at twenty-five hundred waiting for him. Few yet knew what had happened in Memphis. Destiny at hand, Kennedy climbed onto the back of a truck, looked out at the throngs, and improvised. "I have some very sad news," he began, sick with horror. "And that is that Martin Luther King was shot and killed tonight. Martin Luther King dedicated his life to love and to justice between his fellow human beings, and he died because of that effort. In this difficult day, in this difficult time for the United States, it is perhaps well to ask what kind of a nation we are and what direction we want to move in."

The rest of the speech came straight from Kennedy's heart, as he confided for the only time in public his inner pain at losing his brother Jack to an assassin's bullets. With a crusading yet self-controlled air, he answered his own question about the future of the United States by honoring the fervid hope that Dr. King had never lost: that homegrown violence and unendurable bigotry could be replaced with "an effort to understand with compassion and love."

That was the moral ideal embraced by the battle-hardened Martin and Bobby, both slayers of evildoers, and it remains a clarion call that has appealed anew to each succeeding generation of Americans, down to our own divided time. Facing a future perilous with uncertainty, it is illuminating to think that history gave us two such men, walking parallel paths and meeting parallel, tragic ends—martyrs for the uplifting of mankind. Though not colleagues, they were compatriots, bound by the clarity and righteousness of their vision and the immense and enduring sense of hope they each came to embody. The story of that bond has never really been told until now, in the pages of this book. It is well past time.

Robert Kennedy never spoke publicly of his brother's assassination until he acknowledged his pain to an Indianapolis crowd the night King died.

# INTRODUCTION
## DAVID MARGOLICK

Back they went to Room 306 of the Lorraine Motel.

Could the grieving disciples of Martin Luther King, Jr., have possibly chosen a grimmer spot to reconvene—the spot where he'd been murdered only a few hours earlier, where his blood still stained the cement on the balcony outside? And yet when they left the hospital in Memphis where King had died on the evening of April 4, 1968, what better place was there to mourn him than where he'd spent much of his last day on earth?

Gathered there, with King's personal effects nearby—his small attaché case, a crumpled white shirt, a can of Hidden Magic hairspray, his Bible, a half-filled Styrofoam coffee cup, a pair of glass tumblers, and the remnants of a dessert—Ralph Abernathy, Andrew Young, and the others grappled with the catastrophe that had just befallen them. What would now happen to their movement? Who could take King's place? What if his murder was only the first of a series that was still under way? Who among them would be next? And how could they help stop the rioting that had broken out in ghettos across America—the violent antithesis of everything for which King had stood?

But the same nineteen-inch Philco Starlite television set that beamed scenes of America aflame that night also brought some consolation, from Indianapolis, where Senator Robert F. Kennedy had spoken shortly after King had been declared dead. Huddled against the cold in his big brother's old overcoat, he told a stunned and edgy crowd in the city's most dangerous neighborhood that

While black neighborhoods in cities across the country burned, the residents of Indianapolis mourned King's murder peacefully, heeding Robert Kennedy's plea.

23

King had just been killed, then pleaded for calm and brotherhood, reminding everyone—as if anyone could not have known—that someone *he'd* loved had also been killed, and also by a white man. And unlike so many other cities that night, Indianapolis had stayed calm.

"We'd wanted to get on television and tell people not to fight, not to burn down the cities," recalled Andrew Young. "We were trying to get the message out to people, 'This is not what Dr. King would have you doing.' But the press didn't want to talk to us. They were right there at the hospital, and all they wanted to do was talk about the autopsy. Or they were going around chasing the kids with the firebombs, trying to interview them. It was almost like they were trying to provoke a riot.

"We were saying, 'Look, Dr. King has gone. The important thing now is for us to keep his work going, and people are out in the streets now doing things that he wouldn't want them to do.' They weren't interested in that. Bobby Kennedy's was the only voice we identified with that night. We were grateful he was out there."

He almost hadn't been. Kennedy's most senior advisers, the ones running his fledgling presidential campaign, had urged him to cancel the event: doing anything political on such a night would look bad, and going into the ghetto was just too dangerous. (Just be sure that in any statement he put out, they counseled, he not suggest he'd been too *afraid* to speak.) So had the mayor of Indianapolis, Richard Lugar, a lifelong resident who'd never set foot around 17th and Broadway, where a couple thousand people, nearly all of them black, had already gathered. So had the Indianapolis police. So had the customarily fearless Ethel Kennedy, who'd gone back to the hotel, praying in the back seat every minute en route.

Even Kennedy might have had second thoughts. While his relationship with King had slowly improved from contentious to careful to respectful over the eight years they'd known each other, and their causes had come increasingly to overlap, the two men had never been close: the racial and cultural divide between them had simply been too broad. They'd become allies, but never had they been friends. Why would Kennedy, of all people, subject himself to such a risk?

And yet, improbably, Bobby Kennedy, a near-total stranger to black America only ten years earlier, felt more at home in it now than any other white politician in America—and more welcome, and comfortable, there than he would have in ostensibly safer and more "respectable" places. When the moment came, he knew instantly what he wanted, and needed, and had promised, to do. So when, shortly after he'd landed in Indianapolis, police officials reiterated their warning, he brushed it aside. "My family and I could lay down in the street there and they wouldn't bother me," he told them with a confidence bordering on bravado that would have been unimaginable from just about any other white person in America. "If they would bother you, you're the one with the problem." That everyone urged him to stay away was, for him, only another reason to go.

The story of Martin Luther King and Robert Kennedy is hard to tell because they left so few fragments of it behind. For two such famous men whose lives and fates were so closely intertwined, there was only a scant paper trail. Lots of what happened between them happened privately, mostly in unrecorded phone calls, beyond the reach of journalists and historians. They evidently wanted it that way. And then, in the last few years of their lives, it trailed off almost entirely into telepathy.

As often as they came to appear together posthumously—in the memorial drawings, photographs, tapestries, and crockery, usually in triptychs with John F. Kennedy, found largely in black homes—there are few photographs of the two, most of them snapshots or group pictures. In none of them can they be seen *engaging*—talking to each other, smiling at each other, shaking each other's hand. Kennedy and King may be linked in a famous song—both freed a lot of people and died young, it says—but they saw little more of each other than either saw of Abraham Lincoln, who's in that song as well.

They were roughly the same age—Kennedy barely three years older. Both had larger-than-life, tyrannical fathers. Both were deeply religious. Both were charismatic. Both were ever in a hurry, for each knew about the capriciousness and brevity of life. But their differences—not just in race and class but in geographic origins, temperament, power, and position—were much more dramatic. Given the distant poles from which they began, it's impressive— inspiring—to see how closely aligned, on the issues at least, they became, and fascinating to ponder what they might have become in a Robert Kennedy administration.

In one sense, Kennedy's journey had been shorter: he'd been born into wealth and fame and never strayed far from it, while King had been born obscure and became one of the most famous people in the world. In another, Kennedy's path was far longer. Early in his career, he'd been better known for his hatred than his love. ("Bobby is as hard as nails. He hates like me," his father, a man who was often reviled and reviled in return, is said to have said.) It came from an anger in him, and an unbecoming certitude, and made him a much tougher sell than his affable and charming older brother. "Jack travels in that speculative area where doubt lives," a family friend, Charles Spalding, once said of these two Kennedy boys. "Bobby does not travel there."

The term for him was "ruthless," and rarely, if ever, has a single word attached itself to anyone so tenaciously. It popped up so often—in virtually every profile—that it became a running joke: he'd call himself "Senator Ruthless" or sign his notes that way. People were forever diagnosing the many, many moments when Robert Kennedy changed out of that. Perhaps that meant he never really did, or had and then relapsed. By the end, though, there was little doubt that he was profoundly altered. "When I first met Bobby Kennedy he was really very naive about most of these things that he ultimately was willing to give his life for," one of his tutors, the labor leader Walter Reuther, once recalled.

King, by contrast, didn't so much change as deepen. Though his faith occasionally faltered, there were few epiphanies. He just grew more famous, ambitious, revered and inspiring, loathed and threatening, angry, bitter, radical, desperate.

As elusive as it was, King's relationship with Bobby Kennedy was much deeper, more personal, and more intricate than his relationship with Jack, and not just because it lasted twice as long. Though there were some exceptions—like the time in June 1963 when John Kennedy escorted King through the Rose Garden and warned him he was under surveillance, a gesture for which King was profoundly grateful—Attorney General Robert Kennedy was usually his point of contact. That meant three years of tense telephone standoffs, telegrammed pleas for protection, stiff, formal, typewritten complaints, and, occasionally, compliments.

For both Kennedys, King meant trouble—a distraction from the things, like managing the Cold War or the American economy, they'd come to Washington to do. "Until the end of 1963, every big demonstration or turmoil that Martin King led was a problem for the president, so that affected the way Bob Kennedy would look at it," Robert Kennedy's key deputy at the Justice Department, Burke Marshall, later said.

It was Robert Kennedy who had helped spring King from jail in Georgia; saved his life (or so he thought) when King huddled in the basement as an angry mob besieged a Montgomery, Alabama, church; pleaded with him to halt the Freedom Rides; and, when King refused to drop two aides with past communist ties, directed that his telephone be tapped. Theirs was an uneven relationship, and for King, a slightly degrading one: he was the black man invariably asking for things, and Kennedy the white man doling them out, but only when his brother's political interests permitted. King was the one to say "please" and "thank you."

King was not without his powers—he'd arguably gotten John Kennedy elected, and he was the custodian of a large chunk of his legacy. And while he hectored, lectured, criticized, and exasperated Robert Kennedy, he also helped educate him. When they'd met, Kennedy had little experience with, or interest in, or understanding of, or empathy for blacks. King helped coax out

Bobby Kennedy's better angels, especially with the 1963 protests in Birmingham that led to the Civil Rights Act of 1964. But a little boy with a distended belly sitting on the dirt floor of a shack in the Mississippi delta may have done more to change Robert Kennedy than Martin Luther King ever did.

The ostensibly spiritual King approached Bobby Kennedy with a hardheadedness that the pragmatic Kennedy would have admired. He had no illusion about Kennedy's instincts, which were viewed initially by the skeptical civil rights community as authoritarian, pragmatic, and not especially sympathetic. But it was Robert Kennedy with whom he knew he'd have to deal, and he ordered his colleagues, most notably Harry Belafonte, to go find Kennedy's moral center, and not return until they had.

Following President Kennedy's assassination, much changed between the two. As a United States senator, Kennedy no longer lorded over King and had fewer plums to dispense. He was freer to identify with King, or to distance himself from him, and did both. And King had fewer favors to ask. Though Kennedy now served himself rather than his brother, his perspective remained political. He sought change, but never at the expense of order and stability. King's remained spiritual; he was, at his roots, a disrupter.

So, over the last four years of their truncated lives, they barely saw each other—maybe only once: at hearings on urban poverty before a committee on which Kennedy sat. Their various underlings sometimes communicated, but that was largely it; even those surrogates didn't know how often, if ever, they got together, or spoke in private. No longer compelled to deal with each other, they didn't. Inveterately social and intellectually adventurous, Kennedy probably invited more blacks to his home—the black essayist and novelist James Baldwin among them—than any white politician of his era, but Martin Luther King was never among them. He surely would have come: he'd have had to. (Had King invited Kennedy, Kennedy probably wouldn't have come, unless it had been done discreetly, and at least for a time, may not even have RSVP'd.) And yet, their preoccupations and goals—ending the war in Vietnam; tackling racial discrimination in the United States, South Africa, and elsewhere; fighting poverty—increasingly overlapped. Kennedy, the columnist Murray Kempton wrote in November 1965, had become "our first politician for the pariahs...our great national outsider." King, of course, had been that from the start.

When, in 1966, Kennedy visited Chief Albert Luthuli, the South African civil rights activist and Nobel Peace Prize winner living in internal exile, he is thought to have delivered a letter from King. After Kennedy toured the poverty-stricken Mississippi delta, King praised him. While Lyndon Johnson remained mum, Kennedy congratulated King for winning the Nobel Peace Prize. King had moved his activism up north to Chicago, in part, at Kennedy's urging. Only three weeks before his flight to Indianapolis, Kennedy vied for King's endorsement as he ran for president.

But that was an exception—a bow to the polyglot politics of California, which was to hold its presidential primary on June 4, 1968. Politically, Kennedy typically took care not to cozy up to King, who by now was the more radical later Martin Luther King rather than the avuncular Martin Luther King of the March on Washington and, eventually, the national holiday. It might not have posed a problem in New York but would have done him no good nationally. King's views on Vietnam—he favored immediate withdrawal—were far too extreme for Kennedy to embrace, as was his larger critique of American foreign policy and culture. Whenever a hostile politician (like Lyndon Johnson) tried connecting the two through a friendly columnist, Kennedy would beat a hasty retreat.

Other factors kept them apart. Some thought the straightlaced Kennedy, a man who threw *Fanny Hill* overboard during a Potomac cruise and barred *Playboy* from his house, was put off by King's sexual indiscretions, minutely chronicled by the FBI under J. Edgar Hoover. (Other Kennedy intimates found that laughable, given the womanizing of his father and brother.) Paradoxically, King's saintliness was also hard to take. "Doc was a moralist," a Kennedy backer, referring to King, once told the pioneering black journalist Simeon Booker. "A politician just can't honeymoon with this kind of guy. Sooner or later, there has to be a falling out." Stylistically, Kennedy seemed to prefer the company of grittier black leaders, like the ones who'd organized the rally for him in Indianapolis. Kennedy might have been bitter over King's sex-laced wisecracks about his late brother and his wife, overheard and recorded and then gleefully transmitted to him by Hoover's FBI. But guilt too, may have been a barrier. Just how do you befriend someone you've wiretapped, especially if, as former attorney general Ramsey Clark has speculated, Kennedy was ashamed of what he had done?

For his part, King never got in bed with politicians, even the most promising, and sympathetic: invariably, they'd disappoint him. Unless he kept them guessing, and bidding for his support, they'd take him for granted. "Sometimes you can't dine with the president and represent vigorously black people in America," King once said. The rule applied even to the Kennedys, whom King liked, and especially to Bobby, who'd evolved so startlingly.

Then there was always the question of just how independent Bobby Kennedy really was. "We considered him our number one ally but we also knew that Hoover had more on him than he had on us and we never knew when he'd try to pull the string," said Andrew Young. "Bob Kennedy, like his brother, respected courage enormously," Ramsey Clark said. "Most people don't think about courage that much. They like it when they see it. But it was a compelling force and idea in their lives. And there is no question in my mind that he thought Dr. King was an extraordinarily courageous man because he saw him, so to speak, walking in the shadow of death most of his adult life, and if he feared it, he didn't show it. His courage was palpable and Bob respected that." But, always, they kept their distance. "I don't know what it was, but they just were not pals," said a longtime Kennedy aide, Peter Edelman. "They were shadow-boxing a lot of the time," recalled William vanden Heuvel, a key Kennedy aide who was close to King as well. "Wary" is the word most frequently invoked to describe them.

"They were friends, and didn't even know that they were friends," said U.S. Representative John Lewis, who worked with them both.

It's ultimately in the eyes of their common detractors and admirers that Martin Luther King and Robert Kennedy were most closely connected, at least during their lifetimes. John Lewis fell squarely into the second category. "When I was growing up," Lewis said, "I would ask my mother and father and grandparents and great-grandparents, 'Why this?' 'Why that?' And my mother would always say, 'Don't get in trouble, don't get in the way.' But individuals like Robert Kennedy and Dr. King inspired me to get in the way. Dr. King used to say, 'You have to be maladjusted to the problems, to the issues that you see around us.' Robert Kennedy was 'maladjusted.' Martin Luther King, Jr., was 'maladjusted.' "

King would probably not have endorsed Kennedy in 1968 — he never endorsed anyone — but would have made it clear Kennedy was his choice. In other ways, he was moving toward Kennedy, like in the mass protest he was planning in Washington when he was killed. "Andrew Young... dropped by to see me today," Arthur Schlesinger, the historian and veteran Kennedy confidant, wrote in his journal in January 1969. "He said that King had conceived his role as that of mobilizing mass opinion and that he intended the Poor People's March of last spring to lay the basis for a Kennedy Presidency; he thought that it would make it easier for RFK to do as President the things that ought to be done."

The prospect of such a Kennedy-King alliance, one that was emerging as Kennedy assembled his electoral coalition, was, Harry Belafonte theorized, the right wing's greatest fear. Until Memphis on April 4, 1968.

"What do I say?" Kennedy had asked his press secretary, Frank Mankiewicz, on the flight into Indianapolis that night. Should he use what his speechwriters had hastily prepared for him, or go with his gut, even though he had never been the gifted orator his brother was, and rarely spoke extemporaneously, and had never talked of King publicly before? In fact, as was often true when Kennedy asked such questions, he already had his answer.

Standing on the back of a flatbed truck at 17th and Broadway, he spoke for seven minutes. He held some notes, but after glancing at them at the beginning, he never referred to them again. As moving as his speech that night in cold and drizzly Indianapolis had been, it elicited little commentary afterward: it came too late for the morning papers, and, like King's equally memorable remarks the night before—his last speech, the one about having been to the mountaintop—it was lost in the enormity of the assassination. But in Room 306 of the Lorraine Motel, Kennedy's words were duly noted.

"He was in the middle of a totally black community, and he stood there without fear and with great confidence and empathy, and he literally poured his soul out talking about his brother," Young later recalled. "The amazing thing to us was, that the crowd *listened*. He *reached them*." The relationship between the two men had entered its latest, penultimate phase, one that would last two months.

Kennedy could never replace King. But to his disciples back at the Lorraine Motel that night, and throughout the black community, he had picked up his torch. In him, everyone in that room at that grim moment seemed to agree, resided pretty much all of whatever hope remained. There was but one question about that torch: how long Bobby Kennedy would get to hold it. "I don't know, I almost feel like somebody said, 'He's probably going to be next,'" Young later recalled. "I can't *remember* that. But that was the feeling that many of us had."

The balcony outside King's room at the Lorraine Motel in Memphis the night he was killed, April 4, 1968.

Robert Kennedy was actively campaigning for the presidency at the time, crisscrossing the country in state primaries. To many in the struggle, the torch passed to Kennedy that night, until he, too, was slain by an assassin's bullet later that spring.

# ONE

# HISTORY WOULD KEEP THEM TOGETHER

By the beginning of 1959, the Reverend Dr. Martin Luther King, Jr., was the most famous black preacher in America. Apart from assorted athletes and entertainers, he may have been the most famous black *man* in America. In most circles, he had become more widely known than the white religious figure after whom he had been named. And he was surely the most famous man, black or white, in Montgomery, Alabama. But when Robert F. Kennedy, already a man of considerable fame himself, flew into town on February 2, 1959, it wasn't to see King but to hobnob with King's wealthiest and most powerful opponents.

The Whitley Hotel, where Kennedy was to be the luncheon speaker that day, and the Dexter Avenue Baptist Church, the prestigious, even snooty, house of worship where King held the pulpit, were only a few minutes' walk from each other. But in a segregated southern city like Montgomery, they could just as easily have been in different constellations. Kennedy, then counsel for the Senate Rackets Committee in Washington, hadn't planned to look up King, nor would he have just run into him (King was in fact speaking in Philadelphia that day), and that would probably have been fine with them both.

Winton "Red" Blount, a wealthy local businessman and, later, a member of Richard Nixon's cabinet, had dispatched his private plane to fetch Kennedy from Atlanta, then escorted him to the

In September 1954, Reverend Martin Luther King, Jr., took his first and only full-time pastorate at the Dexter Avenue Baptist Church in Montgomery, Alabama, where he remained until his move to Atlanta in 1960.

Whitley, where, undeterred by the rain, more than seven hundred fifty people—the largest crowd ever for such an event—had gathered for the Chamber of Commerce's annual membership dinner. They filled up the hotel's Blue and Gray Room and spilled over into the State Room, where latecomers could watch Kennedy on closed-circuit television.

Introducing him was Alabama governor John Patterson, an arch-segregationist who had effectively banned the NAACP from the state a couple of years earlier. After thanking him, Kennedy went on to describe the fetid, corrupt state of America's unions, the object of his prosecutorial zeal back in Washington and a popular message in a state built on cheap labor. Those who missed Kennedy could read all about him on the front page of the next day's *Montgomery Advertiser* and see a giant photograph of him, a boutonniere in his lapel, flanked by two local burghers. Inside the paper, there was yet more about Kennedy, with his "broad smile" and "piercing blue eyes." Here was one Yankee who was welcome in these parts.

Even had he been in town, King would not have attended that evening. For as famous as he'd become, all Montgomery—its Chamber of Commerce, its hotels and restaurants and schools and water bubblers—remained segregated. So, too, for the most part, were its buses, though thanks to the dramatic campaign King had led three years earlier, it was now by tradition rather than by law: "Whites Only" and "Colored" signs still hung all over town. But while Kennedy and King wouldn't cross paths that rainy winter day, their lives would soon be very much entangled.

Notwithstanding the chasm between the two—a fabulously wealthy and privileged white boy from Massachusetts and the son of a black preacher in Jim Crow Georgia—Robert Francis Kennedy and Martin Luther King, Jr., had a surprising amount in common beyond their age and fame and precociousness. Both had overbearing, even grandiose, fathers: Joseph P. Kennedy, the ambitious businessman, former government official, and ambassador to England; and the Reverend Martin Luther ("Daddy") King Sr., pastor of Atlanta's Ebenezer Baptist Church. Joe Kennedy had decreed that one of his sons would be president, and nothing short of that goal would do: "For the Kennedys, it's the castle or the outhouse. Nothing in between," he once said. And Daddy King did something even Joe Kennedy hadn't contemplated: renaming both himself and his five-year-old son, each of whom had been called "Michael King" at birth, after one of the seminal figures in Western religious history.

Yes, the sizes of their respective fortunes varied vastly, but each was affluent in his own community: Daddy King had vowed that none of his children would ever have to go to school smelling like a mule, as he had in rural Georgia, and this he accomplished. Neither Kennedy nor King had had to work his way through college; in graduate school, King even had a white maid. Both were highly educated and public-spirited: neither ever considered careers in commerce. Neither came from gentry; the family of each had clawed its way to respectability in a couple of genera-tions. Both were gutsy, determined, and diminutive (King was under five feet seven inches tall, and Kennedy, five feet nine)— though King, characteristically, took his size in stride, while Kennedy took it as a challenge. Their stature and persistent youthfulness provided ammunition to their detractors.

To Thurgood Marshall of the NAACP, King was a "boy on a man's errand." While King's size was to some yet another source of affection—"I remember feeling, rather as though he were a younger, much-loved, and menaced brother, that he seemed very slight and vulnerable to be taking on such tremendous odds," James Baldwin once said—for Kennedy's many detractors it provided yet another hook from which to hang their resentment or contempt—as if what they so loathed about him was all the more noxious for being so concentrated. To Lyndon Johnson, Bobby Kennedy was a "little shitass" and a "snot-nosed kid"; and to the Teamsters' Jimmy Hoffa, he was simply "the little bastard." Both married young. Both were anticommunists. Both believed, fervently, in God.

But had they met that evening in Montgomery, they'd have been reminded that their differences were far more profound. King was capacious, adventurous, imaginative, independent, progressive, tolerant. Kennedy was sullen, angry, conventional, conservative, close-minded. King had the buoyancy and confidence of an eldest child; things came easily to him. Kennedy, the seventh of nine children and the younger brother of two handsome and charismatic superstars, had to work at everything. Notwithstanding its color and all the disadvantages it brought, King was far more comfortable in his own skin.

Young King — his oldest, pre-"Martin" friends called him "Mike" — had been an assiduous student, reveling in the life of the mind, forever spreading his wings. He was a rebel, delightedly tweaking his pious father by playing pool and smoking cigarettes in his presence and flirting with other careers. Even when he'd settled on the ministry, his was a career of ambitious activism — one that discomfited and worried Daddy King. He was a gifted orator who spoke mellifluously, sometimes too much so, rattling off extended metaphors and twenty-five-cent words. His heroes were rarefied philosophers and theologians like Paul Tillich and Reinhold Niebuhr.

Robert Kennedy, by contrast, was a plodding student who attended school dutifully and would probably have hidden whatever erudition he had. He followed his father's diktats dutifully. (To other people, he referred to him deferentially and maybe a bit pompously as "The Ambassador.") Never did he rebel or even chafe: he effectively skipped that stage in his development until the last few years of his life. His religion, a strict brand of Catholicism inherited wholesale from his pious mother, was more dutiful and ritualized and rigid than King's, and not, like King's, a call to arms. He went to Mass many mornings, crossed himself when he passed a church, held a Mass for his late sister Kathleen every year on her birthday. "Bog-Irish, with bleeding hearts of Jesus on the wall: a true primitive," was how his distant in-law (and constant, harping critic) Gore Vidal once described him. His heroes weren't thinkers but men of action, like Douglas MacArthur and J. Edgar Hoover. He would have made a great soldier, a longtime family friend once offered, something no one would ever have said about King.

Until the Montgomery Bus Boycott began in late 1955, King had never been especially political. He'd rejected communism, but only after a thorough excursion into Marx. But King's contempt for Soviet communism never extended to American communists, whom he knew had been among the most racially progressive white people out there. It was a distinction which, tragically, his detractors never accepted. Kennedy had been steeped in politics — "I can hardly remember a mealtime when the conversation was not dominated by what Franklin D. Roosevelt was doing or what was happening in the world," he once recalled. But his political views were strictly derivative: his overarching, knee-jerk anticommunism was a carbon copy of his old man's.

Before opting for Gandhian asceticism, King had been stylish — boyhood friends dubbed him "Tweed" — and epicurean, sensual. (His childhood pals were amused by latter-day portraits of his saintliness, noting that in his younger days he'd been plenty able to defend himself, sometimes with fisticuffs. "Tweed hadn't heard about Mahatma Gandhi then," one recalled.) He dated lots of women, white and black, before marrying (in June 1953) Coretta Scott, whom he'd met in Boston. While black and accomplished — she'd graduated from Antioch College, then studied voice at the New England Conservatory of Music — she was from small-town Alabama, and lacked the high-class Atlanta pedigree Daddy King had wanted. Young Martin King had a ribald sense of humor. He was popular and charismatic, elected president of his almost entirely white class at the Pennsylvania seminary he attended, gathering disciples throughout.

The only student office Bobby Kennedy ever held was head of the speakers' bureau at the University of Virginia Law School, a sinecure he won principally because he could stock the schedule with his father's friends. Outside his close and loving family — in the many, many portraits of them together, everyone is invariably smiling—Kennedy was tightly wound and angry. Ethel Skakel, whom he married in 1950, not only matched all the family's expectations (wealthy, Catholic) but even looked like him. He favored ratty sweaters and frayed cuffs and collars in a way only scions can afford.

Kennedy thrived on sports, earning the Harvard football letter his bigger big brothers never managed to, playing one game briefly on a broken leg until Kenny O'Donnell, his teammate and future key Kennedy adviser, sent him to the sidelines on a stretcher. "I think he could have creamed both [of his older brothers if] given half a chance," Arthur Krock of the *New York Times*, a family confidant and retainer, once said.

King's worst faults, like indecisiveness or ego, weren't matters of character. With Bobby Kennedy, it was different. Already by the 1950s, one word had attached itself to him with astonishing frequency and tenacity: *ruthless*. No person and adjective were ever so inseparable.

But the most fundamental difference between Kennedy and King concerned race: their consciousness of it; their experiences with it; their attitudes about it.

Kennedy's posture was beautifully illustrated in December 1964 while he prepared to give the John F. Kennedy Library an oral history on his time as attorney general. Before his interrogator, Anthony Lewis of the *New York Times*, managed to ask a single question, Kennedy preempted him with what he somehow sensed would be the issue foremost on Lewis's mind: *"When did you first hear of civil rights?"*

Even from the printed page, one can detect notes of amusement, weariness, self-pity, impatience, defensiveness, and disgust. More than a year after John Kennedy's assassination, Robert Kennedy was in his latest transition—in a few days, he'd be the junior senator from New York—but he knew that, come what may, this question would always be asked.

"I don't think it was a matter that we were extra concerned about as we were growing up," he said. "There wasn't any great problem." In Massachusetts in those years, he seemed to suggest, there just weren't enough blacks to worry about. (Or, as Martin Luther King later marveled, in Massachusetts, even the maids were Irish.) So, whether because they didn't have to or didn't care to, the Kennedys never did. "I never saw a Negro on level social terms with the Kennedys in all my years of acquaintance with them," Arthur Krock recalled. "And I never heard the subject mentioned.... There was no concern I ever heard over the plight of the Negro." "I won't say I stayed awake nights worrying about civil rights before I became attorney general," Kennedy went on. His world was not just color blind, but color oblivious.

Young Robert had actually known some blacks: he played with the Bell brothers, sons of their white laundress and her black husband, who were about his age and lived just down the street in Hyannis Port. "I know it's the worst thing in the world to say that some of your best friends are...," he told Lewis. "As I was growing up, I suppose two out of my four best friends were Negroes, and so it was all sort of accepted.... There was never any thought about the fact that there was anything different."

"I think he was a misfit at school, and I think he was a misfit all the way through his whole career," his prep school classmate David Hackett later said. Drilled into him as a child, Kennedy recalled, was "the idea that there were a lot of people that were less fortunate. And white people and Negroes were all put in the same category. And that you had a responsibility to try and do something about it. But as far as separating the Negroes for having a more difficult time than the white people, that was not a particular issue in our house."

That had been true in 1948, when, shortly after graduating from Harvard, Bobby Kennedy managed his brother's reelection to his House seat in Cambridge. The district included blacks, but so powerless and numerically insignificant were they that they didn't even warrant campaign promises. "You never had to say

Children often proved the movement's heroes: six-year-old Ruby Bridges integrated New Orleans's William Frantz Elementary School, November 1960.

you were going to do anything on civil rights; you never had to say you were going to do anything on housing," Bobby continued. "It was mostly just recognition of them.... The Negroes were a relatively small population, and we weren't thinking [about] the Negroes in Mississippi or Alabama, what should be done for them. We were thinking of what needed to be done in Massachusetts." Surely, a skeptical Lewis pressed, there must have been times when race had come to loom larger to him. No, there *hadn't* been, Kennedy insisted. He stressed the point, though whether to expose or excoriate himself for his early insensitivity or to highlight his hardheadedness and evenhandedness (either would be in character) is not clear.

In any case, he was selling himself short. In 1947, one of Kennedy's Harvard football teammates was a black man named Chester Pierce. Kennedy, along with the others, convinced the administration to insist that if the University of Virginia refused to play against Pierce, it wouldn't play Harvard at all. (Pierce did get to play in Charlottesville. Harvard got clobbered, 47-0. An injured Kennedy listened to the game back in Cambridge.)

If Kennedy were at all put off by the whiff of Jim Crow attitudes in Charlottesville, it didn't keep him from going to law school there, though his undergraduate grades very nearly did—not an easy feat for someone of Kennedy's wealth and background. "It is, I think, only fair to tell you that in view of your record at Harvard College, you are unlikely to be admitted to this Law School, unless you do well on the Aptitude test," the chairman of the admissions committee there wrote him in April 1948.

That was enough to prompt Kennedy to enlist James M. Landis, who'd succeeded Joseph Kennedy as chairman of the Securities and Exchange Commission and later became dean of Harvard Law School. In his letter to the committee, Landis suggested that one of young Kennedy's greatest credentials was that he was like his old man. "My own acquaintance with Robert Kennedy has been intimate enough to confirm my impressions that he had a number of those qualities that have worked so much for the success that his father has made in business, in government and in diplomacy," he wrote. "I realize, of course, that his academic record at Harvard is none too impressive. But some men only reveal capacities for work and achievement when they hit the impact of a professional school."

More impressive than sticking up for a black teammate at Harvard, at least implicitly, was how in 1951 Kennedy managed to bring the black diplomat Ralph Bunche (who, the year before, had become the first black to win the Nobel Peace Prize) to the still-segregated Charlottesville campus. Bunche refused to speak before the segregated audiences state law still insisted upon. Kennedy first overcame resistance from fellow students, southerners with political aspirations. And then, citing the Bill of Rights, the United Nations Charter, America's mission in World War II, and the ongoing propaganda war with the Soviets, he persuaded the university president to come around, too. So Bunche spoke to an audience with numerous blacks who sat wherever they pleased.

Undoubtedly with a prod from Joe Kennedy, even the famed New York gossip columnist Walter Winchell took note. "Ex-Ambassador J. P. Kennedy's son, Robert, did what liberals flopped at," he reported to Mr. and Mrs. America and all the ships at sea on April 2, 1951. "Although Virginia has a segregation law—the univ. prexy forgot it.... The univ. president and Dr. Bunche paid tribute to Bob, 'A young student with no ax to grind—a true liberal.'" It was Robert Kennedy's debut in the national press.

Whether intentionally or not, Winchell struck a note Kennedy himself repeatedly sounded in his career: that for all their piety, liberals often accomplished less than tough-minded pragmatists like him. "Liberal" was a label he adamantly—even gleefully— avoided all his life, and from liberals, whom he considered hypocritical and self-indulgent as well as ineffective, he was forever distancing himself. But Kennedy's encounters with blacks remained aberrational, and glancing, and his sense of injustice, retail. "He had always acted with impetuous decency when racial discrimination forced itself on his attention," his most sympathetic biographer, Arthur Schlesinger, wrote. "But this was [a] response to individual wrong, not to national shame." His lack of any substantial interaction with the black community would fuel charges of hypocrisy from southern critics. The editor of the *Albany* (Georgia) *Herald* would later describe the Kennedy brothers as "two ambitious Bostonians, who have been as practically connected with the American Negro in their lifetimes as Eskimos are to the Congo Democrats."

Kennedy graduated from the law school, fifty-sixth in his class of one hundred twenty-four, in 1951. While not a "mental genius," one of his professors attested, Kennedy was "an extremely well-rounded young man possessing an average knowledge of the legal profession coupled with an acute interest in social and international affairs."

Anthony Lewis's questions to Kennedy about race were ones he could never conceivably have posed to King. The largely segregated world of King's childhood may have afforded him some temporary protection from American racial realities, and his family's wealth and status a bit more, but no black person of King's generation was insulated for long. King lost his innocence when he was six and learned that a white playmate would no longer see him. As the boy's mother explained, her son was "getting too big to play with a nigger anymore." Talking it over with his mother (who was a schoolteacher and good at explaining things) or at dinner that night (the stories varied), King recalled that "for the first time I was made aware of the existence of a race problem. I had never been conscious of it before."

Then came the regular reminders: the clerk who refused to sell shoes to him or his father until they moved to the back of the store (something his father had refused to do); the white woman who slapped him and said, "You're the nigger who stepped on my foot"; the boss at the Railway Express Agency office who called him a "nigger"; the segregated bus he rode to elementary school; the curtains that separated the black and white sections of the dining cars on trains; the long bus ride back from a public speaking contest in South Georgia, when he and his teacher had been made to stand after some whites had demanded their seats. ("Black sons of bitches," the driver had called them when they failed to move quickly enough.) Aroused once by alarmist whites warning of the perils of race mixing, King, having just finished his sophomore year at Morehouse College, sent a letter to the *Atlanta Constitution*. "It is fair to remember that almost the total of race mixture in America has come, not at Negro initiative, but by the acts of those very white men who talk loudest of race purity," he wrote. "We aren't eager to marry white girls, and we would like to have our own girls left alone by both white toughs and white aristocrats." It was a rare early example of King's race consciousness and, to his parents, an intimation of his "developing greatness." (A decade later, he made pretty much the same point to a young journalist named Mike Wallace. "Many of the most violent segregationists in the South have fathered children with Negro women—and their guilt makes them scream the loudest," he said.)

Prejudice followed him up north at Crozer Theological Seminary, where the vegetables served to him at a Stouffer's restaurant in Philadelphia had been laced with sand, and even into married life. With accommodations in Alabama still very much segregated, King and his new wife spent their wedding night in a black-owned funeral parlor. There'd been periods when he'd hated all whites. But for reasons rooted in his personality—his strength or open-mindedness or disposition, or the serenity and perspective that came from studying and learning, especially about nonviolence—somehow this hatred never congealed.

In Boston—whose baseball team was the last in the major leagues to integrate, nearly a decade after King got there—the discrimination continued. "I remember very well trying to find a place to live," King, who had enrolled in Boston University's School of Theology, later recalled. "I went into place after place where there were signs that rooms were for rent. They were for rent until they found out I was a Negro and suddenly they had just been rented." But the experience did not jolt him into activism. King "never talked much about civil rights as a student," one of his professors there later recalled.

The newlyweds could have remained in the (relatively) racially enlightened North after King graduated from B.U. in 1954. (He was awarded his PhD the following year.) Instead, at his insistence, they returned South, to Montgomery. Coretta opposed the move. "They came back as natives and not just as missionaries," the journalist Murray Kempton, who, primarily as a columnist for the then-liberal *New York Post*, followed both King and Kennedy closely throughout their careers, was to write. "It is very hard for the North to understand, but to the Negro, 'new' or 'old,' the deep South is his country. Here he was born and here he will stand." King took over the Dexter Avenue Baptist Church, a redbrick

Rosa Parks was an activist for more than a decade before refusing to yield her seat to a white passenger in 1955. The 54-week Montgomery Bus Boycott, which was led by Martin Luther King, Jr., thrust the young pastor into the national spotlight.

building located a "hymn sound away," as one journalist put it, from the Capitol Building, where Jefferson Davis had been sworn in as president of the Confederacy. It was Montgomery's "uppity" black congregation, filled with professionals, where it was frowned upon to shout "Amen." Two weeks after he formally accepted the pastorate, the Supreme Court handed down the *Brown v. Board of Education* decision, which declared state-mandated segregated public schools unconstitutional and cast doubt on all forms of legalized segregation everywhere.

King was chosen to lead the Montgomery Bus Boycott in early December 1955, only a few days after a black seamstress named Rosa Parks was arrested for refusing to give up her seat to a white passenger. (When she'd first met the boyish King, Parks thought he was a college student. His youthfulness was one of the reasons he preferred being called "Dr. King.") Its goals were actually quite modest: not to end segregation per se, but only to make it more tolerable in those instances where seats were scarce. Even King thought its objectives inadequate. "Frankly, I am for immediate integration," he said. "Segregation is evil, and I cannot, as a minister, condone evil." And yet no one missed what was really at stake. Montgomery had become, as Joe Azbell of the *Advertiser* put it, a "national guinea pig for integration." If King and his allies got what they wanted, the campaign for integration would "spread and spread and spread."

Blacks understood this better than whites, Azbell wrote. In fact, blacks were outsmarting whites in every which way; they had to: "The Negro understands the white man pretty well, but the white man doesn't always understand the Negro. Many whites will believe the Negro who tells him he is opposed to the boycott, but walks five miles to work. Many whites will believe the Negro who says he is scared to ride the buses, but sings and shouts at the mass meetings. Few Negroes are going to admit to a white employer who may be a White Citizens Council member that he is in favor of the boycott."

In black Montgomery and Alabama, King quickly established himself. The future congressman John Lewis, then fifteen years old and living in rural Pike County, heard him over a black soul station that broadcast preachers on Sunday mornings. But so complete was its color line that white Montgomery was slow to learn just how important King was. A few days into the protest, *Advertiser* editor Grover Hall referred to him simply as "a Negro spokesman," albeit one who spoke "with no little authority."

The elderly black domestics constituting the boycott's backbone revered King, seeing in him not just a natural leader but the embodiment of everything they hoped to become themselves. "He makes up to me for all my two boys didn't do," one of them told the trailblazing *New York Post* black journalist Ted Poston, who had—in the northern white press at least—the real story of the boycott pretty much to himself, except for Kempton, who watched King from the loftier perch of columnist. He attended a rally four months into the boycott during which someone predicted "their children's children's children's children would one day remember what they'd done." (That was several generations too pessimistic.) "The deep South has come face to face with the cruel fact that one side possesses the privileges and the other all the saints," Kempton wrote. At one rally a few months later, King was in fact introduced as someone "blessed with immortality while he is still among us."

Up to this point, litigation had been the principal weapon in the civil rights movement, and advocates of that approach, like Roy Wilkins and Thurgood Marshall of the NAACP, questioned King and his tactics. ("All that walking for nothing!" Marshall had once said, claiming they could have waited for a court to throw out the local ordinance. But within a matter of weeks—and much to the chagrin of these more established figures—King became the most prominent black leader in the country. On March 21, 1956, the *New York Times* made King its "Man in the News." ("Dr. King is a rather soft-spoken man with a learning and maturity far beyond his twenty-seven years," the *Times* wrote. "Dr. King is a Baptist preacher in a great southern tradition of resounding, repetitive rhetoric. And he can build to his climax with a crescendo of impassioned pulpit-pounding that overwhelms the listener with the depth of his convictions.")

The liberal southern writer Lillian Smith called for a white civil rights leader to be as great as King. Traveling to a black church in New York in late March 1956, King received the kind of welcome usually reserved for the Brooklyn Dodgers, as one paper put it, winning over parishioners with his passion, eloquence, humility, and wit. If Alabama were, indeed, the "Cradle of the Confederacy," he told them, then for the first time in years "the cradle was rocking."

King's decision to complement the NAACP's legal assault on segregation with the direct nonviolence of Gandhi thrilled *New York Post* columnist Max Lerner. "Outwardly it would seem that there isn't much left for the Negroes to try," he wrote, noting how they'd already attempted the nationalism of Marcus Garvey, and communism, and jazz and bohemianism, and the New Deal and the courts. The black community had lacked a unifying figure, but suddenly there was "a feel of Negro greatness in the air, and it comes from Negro churches and campuses and committees and plain Negro people in towns like Montgomery." Reading King's New York speech, Lerner continued, "I got the feeling that new shoots of grass are springing up out of the soil in the South, different from anything we have had thus far."

In February 1957, *Time* put him on the cover. (In Montgomery, white diehards ostentatiously tore up the magazine in front of black bystanders; black newsstands there bought hundreds of extra copies and still couldn't meet the demand.) And yet, noted Kempton, King could not get his hair cut at any hotel in Montgomery. Three months later, King spoke to twenty five thousand people in a prayer pilgrimage from the steps of the Lincoln Memorial. King, wrote James L. Hicks of the *Amsterdam News*, had emerged "as the No. 1 leader of 16 million Negroes," adding "at this point in his career, they will follow him anywhere." There were reports later that year that Hollywood was going to make "The Montgomery Story," with Harry Belafonte as King.

The Montgomery Bus Boycott changed another thing: for the first time, King faced the risk, and even the likelihood, of a violent death. His house was bombed. Another time, dynamite was found on his porch. The telephone threats were unrelenting. Through it all, he remained stoic—and fatalistic. If anything happened to him, he told people, there'd be others to take his place. In 1960, the *New York Times* assigned its first advance obituary of King and set it in type, leaving only the dateline and the lead paragraph, with the time, place, and gory details of his death, incomplete. King was all of thirty-one years old.

Later on, and especially after the assassination of John F. Kennedy, it became commonplace to say that both King and Bobby Kennedy knew they were doomed. Kennedy was no stranger to premature death even before his brother's murder—by age eighteen, he'd lost an older brother and a sister—but only for a few years did death stalk him. It loomed over King far longer—so long that he had a chance to devise and polish what he said about it. "So I'm not afraid of anybody this morning," he said. "If I had to die tomorrow morning I would die happy because I've been to the mountaintop and I've seen the promised land." It sounds like April 1968 in Memphis. In fact, it was January 1957 in Montgomery.

The boycott ended, after thirteen long months, in late 1956, when the federal courts declared Montgomery's laws on segregated public transportation unconstitutional. Shortly before six o'clock on the morning of December 21, King, joined by Rosa Parks, his colleague Ralph Abernathy, and a few others, boarded a bus outside his house and took a seat near the front. "We are glad to have you," the driver told him. Initially, blacks and whites remained among their own, but now it was a matter of preference rather than compulsion. King had always squirmed a bit over his highfalutin name. After Montgomery, he allowed that perhaps he'd earned it.

His suddenly enhanced stature explained why, when the Highlander Folk School celebrated its twenty-fifth anniversary in September 1957, it asked King to give the closing address. The school, halfway between Nashville and Chattanooga, was a kind of Chautauqua Institution for labor officials and civil rights advocates, teaching them how to run programs in community organizing, voter registration, and literacy skills. It had somehow managed to survive unremitting hostility throughout its history, aimed as much at its unconventional mores as its objectives: the center was one of the only places in the South where whites and blacks could work, and learn, and square-dance, and swim, together. (Rosa Parks had attended a program four months before her fateful bus ride.)

For decades, southerners who equated integration with communism had depicted Highlander as a Red colony; the FBI entertained their complaints, but concluded that while communists participated in its programs, they didn't control the place. Among its supporters, in fact, were Eleanor Roosevelt, Walter Reuther, and Reinhold Niebuhr. "Certainly there was the discontent of the working class expressed in the 1930's, just as in the 1950's there was discontent expressed by Negroes who were beginning to struggle for equal rights," wrote Nat Caldwell of the *Nashville Tennessean*, who'd periodically stopped by. "But there was never the feeling that this was subversive or un-American, even when some ideas which seemed impractical, hair-brained, or half-baked were offered."

It was a heady time for King. During his hour-long visit that day, he gave a rousing address tracing American progress in race relations. "To put it in biblical terms," he said, "we have broken loose from the Egypt of slavery. We have moved through the wilderness of 'separate but equal,' and now we stand on the border of the promised land of integration."

"The future is filled with vast and marvelous possibilities," King told his audience. "This is a great time to be alive." He then went into a jaunty bit of Freudian analysis. Normally, one wouldn't want such a diagnosis, he said, but in some instances, one should *want* to be maladjusted: who'd want to be adjusted to the viciousness of segregation? "It may be that the salvation of the world lies in the hands of the maladjusted," he said—as maladjusted as Lincoln or Jefferson or Jesus of Nazareth.

But even in his midst that day, there was peril: seeking to reveal "where some of the South's racial troubles originate," Georgia Governor Marvin Griffin sent a photographer to document the session. Soon the Georgia Commission on Education would claim in a brochure and at a public hearing that Highlander was a nest of communists. The commission printed up a quarter million brochures entitled "Martin Luther King at Communist Training School" featuring a photograph of King taken during his visit. That picture was destined to become one of the most durable, widely circulated, and misrepresented images of King ever—as ubiquitous a symbol of white resistance as the photographs of blacks fighting off dogs and fire hoses would soon be to the civil rights movement.

For all his optimism, there was so much more to do, as King seemed to acknowledge to law professor and civil rights activist Harris Wofford when the two went into a whites-only bathroom at the Atlanta airport in late 1957 and the anxious black attendant working there tried to shoo King over to the room for "coloreds." "Do you mean that every time you need to go to the bathroom you go out of here and all the way to that other room?" King asked him. "Yes, suh, that's the place for colored," he replied. "Martin Luther King, Jr., walked out in exasperation and said to me, 'That's the way most of the Negroes of Montgomery acted before the boycott,'" Wofford later wrote. And, both inside and outside of Montgomery, still would.

In all likelihood, Robert Kennedy was paying Martin Luther King and the epochal events taking shape around him absolutely no mind. His energies, and passions, lay elsewhere. After graduating from law school in 1951, and thanks to his father, he'd worked briefly in the Justice Department. Then he'd managed his brother's successful Senate campaign in 1952. That was when he first met the *Washington Star*'s Mary McGrory, who among many other things went on to spend a career chronicling the Kennedys. She'd liked him from the start: he was less attractive but more appealing than Jack, more raw and straightforward and warm and vulnerable. "He is unassimilated, isn't he?" Robert Lowell said to her after meeting Kennedy at a party.

In early 1953 Kennedy joined the staff of the Permanent Subcommittee on Investigations of the Senate Government Operations Committee, the unwieldy name for Senator Joseph McCarthy's panel investigating domestic subversion. It was a good fit: McCarthy was a Kennedy family friend who'd taken money from Bobby Kennedy's father—$50,000, Drew Pearson once reported, to further his investigations—and dated a couple of his sisters. And his anticommunism mirrored Bobby Kennedy's: America's security was under threat, and McCarthy seemed to be the only person doing anything about it. For someone who'd imbibed his father's own conservative politics, it was for young Kennedy a comfortable ideological fit. "Kennedy has worked for his liberalism," Senator Daniel Patrick Moynihan observed many years later. "It's not something he learned at the Bronx High School of Science. The things he learned first were conservative things. The things he learned second were liberal things."

In fact, Kennedy investigated other matters, like businesses trading illegally with Communist China, and played little part in the witch hunts. Disapproving of McCarthy's methods and loathing his cocounsel, Roy Cohn ("Bobby either hated people or loved people, there was never any in-between ground," Cohn later said), Kennedy quit after six months, in July 1953. But it was long enough to stigmatize him among liberals for the rest of his career. "I never thought that either Jack or his brother Bobby felt the sort of outrage that many other people felt at the time about McCarthy's methods and purposes," McGrory later recalled. This was especially apparent after leaving the post: when Edward R. Murrow criticized McCarthy in a dinner speech, Robert Kennedy walked out; he visited McCarthy when he was dying and then attended his funeral. But it also illustrated one of Kennedy's most talked-about traits: what Kenneth O'Donnell called his "outrageous loyalty," which trumped fashion and political expediency. Longtime family friend Kirk LeMoyne "Lem" Billings observed, "Bobby was tender-hearted, and it was typical of him to go and see somebody in trouble."

And his loyalty persisted, even when it cost him politically. It reflected an ornery, contrarian quality in him: he hated doing what everyone else did, or what everyone else expected, even when it might make him look better in some eyes. "I felt sorry for him, particularly in the last year, when he was such a beaten, destroyed person—particularly since many of his so-called friends, realizing when he was finished, ran away from him and left him with virtually no one," he once said of McCarthy. Running for office, nothing changed. "Nothing would be easier than to agree

Kennedy's short-lived association with Senator Joseph McCarthy earned him national recognition but cost him the trust of many liberal voters.

with all the attacks on McCarthy—it makes you very popular," he said years later. "It's easy to sit here and attack McCarthy as an SOB. I'm not going to do it." Just about the worst thing he ever said about the man was that "at times he was terribly heavy-handed."

His McCarthy ties left black intellectuals even warier than their white counterparts. Many of their most heroic figures, like W. E. B. Du Bois and Paul Robeson, had had communist ties. American communists had denounced lynching and baseball's color line longer and louder than just about anyone. To these people—like Harry Belafonte—"anticommunism" was racist code. In Kennedy's case, it was something Belafonte, one of the handful of people ever to grow close to King and Kennedy both, had to overcome before he and Kennedy could become confidants.

For his work in McCarthy's office, the Junior Chamber of Commerce made Kennedy one of its "Ten Outstanding Young

Persons" (the aviator Chuck Yeager was another) for 1954. The award was arranged for by his father. That same year, the Democrats regained the Senate, and Kennedy returned to the subcommittee, now led by Senator John McClellan of Arkansas, as majority counsel. As King made history in Montgomery, Kennedy became the scourge of corrupt union chiefs like Dave Beck and Jimmy Hoffa of the Teamsters on what was popularly known as the Senate Rackets Committee. Millions watched him and Hoffa go at one another on national television. To Hoffa, Kennedy was "a young, dim-witted, curly-headed smart aleck, a ruthless little monster, a spoiled young millionaire who never had to go out and find a way to live by his own efforts — and he cannot understand resistance to what he wants." But he did find one thing in Kennedy to admire: "His willingness to work and to fight to win."

Going up against Hoffa was perhaps the first of the many transformative moments people spotted in Kennedy's life. He "recognized in Hoffa a general fanaticism for evil that could be thought of as the opposite side of his own fanaticism for good, and therefore involved direct combat," Murray Kempton once wrote. Pre-Hoffa, Bobby Kennedy was "really a very cross, unhappy, angry young man," Lem Billings recalled. Then suddenly, he "wasn't the angry man anymore." If that were so, it was only to family intimates. Others had trouble spotting the suddenly more contented Robert Kennedy. To his critics, his crusade against Hoffa became one more item on the bill of particulars. As *Esquire* later had it, by pursuing Hoffa so relentlessly, Kennedy pulled off "the truly stupendous feat" of making many people feel sorry for the corrupt union leader.

Though Mary McGrory might have liked him at first, for Anthony Lewis — "Hardly knew him and didn't like him and thought he was callow and tough" was how he remembered him at Harvard — and many other people, Bobby Kennedy remained an acquired taste. He finished last in first impressions. "A long, rather sullen and ominous presence" was Arthur Schlesinger's. "Kennedy and I regarded one another with great suspicion and barely spoke." To the Tennessee newspaperman who became one of his closest aides, John Seigenthaler, Kennedy at first blush was a "rich little snob." Harris Wofford, who later worked closely with him on John Kennedy's presidential campaign, found him to be precisely the "arrogant, narrow, rude young man" he'd been warned about, and "insufferable" to boot. (Wofford recalled how shocked Kennedy was to learn he'd graduated from the all-black Howard Law School; it was OK to *teach* them, an incredulous Kennedy said, but *go to school with them?*) "No one became a friend of Bob Kennedy at first meeting," Edwin Guthman, the veteran newspaperman who later became his press secretary, once wrote. "You had to go through something with him, to test and be tested. But once the bond was formed it was indestructible."

At the same time, Kennedy had a knack for picking up older mentors, often friends of his father's. Two were named Hoover: Herbert, for whom he worked briefly, and J. Edgar, whom Joe Kennedy once tried to lure away from the FBI with a generous offer of employment, presumably in security. Robert Kennedy invited the second of the Hoovers to his wedding (he declined), sought his counsel from time to time, and sent him fan mail. "You have established a record of which the whole country is very proud," he wrote him in September 1956. "I hope the United States continues to enjoy your leadership for a long period of time." A friend of his from the bureau, Courtney Evans, gave Kennedy a copy of *The FBI Story* for his birthday, only to get it back. "He said it was a present which he greatly appreciated receiving but that he would cherish it even more if the Director would autograph it for him," Evans later wrote.

Kennedy's enthusiasm wasn't always reciprocated. After one professional encounter with him in 1954, Hoover wrote to a colleague, "The attitude of Kennedy in this matter clearly shows need for absolute circumspection in any conversation with him." The following year, Hoover felt Kennedy hadn't shared some information he'd developed on the McClellan committee as quickly as he might have. "Kennedy was completely uncooperative until after he had squeezed all the publicity out of the matter he could," Hoover complained.

Kennedy had also stopped in to see Hoover both before and after taking a six-week tour of the Soviet Union in the spring of 1955 with another mentor (and friend of his father), Supreme Court Justice William O. Douglas. The invitation was largely a favor to Joe Kennedy, for whom Douglas had once worked at the SEC, and to whom he thought he owed his seat on the Supreme Court. They spent most of their time in the Central Asian provinces of Kazakhstan, Turkmenistan, Uzbekistan, Tadzhikistan, and Kirghizia, though they reached Moscow and Leningrad, too. Douglas found Kennedy's paranoia and political dogmatism exasperating: refusing to eat Soviet food or be treated by suspect Soviet doctors—according to the columnist Drew Pearson, he'd practically died for lack of proper care while there—forever trying to convince Communist Party apparatchiks they were wrong. But Kennedy studied hard and, Douglas believed, abandoned some of his rigid orthodoxies. Afterward, he described to *U.S. News and World Report* a world of unrelieved bleakness, disinformation, surveillance, and religious oppression, including—this seemed especially offensive to him—a museum in Leningrad devoted solely to ridiculing God.

It was in the USSR, oddly enough, that Kennedy first addressed institutionalized racism in America, and only because he was challenged repeatedly about it by the people he encountered there. His response, in effect, was that in their discrimination against indigenous peoples, the Soviets were even worse. He thought a fine way to counter calumnies about American racism would be to have the Harlem Globetrotters tour Russia.

In September 1956, as the bus boycott in Montgomery reached into its tenth month, Kennedy found himself on the hustings nearby in Little Rock. As part of his ongoing political apprenticeship, he tagged along with the presidential campaign of Adlai Stevenson, then facing Dwight Eisenhower for the second time. "He was watching how presidential campaigns should be run, or should not be run," Schlesinger recalled. "And, also, Stevenson wanted him there. As you brought a Negro along, you brought an Irish-Catholic and all that. And he was also a symbol of his brother, who'd made a great impression at the Convention." What he meant was that John F. Kennedy had very nearly gotten on the ticket, thanks largely to southern support. It wasn't that they loved Kennedy so much as they wanted to stop Senator Estes Kefauver of Tennessee, even though, as a southerner, he was one of their own. In fact, he was the one thing they loathed: a racial moderate. "We'd be for anyone against that damned, nigger-loving Kefauver," a Mississippi delegate told Ralph McGill of the *Atlanta Constitution.* John Kennedy's move had been perfectly executed; he'd gained national exposure, undermined old notions that Catholics couldn't win, spared himself from certain defeat in November, and set himself up nicely for the real prize next time around.

Thus, when Robert Kennedy spoke at one of Stevenson's events in Little Rock, his message was one of party loyalty and gratitude, especially to the southerners who'd backed his brother. He saluted Arkansas's two Democratic senators: first his boss, John McClellan, and then J. William Fulbright, each unremittingly hostile to civil rights. He then praised Governor Orval Faubus, who within a year would block nine black students from entering Little Rock Central High School.

"Since the convention in Chicago, we in Massachusetts look upon the states of the South as our second home," he joked. "As a matter of fact, we Kennedys have taken to singing 'Dixie' before breakfast every morning." He may have cribbed the line from his older brother, who'd told Arthur Krock he was "going to sing 'Dixie' for the rest of my life." But his further embrace of the region was his own. "Our admiration for the South isn't really something new," he continued. "We were brought up to admire the great traditions of the South, its courtesy, the great moral strength and the courage. Nothing personifies these traits so much as the activities of the Southern soldier during and after the War Between the States. When I was young I used to hear this story of these —." The paper trail ends there — only portions of Kennedy's handwritten notes of the speech are publicly available, the rest having fallen into private hands — but it's easy to imagine where it went: to tales of Confederate heroism. Mindful of southern sensibilities, he'd even avoided that much-loathed Yankee locution: the "Civil War."

But Kennedy's attitudes are often complicated, and even at this stage, he showed contrary — one might say, "Union" — impulses. His stint with the Stevenson campaign also brought him, for the first time, to Springfield, Illinois, where he asked one of Stevenson's aides, Newton Minow (later commissioner of the Federal Communications Commission during the Kennedy Administration) to take him to Abraham Lincoln's house. "Newt said RFK was very silent, obviously deeply moved," Arthur Schlesinger later recalled. "For the first time," Minow "understood that there were depths of feeling in him I had never suspected." People were always able to pick up things in Robert Kennedy they had not suspected, which speaks of course not just to Kennedy's surprising depth, but to the depth of the belief that he was shallow.

As the work on the Rackets Committee proceeded, Kennedy's fame only grew, as did his Southern appeal. In the spring of 1958, he was the keynote speaker at the annual Law Day banquet at the University of Alabama Law School, where he described how a cunning, highly financed, and well-organized underworld was infiltrating organized labor. And then, in February 1959, he came to Montgomery for that triumphant appearance before the local Chamber of Commerce.

Even friends conceded that public speaking wasn't Robert Kennedy's forte. "He just didn't have it," said Lem Billings, who'd sat suffering for his young friend a couple of times as he described his Soviet adventure. "I heard him in Palm Beach and I heard him in Washington and they both were terrible," he said. Knowing Bobby Kennedy as he did, he guessed that Kennedy had sought expert help for his deficiency, and rehearsed in front of mirrors—both of which he in fact did when he was attorney general. (He abandoned the lessons when he thought the teacher was over-charging him.) "Bobby gave the worst speech I have ever heard in my life," Sander Vanocur of NBC News, one of the many journalists whom Robert Kennedy befriended over the years, recalled of a performance he'd witnessed in Wisconsin during the 1960 presidential campaign. "It was just disastrous—he couldn't speak and he was faltering and sweating and rubbing his palms." The public speaking itself gradually improved, but the anxiety—the hands and legs shaking under the table—never eased. And reporters never ceased to be amazed when they spotted it.

But in Montgomery, no one seemed to notice—or care. Young Kennedy that day "spoke without notes, reeling off names and figures by the dozen as he told the story of labor racketeering, mostly in the Teamsters Union, all over the country," the *Advertiser* reported, then "urged his listeners to contact their members in Congress to support legislation to curb the corrupt practices now seemingly rampant in labor." Days later, they were still talking about him. "Understand there were 750 present to hear the brilliant young speaker, Robert F. Kennedy of Washington," the paper's gossip columnist, "Go Peep," noted later in the week. "I only wish there might have been 700 more!"

Kennedy played more roles that day in Montgomery than the bane of corrupt labor unions; he was also manager of his brother's gestating presidential campaign. Now as always, the South—the *white* South—was crucial to any Democratic candidate. In Alabama, his concern was politicians like the man who introduced him that day, Governor Patterson (who found him "energetic and impetuous and full of good ideas"), to whom he sent a handwritten thank-you note afterward. "I hope on your next visit to Washington you will let me know and that if you can take the time you will come and have dinner with us at home just outside the city," he said.

Before that could ever happen, in June, John Kennedy invited Patterson, whom he'd met in 1957 and had since hosted a couple of times in his Senate office, to breakfast in his Georgetown home. Joining Patterson was Sam Engelhardt, a member of the state's segregationist White Citizens Council, who doubled as his highway director, and who'd once said that the bombing of King's home had been staged. "A friend of the South," Patterson called Kennedy after their visit. Still largely disenfranchised in Alabama and throughout the Deep South, black voters would have mattered little to Robert Kennedy that day in Montgomery. Had he thought about it, he'd have realized then that black votes could help determine who won several crucial Northern states in the general election, votes that for the first time were really up for grabs. And, more than anyone else, Martin Luther King might be the key to grabbing them.

Throughout his career, RFK was known for his ferocious devotion to his brother's political well-being. "I don't care if anybody around here likes me," he said at Kennedy headquarters, "as long as they like Jack."

# TWO

# LOOK THE ENEMY
# IN THE EYE

Anyone who becomes world famous at twenty-seven has a tough act to follow. "Frankly, I'm worried to death," King confided to a mentor. "People will be expecting me to pull rabbits out of the hat for the rest of my life." Everything else that followed for him would be anticlimactic, he told the *Saturday Evening Post*. (It was the same magazine which, in its September 7, 1957, issue, declared that admirers of the Kennedys "confidently look forward to the day when Jack will be in the White House, Bobby will serve in the Cabinet as Attorney General, and Teddy will be the Senator from Massachusetts.")

When James Baldwin, also a preacher's son, met King in 1957, he was pleasantly surprised. "It is rare that one *likes* a world-famous man — by the time they become world-famous they rarely like themselves," he wrote. But King lacked "the hideous piety" that plagued his profession, wrote Baldwin, plus the "ghastly self-importance which until recently, was all that allowed one to be certain one was addressing a Negro leader." Nor, he said, was he one of those famous black men "who always seem to be giving an uncertain imitation of some extremely improbable white man."

At the time of the 1957 "prayer pilgrimage," wrote James Hicks of the *Amsterdam News*, King could have taken over any of the top black organizations, including the NAACP and the National Baptist Conference. "There is a saying that if you can't whip a

Misdemeanor offenses plagued King wherever he traveled as local law enforcement sought to thwart his cause. Between 1955 and 1967, he was jailed twenty-nine times.

man, you should join him," he wrote. "Negro leaders can't whip Martin L. King. The people are praying they will be wise enough to join him." But King opted to create his own niche, a consortium of church and civic groups he called the Southern Christian Leadership Conference. Its cofounder was his close friend Ralph Abernathy, also a minister and a key collaborator on the Montgomery Bus Boycott. Among King's key advisers on the SCLC were a white ex-communist Jewish lawyer and businessman, Stanley Levison, and a pacifist ex-communist gay black man, Bayard Rustin—collaborations that simultaneously showed King's wisdom, discernment, courage, imagination, tolerance, arrogance, recklessness, dependency, and desperation.

For all his eminence, King struggled to remain relevant and visible. Spreading what he called "the Montgomery experience" wasn't easy. King needed to tend to the more mundane but essential tasks of raising money and building his organization. For a time the launch of Sputnik in 1957 distracted everyone from everything earthbound, including civil rights. As if to catch its collective breath, in the late 1950s, things grew temporarily quiet on the racial front, and King receded from view. "It is a curious fact that, between crises, [King's] place in the civil-rights struggle seems to slip," Reese Cleghorn was to write in the *Saturday Evening Post*. Following the bus boycott, "he passed through a period of limbo." When civil rights reemerged, the cutting edge lay not with King but with the young black activists, mostly college kids, staging sit-ins at segregated southern lunch counters, who sat stoically as young thugs in ducktails poured scalding hot coffee, or ketchup, or sugar, on their heads or down their backs until the black students—and not their assailants—were arrested.

King's most sensational appearance during this period came in September 1958, when at a book signing in a Harlem department store a mentally unstable black woman named Izola Ware Curry stabbed—and very nearly killed—him with a letter opener. The blade lodged near his aorta—a sneeze, it was said, would have been the end of him—and only after hours of delicate surgery was it

THE PROMISE AND THE DREAM

removed. The liberal press closely followed King's convalescence. Meantime, a group of whites in Cartersville, Georgia, sent a cash contribution to Mrs. Curry.

In late 1959 King announced plans to move back to Atlanta, and to Ebenezer Baptist Church, where he'd share the pulpit with his father. Whose arrival anywhere else in America could have been more heralded, and feared? Ralph McGill, the crusading liberal editor of the *Atlanta Constitution*, likened local whites apprehensive over King's relocation to "citizens of medieval walled cities who heard that the great plague was coming." "Wherever M. L. King, Jr., has been there has followed in his wake a wave of crimes including stabbing, bombings, and inciting of riots, barratry [bringing bogus lawsuits], destruction of property and many others," the state's governor, Ernest Vandiver, Jr., warned. "For these reasons, he is not welcome to Georgia." But come back he did, and just as the 1960 presidential campaign was heating up.


The black community's traditional ties to the "Party of Lincoln" — along with the Republican Party's claim to any such historical connection — had long since frayed. But Dwight Eisenhower, personally appealing and a war hero, had won back a majority of the black vote in 1956 for the GOP, and despite his personal discomfort with blacks, he'd won them some victories: the desegregation of Little Rock Central High School; the Civil Rights Act of 1957; and — freed from having to kowtow to southern senators in his own party — a host of progressive federal judges and justices. What was unclear was whether Eisenhower had reversed black America's long-term desertion of the Republicans, a process that began during Franklin Roosevelt's presidency, or if he'd only delayed the process. In that question lay the fate of such key states as New York, New Jersey, and Illinois and quite possibly the 1960 election. In other words, for the first time, except, possibly, during Reconstruction, black voters may have held the balance of power.

There was one more question: whether black goodwill toward

Ike would carry over to his vice president, and the 1960 Republican standard-bearer, Richard Nixon. Going into the campaign, Nixon was in many ways more enlightened and engaged on racial matters than some of the Democrats battling in the primaries (John F. Kennedy among them). But like so many others, King never quite trusted him. ("Nixon has a genius for convincing one that he is sincere," he'd said. "He almost disarms you with his apparent sincerity.... If Richard Nixon is not sincere, he is the most dangerous man in America.") As vice president, Nixon joined the NAACP and visited Africa, where, in fact, he'd first met King. When the black press association in Washington made King its "Man of the Year," Pat Nixon collected the award with him. The publisher of *Ebony* and *Jet* backed him, as did Daddy King, as did the organization of Baptist preachers in Atlanta.

Compounding John Kennedy's ignorance about blacks was his indifference: as with Bobby, they didn't much interest him. "The Kennedys just never crossed those areas that I covered," the Washington editor of *Jet*, Simeon Booker, remembered. In fact, it was worse than that: Kennedy had supported a key provision of the 1957 statute guaranteeing jury trials to officials accused of blocking voting rights, pretty much ensuring they'd get off scot-free and thereby negating the intent of the legislation. A "compromiser with evil," NAACP executive director Roy Wilkins called him for that vote. For the convenience of its readers, the *Amsterdam News* enumerated "Your Friends" and "Your Enemies," based on senators' votes on that measure, and lumped Kennedy in the latter.

Bobby Kennedy shared in the blame. "The whisper is around that the young lawyer on Capitol Hill who painstakingly dug up all the old statues [sic] in reference to civil rights and gave them to the southerners to use as ammunition to gut the bill of its most potent parts was Robert Kennedy, counsel of the McClellan committee," the *Chicago Defender* reported.

John Kennedy's June 1960 breakfast with Governor Patterson and his segregationist pal hadn't helped: "Two of the worst Negro haters and enemies of the Constitution to be found in public life today," Jackie Robinson, the former baseball star and *New York Post* columnist, called them. John Kennedy's rejoinders—that he'd been roped into the meeting, that he'd made no promises, that he'd eaten with Thurgood Marshall a few days later—weren't reassuring. That he'd donated his Pulitzer Prize winnings from *Profiles in Courage* ($500) to the United Negro College Fund didn't mollify anyone, either.

White southerners were skeptical of John Kennedy, too, despite their support for him at the 1956 convention. To Grover Hill of the *Montgomery Advertiser*, Kennedy's efforts to appeal to the South were phony. In fact, he insisted, Kennedy was busy "delousing himself of Dixie ticks" and looking elsewhere: "the eminent saint, King," he'd read in *Newsweek*, was forming "Negroes for Kennedy." That wasn't the case, but it is an indication of how influential King was.

Reporters came to view Robert Kennedy as a stripped-down, unevolved, unrestrained version of his older brother: John Kennedy's id. In the *New York Post*, Irwin Ross described him as "an intense young man with a personality alternately abrasive and good-humored, and a churning, restless energy which is both infectious and wearying. His conversation is a breathless, eager rush of words. He chews gum at a furious pace. He runs up stairs when he has no need to hurry. Even in moments of repose, he can be observed impatiently drumming with his fingers against the side of the chair." The younger Kennedy was lean and muscular, tanned and windblown like his brother, but easier to read. "He has the same bright, flashing smile and easy geniality, but there is a flinty hardness in Bobby, a visible wariness beneath the cordiality," Ross wrote. Some called Robert Kennedy "Raul"— a reference to Fidel Castro's loyal, shadowy younger brother. Or, he was, in the words of Martin Luther King's longtime lawyer, Clarence Jones, John Kennedy's "consiglieri."

"To the extent that he had any center—I'm not even going to use the word 'moral center'—it was wholly based on what was in the political best interests of his brother," Jones said. Bobby did some occasional campaigning for his brother, but he wasn't a natural glad-hander and mostly stuck to the behind-the-scenes work of running the campaign. "I'm not running a popularity contest," he once said. "It doesn't matter if they like me or not. Jack can be nice to them." "He couldn't stand to be touched," a campaign aide, Paul Corbin, remembered. "I used to tease him by touching him as he went by." And black neighborhoods posed a particular problem for him. "What shall I say to these people?" he beseeched Corbin before campaigning for his brother in Milwaukee's largely black Sixth Ward during the Wisconsin primary in April. (Corbin recalled how, campaigning in rural, Protestant Wisconsin, Kennedy had asked the proprietor of the motel in which they were staying where he might find a Catholic church so he could attend Mass in the morning. To the hard-boiled Corbin, it was a dumb move: why would he flaunt his Catholicism in the middle of Lutheran Wisconsin? He didn't care whether his brother won if it meant giving up his religion, Kennedy replied— loudly enough, apparently, for the motel keeper to hear him. Kennedy's religious devotion so impressed the man that the next morning, while Robert Kennedy was off worshipping, the owner told Corbin he was voting for John F. Kennedy.)

The Kennedys mobilized to win over black delegates, and then black voters. Running the effort was R. Sargent Shriver, the Kennedy brother-in-law and the family's resident progressive. (The Kennedy family called him the "house communist." Assisting Shriver was Harris Wofford, a law professor and civil rights activist who'd become a King acolyte during the bus boycott. "We're in trouble with the Negroes," Robert Kennedy conceded to him. "We really don't know much about this whole thing. We've been dealing outside the field of the main Negro leadership and have to start from scratch."

The Kennedys initially reached out to the black world the customary way—"using that old stereotypical appeal, taking Negro athletes or stage people," as Booker put it. The prime target was the beloved Jackie Robinson, who was a Republican. John Kennedy met with him and pleaded for time to prove his mettle,

1960 marked the first national election in which black voters held sway; the Kennedys' efforts in getting King released from prison helped secure their support.

only to look on with horror as his combative kid brother charged on a popular radio show that Robinson had helped block the unionization of Chock full o'Nuts, where Robinson was an executive. To take on Robinson within shouting distance of Ebbets Field, recently abandoned and already mourned, was outrageous — and, Robinson insisted, unfair. Bobby Kennedy "must really have a low impression of the intelligence of Negro Americans" to make such a charge, he wrote in the *Amsterdam News*, and proved he "will not hesitate to use lies, innuendos and personal attacks on those who disagree with him to get his candidate into the White House."

Just as offensive to Robinson was the way Bobby Kennedy had called America's eighteen million blacks "his Negroes" — meaning Robinson's. "Apparently young Bobby hasn't heard that the Emancipation Proclamation was signed 97 years ago," Robinson fumed. "I don't run any plantation, and I suggest to Kennedy that he stop acting as if he did. Negroes in the U.S. don't belong to anybody but themselves. This latest episode convinces me all the more that this bunch has no business at the helm of the U.S.A."

Television reporter Sander Vanocur was with John Kennedy as he read Robinson's column. "He put his head in his hands, rested his elbows on his knees, then called [his spokesman] Pierre [Salinger] and said, 'Get a hold of Bobby and tell him we're not running against Jackie Robinson,'" Vanocur recalled.

Bobby kept rubbing people the wrong way, Wofford remembered. "For him, everything was black and white. . . . He had these moral judgments, but I didn't have great confidence in his wisdom about them." "Whenever you see Bobby Kennedy in public with his brother, he looks as though he showed up for a rumble," Murray Kempton wrote.

Tough, pragmatic, and much loathed himself, Joe Kennedy contrasted his two eldest surviving sons. It remains unresolved whether Joseph Kennedy really did say, of his fourth son, that "he hates the same way I do," but no one disputes that it was true. "My father had warned me not to become too emotionally involved with people," Bobby Kennedy once said. At Jack's request, John Seigenthaler dropped off Bobby at the Mayflower Hotel one day to see Harry Truman, who was in town for a visit. "Truman scolded him a little bit and told him he should stop being so presumptuous and that he should stop trying, in effect, to make people mad, and that everybody thought he was a son-of-bitch," Seigenthaler recalled. It's unclear whether John Kennedy knew what Truman was going to say and considered it something his younger brother should hear.

What *is* clear is that the former president had wasted his breath. "Bob said he told him that he thought [the stories about him] were largely exaggerated and that he didn't think he was a monster, a bogeyman," Seigenthaler added. Perhaps, but during the race he further burnished his reputation for ruthlessness. Perhaps the lowest blow in that campaign came in West Virginia, when one of John Kennedy's surrogates, Franklin D. Roosevelt,

Jr., accused Hubert Humphrey of dodging the draft during World War II. (Years later—oddly enough, at the White House on the night John Kennedy was assassinated—Roosevelt reminded Robert Kennedy that it was he who'd put him up to it.)

Having lost Jackie Robinson, the Kennedys set out to find another black celebrity and cast their eyes on Harry Belafonte. Even he knew he'd been designated to, as he put it, fill "that space that Jackie left." He was skeptical, especially of Robert Kennedy because of his McCarthy ties. With Belafonte and other blacks on the left, the problem with McCarthy wasn't that he accused people of having communist ties indiscriminately, but that he castigated American communism. "There's no way to champion the cause of black people in this country and our struggle and not be in the shadow of some of the tenets of the Communist Party," Belafonte later said. "The black cause was the main article of debate for the Communist Party." And, by affiliating with McCarthy, he said, Robert Kennedy "came from the anti-black, anti-communist side of the equation."

"Not only did I feel he was someone that could not be trusted, I thought he had to be dealt with very carefully because he was not just somebody we didn't know," Belafonte went on. "What we did know about him was not favorable to our cause." Belafonte felt that in addition to being hostile to blacks, Robert Kennedy was ignorant of them. "Bobby was not only not comfortable, he had no reference," he recalled. "He really didn't know quite what to say. He didn't have our vocabulary. He didn't speak to our cause."

John Kennedy carried less of this baggage than his kid brother, and Belafonte agreed to meet with him and, as it turned out, to become his matchmaker. He told Kennedy that courting Robinson was, in any case, retrograde: as the campaign for equal rights had escalated, a different kind of hero had emerged. If Kennedy could tie himself to Martin Luther King, Belafonte advised, and get his counsel, *that* would make a difference. Belafonte then recommended to King that he see John Kennedy, as did Wofford.

A few weeks later, the two men met at Joseph Kennedy's apartment on Central Park South in New York. John Kennedy struck King as unsophisticated and detached on the matter of black rights, with little sense for what he called their "deep groans and passionate yearnings," but he did appear eager to learn. In the end, while Kennedy's aides impressed King more than Nixon's, the two candidates themselves didn't seem all that different to him, and he refused to endorse either.

It was a truism in the Kennedy campaign: one kind word about one of three people—Jimmy Hoffa, Nikita Khrushchev, or Martin Luther King—and the Democratic nominee could kiss the South good-bye. While John Kennedy could wax eloquent on civil rights—in a speech to African ambassadors, he called for "equal access to the voting booth, to the schoolroom, to jobs, to housing, and to public facilities, including lunchrooms"—Robert Kennedy kept those piercing blue eyes of his on electoral realities.

Ruth Batson, an NAACP official in Boston who, despite serial disappointments, had stuck with the Kennedys since 1952, always remembered something Robert Kennedy told campaign workers. "He came in and he said, 'Listen,' as tough as he could say it, 'there are more issues to discuss around here than civil rights, and don't forget it.' And, I mean, he said it in just that kind of tone. And I said to myself, 'What am I doing here?' You know, 'What is this, the same old same old?'" But of course, it was more complicated than that. That same Robert Kennedy supported the expansive plank on civil rights for the Democratic Party's 1960 platform, arguing for executive action on desegregation and public housing. "Make it absolutely clear how we stand on civil rights," he directed Wofford, who helped draft it. "Don't fuzz it up." King was among those who praised it. "The most positive, dynamic, and meaningful civil rights plank that has ever been adopted by either party," King, who'd again been consulted, called it.

But when it came right down to it, John Kennedy wanted to placate the black community and then move on to things he considered more important. "Now, in five minutes, tick off the ten things that a president ought to do to clean up this goddamn civil rights mess," he asked Wofford from behind the wheel of his red convertible as he drove (too quickly) to Capitol Hill one morning after winning the nomination. While little could be done legislatively, Wofford insisted, much could by executive action: with "the stroke of a pen," as he put it, discrimination in federally funded housing could end. And Kennedy began saying as much on the stump.

Joining what became known as the "civil rights section" of the campaign was Louis Martin, the savvy former editor of the *Chicago Defender*, who immediately ingratiated the Kennedy campaign with the black press by arranging for the Democratic Party to pay off its debts to them left over from the 1956 race. (With characteristic caution, the phrase "civil rights" was stricken from the campaign's public lexicon, and the civil rights department was sequestered from the regular campaign offices.) With the focus still on celebrities, Robert Kennedy—"a pretty tough cat" was how Martin described him— put together a flying caravan of black athletes and assorted names: boxers like Jersey Joe Wolcott and Henry Armstrong and Willie Mays's wife. But a King endorsement was still the biggest catch to capture black loyalties—and votes.

A couple of months after they'd first met, King and John Kennedy had a second encounter, this time at the candidate's home in Georgetown. King was impressed by how much the candidate had learned about black issues in the interim. But he urged Kennedy to do "something dramatic," like campaign down South. Philip Graham, the publisher of the *Washington Post* and another Kennedy confidant, was thinking along the same lines; the time was coming, he suggested presciently, when the Democratic Party would have to choose between blacks and white southerners. "Martin Luther King came to see Jack to say that he thought he would come out for him," Schlesinger wrote in his journal at the end of August. "But he wants Jack to come South and speak in a Negro church in Georgia....Phil said [to Kennedy], 'If you have to choose between [Georgia Senator] Herman Talmadge or Martin Luther King, I hope you will choose King.' JFK seemed to agree."

But only to a certain extent, as Kennedy's choice of Lyndon Johnson as his running mate attested: in June 1960, the NAACP had given Johnson the lowest rating of all the presidential candidates in the primaries, Democrats and Republicans alike. In their opposition to Johnson, and their ultimate impotence on the point, the black leadership and Bobby Kennedy were aligned; the younger Kennedy famously loathed Johnson (the feeling was mutual) and tried to keep him off the ticket.

However spotty John Kennedy's record on civil rights, black voters grew to like him. Simeon Booker sensed things turning after one of the debates, when Kennedy touched on civil rights in a way Nixon didn't. When blacks lined up for him three deep along the streets of Indianapolis, "I think it did something to Kennedy," he said. Kennedy's advance men started scouting black neighborhoods.

In the end, all the careful calibrations of Robert Kennedy and others mattered less than the effect of a dinner Martin and Coretta King had in Atlanta with the writer Lillian Smith several months before the vote. Driving her home afterward, King was pulled over by a local policeman; the borrowed car had expired plates. Then it turned out that several months after moving to Georgia, King was still using his Alabama license, illegal under Georgia law. Judge J. Oscar Mitchell of DeKalb County Civil and Criminal Court fined King twenty-five dollars and gave him a year's probation. Any future arrests would be a violation of parole, and since acts of civil disobedience were a staple of black protests, King had to behave himself. Even so, when future NAACP chairman Julian Bond and other activists from the Student Nonviolent Coordinating Committee in Atlanta asked King to sit in with them at the segregated Magnolia Room in Rich's department store, he agreed.

He was one of thirty-five people arrested that day; after refusing to post bond, he spent his first night ever behind bars.

The others were quickly released, but for violating his parole, Judge Mitchell sentenced King to four months on a road gang. His hands cuffed and his legs placed in irons, he was thrown into the back of a police car and, in the middle of the night, driven to a penitentiary in rural Georgia. It marked what became a leitmotif of the movement: clueless, sadistic white officials playing directly into the hands of black protestors by making martyrs out of them. "People cannot devote themselves to a great cause without finding someone who becomes the personification of the cause," wrote Loudon Wainwright in *Life*. "People cannot become devoted to Christianity until they find Christ, to democracy until they find Lincoln and Jefferson and Roosevelt, to Communism until they find Marx and Lenin and Stalin." His own people had found King long ago, but now King's enemies coronated him.

But first, they had to spring him. A distraught Coretta King, five months pregnant at the time, called Wofford for help. Here, Wofford realized, was the perfect chance for Kennedy to show he cared. With Shriver's connivance—which meant going around Robert Kennedy, who would surely have disapproved—the candidate called and comforted her. The call lasted all of a minute and a half. After Coretta King recounted the call to the press, Robert Kennedy was predictably apoplectic—"fists tight, his blue eyes cold," as Wofford remembered it. "All you freelance bomb throwers had quite possibly cost John Kennedy the election," he fulminated, and he threatened to ground them for the rest of the campaign. But visceral and rigid as he was, Bobby Kennedy followed his own Newtonian laws: upon some reflection, his actions often prompted equal and opposite reactions. In other words, in what was to become a pattern with him, he could change his mind and "grow," suddenly and dramatically.

"Bobby Kennedy landed on me like a ton of bricks," said Shriver. "He scorched my ass on the long-distance telephone from New York. And then he found suddenly that the whole damned thing changed. Within twenty-four hours. The next thing you know he was leading the pack in the opposite direction." On second thought, it seemed, the lawyer in Robert Kennedy was offended: imprisoning a man for a misdemeanor, without a chance to post bail, was disgraceful. Someone, he grumbled, should call the judge to complain. And since no one else would, he did, from a pay phone somewhere on Long Island.

It's dubious that Kennedy's action was as spontaneous as it was later represented to be, which may be why his tone in that conversation—whether supplicating, collegial, or abusive—varies with different recollections. "Bob said he just woke up this morning and he was so damn mad that that cracker judge should put a decent American in jail for driving with an out-of-state driver's license, clearly on the grounds of color, and screwing up his brother's campaign to boot, that he just got the judge on the phone and said to him, 'Are you an American? Do you know what it means to be an American? You get King out of jail!'" went one of them. (In another version of the story, the conversation was entirely amicable. "Bob, it's nice to talk to you," the judge supposedly told him. "And I don't have any objection about doing that." According to Kennedy, the judge even came to visit him later at the Justice Department.)

A day into his four-month sentence, Martin Luther King was released. Louis Martin promptly made Robert Kennedy "an honorary brother." And as the *Pittsburgh Courier* put it, "these white folks"—really, John and Robert Kennedy—"have now made Dr. Martin Luther King, Jr., the biggest Negro in the United States."

(Some time afterward, Deputy Attorney General Byron White asked Wofford whether he thought that even for the man who was to become the nation's top law enforcement officer, calling a sitting judge on a pending case was unethical. Wofford replied that though it didn't warrant disbarment, it was worth at least a reprimand. "Well, you'll be very pleased to know that I'm the one who recommended to Bob that he call the judge," replied a clearly unamused White, whom John Kennedy would soon name to the Supreme

Court. Richard Nixon later said that though King's imprisonment had been a "bum rap," the attorney general had crossed an ethical line he would never have. "It would be completely improper for me or any other lawyer to call the judge," he wrote. "And Robert Kennedy should have known better than to do so.")

King never did officially endorse John Kennedy, but he came very close. ("Neutral against Nixon" was how Wofford put it.) He said he was "deeply indebted" to him, adding a few days later that Kennedy had "exhibited moral courage of a high order." Daddy King wasn't so cagy. True, he'd already endorsed Nixon, largely because *he* wasn't a Catholic. ("Imagine *Martin Luther King* having a bigot for a father!" John Kennedy marveled afterward.) But Kennedy's call to Coretta King changed everything for him. "I'll take a Catholic or the Devil himself if he'll wipe the tears from my daughter-in-law's eyes," he said. "I've got a suitcase full of votes—my whole church—for Senator Kennedy." The one exception was his son, whose official neutrality in electoral matters kept him even from voting.

Making it all the easier was that Nixon—whether waiting on Eisenhower to say something, or afraid of losing southern votes, or just slow on his feet—had said absolutely nothing about King's travails. "It was like he had never heard of me," King recalled. "A couple of phone calls," Ike later lamented, had changed everything. In fact, it was all carefully calculated—and, as it turned out, miscalculated. "All the while the great minds were meeting on this," journalist Ralph McGill recalled, "and they finally said, 'No. We've got a chance to carry Georgia and South Carolina.' So they telephoned around, and of course, then these Southern states said, 'No. We don't have anything to say on behalf of Martin Luther King.' And so the great moment passed."

The white press mostly missed the story; certainly, the Kennedy campaign wasn't about to publicize it. But on the Sunday before Election Day, millions of small, blue pamphlets descended upon black churches nationwide. Some were handed out indiscriminately, others with a more personal touch: had you entered Ebenezer Baptist Church in Chicago that Sunday, for instance, you might have gotten yours from Sargent Shriver, assisted that day by his son, Bobby, and his daughter, Maria. "The Case of 'No Comment Nixon' Versus A Candidate With a Heart, Senator Kennedy," they declared. "You could see the people taking them and carrying them home," Shriver remembered. "It was absolutely remarkable."

In states like Illinois, New Jersey, Michigan, South Carolina, and Delaware, black votes were probably decisive. Black voters had elected a President. So too, in a way, had Martin Luther King. Someone asked Robert Kennedy whether he was glad he'd called the judge. "Sure, I'm glad," he replied, "but I would hope I'm not glad for the reason you think I'm glad." In fact, there's no evidence that the experience either reflected or prompted a fundamental change in Kennedy's racial attitudes. King summarized the situation beautifully. "There are those moments when the politically expedient is the morally wise," he said.


The question now for President-elect Kennedy was what to do with the man who, as Marguerite Higgins of the *New York Herald Tribune* put it, had worked more intensely for his brother "than most people ever work for anything or anybody, including themselves"—or indeed, what Robert Kennedy wanted to do with himself. He looked half-heartedly into taking a teaching job at a Massachusetts university—perhaps as a way to inch into elected office up there. He spoke to a newspaper publisher about a foreign assignment—a reprise of a short gig in the Middle East in 1948 arranged by his father with the *Boston Post*—just to get away for a while. Any administration post at all would bring howls of nepotism. "They'd better retire me with Casey Stengel," joked Bobby, referring to the recently deposed manager of the New York Yankees.

But given his legal and prosecutorial experience, the logical slot was attorney general. One account has Connecticut governor Abraham Ribicoff turning down the job because "he didn't think a Jew should be putting Negro children in white Protestant schools in the South...at the instructions of a Catholic." But according to another, far more plausible, Joe Kennedy had decreed the outcome from the start. "Your brother Bobby busted his ass for you," he is said to have told John Kennedy. "He gave you his lifeblood. You know it, and I know it. By God, he deserves to be attorney general of the U.S., and by God, that's what he's going to be." ("Yes, sir," John Kennedy was said to have meekly replied, at least in one version of the story.) "He can throw all the people Dad doesn't like into jail," Eunice Shriver reportedly said. "That means we'll have to build more jails."

Bobby initially resisted. He was tired of chasing "bad men," he said, and ready to get away from his brother. He also knew that with the chance to pass civil rights legislation at nil, the Justice Department would be the center of things, and that his blood tie to the president would deny either of them cover: everything would be the work of the "Kennedy Brothers." (There'd be no hiding him on an airplane the way Richard Nixon had sequestered Attorney General William Rogers, architect of Eisenhower's civil rights policy, during a campaign stop in North Carolina.) "You would make a whale of a good attorney general," the syndicated newspaper columnist Drew Pearson, whom Kennedy had sought out for advice, told him. But "you would handle so many controversial questions with such vigor that your brother in the White House would be in hot water all the time."

Bobby polled his brain trust of elder mentors, including his old Senate boss, John McClellan; William O. Douglas; and J. Edgar Hoover. Only Hoover encouraged him to take it, and only because, he later explained, he hadn't known what else to say. Kennedy's reluctance — he turned down the job more than once — won praise from influential Washington columnist Joseph Alsop; it was, he wrote, "very unlike the hard, ruthless, and totally unscrupulous fellow Robert Kennedy has been portrayed as being." (Whenever Bobby *wasn't* ruthless, it was news.) But within a few weeks, over bacon and eggs in his brother's house, he relented. John Seigenthaler, who'd been with the two of them that morning, heard John Kennedy explain how he had no close friends in the cabinet, and how vexing race relations would be, and how he needed someone who'd level with him, and how if all these others he barely knew, like Robert McNamara and Dean Rusk and Adlai Stevenson, could sacrifice for him by taking positions with the new administration, then so could he. The president-elect then got up and went into the kitchen, either for effect or for more bacon and eggs. Bobby was about to respond when he returned and said, "So that's it, general. Let's go." Maybe if he appointed his brother in the middle of the night, John Kennedy teased, no one would notice.

But he did it in broad daylight, and some people were predictably outraged. Anthony Lewis, who'd developed an almost proprietary attitude toward the Justice Department while covering it, was "shocked and horrified": the boorish ruffian he'd so disliked at Harvard was taking over the place. The *Times* joined in the attack—an early illustration of what Bobby Kennedy considered its long vendetta against him, one rooted in what he saw as the paper's broader anti-Catholic animus, which was rooted in turn in the prejudices of the intellectual elite. "[The poet and historian] Peter Viereck once said that 'anti-Catholicism is the anti-Semitism of the intellectuals,'" Frank Mankiewicz once recalled. "He liked that." "If Robert Kennedy was one of the outstanding lawyers of the country, a pre-eminent legal philosopher, a noted prosecutor or legal officer at Federal or State level, the situation would have been different," it thundered. (Kennedy would joke about the paper's purported concern about nepotism, noting how the *Times*' publisher, Arthur O. "Punch" Sulzberger, was the son, grandson, and brother-in-law of prior *Times* publishers. "Punch and I both worked our way to the top through diligence and merit," he responded.)

Harris Wofford recalled that he was "appalled" by the appointment; to him, Robert Kennedy lacked "the fair and thoughtful cast of mind required of the nation's chief legal officer." Joining in the criticism was King. "We hadn't forgotten Bobby's role as a twenty-seven-year-old legal counsel to Senator Joe McCarthy in his rabid persecution of suspected communist spies and sympathizers," he recalled. But to him, there was no choice but to try to make it work. "As the head of the Justice Department, he's our number one target for all things we will have to do in our quest for freedom in this country," King told colleagues. "Somewhere in this man sits good. Your task from this moment on is to find his soul, find his moral center, and win him to our cause." In one meeting, Belafonte recalled, King slammed down his hand in frustration when no one could come up with anything good to say about Robert Kennedy. "Well, let's call this meeting closed," King said. It would resume, he went on, only once someone could find something complimentary to say about the guy, because the door to Robert Kennedy's office would be the door through which the civil rights movement would now have to pass.

"I was more wary of Bobby than Dr. King was," Belafonte, who said he reacted to Kennedy's appointment with "great horror," recalled. But here was another aspect of King's nonviolence: "to look the enemy in the eye and establish a mutual humanity." "To us, the chances of doing that with the cold and tightly wound Bobby Kennedy seemed very dim indeed," Belafonte later wrote, but this was King's command. From then on, Belafonte scoured "to find this place in which Bobby Kennedy existed, and to become more intimately involved with who he was."

Conservatives, on the other hand, backed the appointee as one of their own. "When a man builds a career all by himself, is it nepotism if that career received adequate recognition?" the right-wing commentator George Sokolsky asked in his column for Hearst. Back at the *Montgomery Advertiser*, Grover Hall conceded that Robert Kennedy's "seasoning" was "deficient," but that was a minor consideration; John Kennedy had put together a conservative cabinet—the liberals, he wrote, had been "cuckolded"—and Bobby Kennedy was part of that. He was tough and able, as well as the closest man to his brother. "All this we contend, even though the new Attorney General presumably will be more aggressive

As the civil rights movement grew, Ku Klux Klan membership surged; numerous
Klansmen were implicated in bombings and other atrocities of the era.

than any predecessor in race mixing adventures," Hall continued.
"When he impudently intervened in Georgia on behalf of the latter-
day Christian martyr Doctor King, you got the feeling he would
have, if possible at the time, dispatched a cavalry squadron to
rescue him from the pagans."

The January 1961 confirmation hearing was billed as Spartacus
facing the lions, Mary McGrory wrote in the *Washington Star*. The
Robert Kennedy who showed up for it, she wrote, "looked suitably
pale and tense, rather like a schoolboy about to undergo his orals.
He had a slightly rumpled air, and a wave of blondish hair falling

over his brow did not add materially to the impression that here was the soon-to-be legal officer of the republic." But the sailing was all smooth. When Republican senators alluded, very gently, to Kennedy's lack of experience, southern Democrats like James Eastland of Mississippi and John McClellan leaped to his defense. "The only thing I can think that I can say about Bob Kennedy is that he is young, and that is something he can cure," purred Sam Ervin of North Carolina.

Civil rights came up in the hearing, but just only briefly— disconcertingly so to Louis Lautier, who covered Washington for the National Negro Publishers Association. Kennedy was "very cautious and dexterous in bobbing and weaving," he said. James Reston of the *New York Times* agreed. "Mr. Kennedy was extremely careful not to say anything about civil rights that would trouble the South," he observed. Kennedy was promptly confirmed by voice vote. "All the Southerners were very much in favor of my being Attorney General," Kennedy later said. "The strongest support I received as Attorney General came from Southerners." And no one supported him more stalwartly than Eastland, the arch-segregationist head of the Judiciary Committee, who became a mentor and confidant to him during the civil rights crises he encountered at the Justice Department.

"I found it much more pleasant to deal with him than any of the so-called liberals in the House Judiciary Committee, or in other parts of Congress and the Senate," Kennedy was to recall, with the perverse, even sadistic, pleasure he often got from tweaking progressives. His southern senator friends might have felt slightly less fraternal with Kennedy had they known that, as the longtime editor of the *Washington Post*, Ben Bradlee, later asserted, Kennedy had sabotaged the possible appointment of one of their own, J. William Fulbright, to secretary of state. Bradlee was convinced Kennedy had leaked word that the Arkansas segregationist was under consideration to the *New York Herald Tribune* to scuttle an appointment which, as Bradlee put it, would have been "a terrible kick in the teeth to the Negroes."

Optically at least, the inauguration of John F. Kennedy marked a new beginning for black America, with blacks visible as never before. For thirty-six hours, anyway, the Kennedy administration didn't worry about offending southern sensibilities. "Only Jim Crow Will Be Absent," the *Amsterdam News* boasted. The show on inauguration eve featured Belafonte, Nat King Cole, and Ella Fitzgerald; Mahalia Jackson sang "The Star-Spangled Banner." *Jet*—its three photographers carrying fourteen cameras between them, it bragged—was kept busy documenting all the black dignitaries, celebrities, and campaign officials in attendance. One of Kennedy's black advisers had a chauffeur-driven car at his disposal, and in another "unprecedented advance," Simeon Booker got to follow the new president all Inauguration Day. According to Booker, "a widespread feeling that Kennedy will become the first Chief Executive to be sensitive to racial matters" brought "a lavish show of affection from Negroes." The new president even danced with black women on inauguration night. The Kennedy administration was to become known as the "New Frontier," a phrase cribbed from John Kennedy's acceptance speech at the 1960 Democratic National Convention and suggesting a dynamic new approach at home, abroad, and even in space after the somnolent Eisenhower years. Having helped bring it all about, the black community had every reason to think that it would be a key component, and beneficiary, of this national reinvigoration.

But for all its soaring rhetoric, Kennedy's legendary inaugural address did not mention civil rights or race. (It nonetheless inspired a black Air Force veteran named James Meredith to apply to the segregated University of Mississippi.) And nowhere to be seen at any of the commemorations were Sammy Davis, Jr., and his white (and pregnant) Swedish-born wife, May Britt. The gossip columnist Dorothy Kilgallen had it partially pegged: "Sammy's omission from the star-studded bill is generally regarded as a gesture of appeasement to the anti-integrationists," she wrote. (In fact, Joe Kennedy had weighed in on that as well.) From the outset, the Kennedys were in a bind: blacks had catapulted them into office, but southern segregationists would determine their effectiveness.

Though invited to the inaugural events, King did not attend. But for him, something even bigger loomed: a giant tribute in Carnegie Hall a week later, featuring many of the same black stars *and* Sammy Davis, Jr. It was Davis, along with Frank Sinatra, who'd come up with the idea several months earlier in a Las Vegas steam room during the filming of *Ocean's 11*. "I told Sinatra, 'We've got to do a benefit.' And Sinatra replied, 'Great! Dr. King deserves it. Let's do it in January.'" It was set for the 27th.

A letter went out from Belafonte listing the event's organizers (all the Rat Pack regulars: Sinatra, Dean Martin, Joey Bishop, Davis) and various sponsors (Sidney Poitier, Eleanor Roosevelt, Adam Clayton Powell, and Leonard Bernstein, among them) and promising "an unprecedented Theatrical Tribute to the greatest civil rights leader to emerge in the South since the Civil War." The object was to help King continue extending "the frontiers of liberty" into the "heartland of segregation." Tickets began at a few dollars; a hundred bucks got you two box seats plus the chance to meet King afterward.

At the gala itself, Poitier introduced Mahalia Jackson, who again sang the national anthem. Then came Count Basie, Tony Bennett, and a host of black performers who, as Henrietta Leith of the Associated Press put it, "are so good they don't get out of town—and sometimes don't even get out of Harlem." Belafonte read telegrams from President Kennedy and Eleanor Roosevelt and then introduced King. Any tribute to him, King said, was really a tribute to all those black people who'd walked in Montgomery and been jailed at the sit-ins, as well as to their "hundreds of thousands" of white allies. ("Several thousand of the latter were in his audience," noted Leith, "for it was overwhelmingly white.")

After going through his usual impressions—James Cagney, Cary Grant, et al.—Davis solemnly announced that "The Leader" had arrived, accompanied by "his drunken Italian friend." Dean Martin then sang a few numbers. And then, as Davis did an impersonation of Sinatra, the Chairman of the Board himself ran down the aisle toward the stage. He performed six songs of his own before all the others joined him. "They interrupted each other's songs with insults—sometimes slightly smutty—from mikes off stage; rolled in a cart loaded with liquor bottles and poured each other drinks; paraded on and off while one of the pack was trying to perform, generally living up to Davis' introduction: "Now comes the tumult," he'd said. It hardly comported with King's image of rectitude, but he was no prude and had to be pragmatic. Finally, the evening ended, nearly five hours after it began. Even those in the fancy seats had gotten their money's worth.

The night was a great financial success, putting $20,000 into the SCLC's shallow coffers, which came on top of the $37,000 raised during King's brief imprisonment. In the white South, though, the reviews were harsh. "A study in bottle diplomacy," a paper in Alexandria, Louisiana, called it, in an editorial titled "Rats in Carnegie Hall." "Such alcoholic antics to raise funds for the 'Committee to Aid the Southern Freedom Struggle' gives rise to questions on what manner of people these 'committeemen' be, and to what manner of 'reverend' Martin Luther King professes to be," it huffed. "It also may be wondered if Carnegie Hall will sponsor a benefit to focus attention on nearby Harlem with its filth, crime and corruption."

For Robert Kennedy and Martin Luther King, a new and promising era was beginning. But even if they were allies, they were tentative, wary. Meantime, the opposition was entrenched— and fierce.

In February 1960, two months after the Kings moved from Montgomery to Atlanta, members of the KKK left a terrifying message on their front lawn.

# THREE

# THE FACE OF COURAGE

"Please." "We urge you." "Must." "It is essential that." "Request immediate investigation of." "Situation desperate." "Gross violation." "Tragic and devastating racial holocaust." "Shames all decent Americans." "Reverend Abernathy and I earnestly hope." "Am greatly disturbed by." "A reign of terror exists in the state of Mississippi." "Dangerous." "I shudder to think what our nation has become." "Calamitous." "Irreparable."

"No." "Not now." "Not yet." "Impossible to make any commitments on the President's schedule." "Wait." "Wait a few months." "Wait until after the election." "Wait a few more years." "Please be assured that." "Not a matter in which this Department has jurisdiction." "No." "Can't." "No authority." Silence. Silence. Silence. Silence. Silence.

From the outset of the Kennedy administration, Martin Luther King and Robert Kennedy both collaborated and collided. They were largely interdependent, with all of the solicitude and manipulation and resentment that interdependence generates. King needed Kennedy's help, or at least his protection, to sustain and advance his movement. Kennedy needed King's cooperation to keep things from getting worse or undermining his brother's presidency. For King, Kennedy was an ally and an obstacle. For Kennedy, King was an ally and an irritant and maybe an embarrassment, reminding him of his own shortcomings.

JFK's most contentious appointment was his pick for attorney general: his brother, who had never written a trial brief or handled a federal case.

Their positions were asymmetrical. When they did interact, King was usually asking for something. But if Kennedy had more power, King had more autonomy: for all his problems, he was his own man, rather than one who served someone else. They had dramatically different mandates. King had a movement to run and a people to represent, while for Kennedy, civil rights was a subset of a subset, a small part of his official job, which was, in turn, a small part of his portfolio in the Kennedy administration. Civil rights were a crusade to one and a problem to be managed for the other. Whatever turbulence both men experienced, each was sure he was right. The tensions between them at the outset only intensified as the stakes rose; that was a sign that, separately and together, they were succeeding.

King's path was largely predictable—those who loathed him or admired him loathed him or admired him more. Kennedy's was surprising: former admirers quickly felt betrayed, while at least some skeptics slowly became more respectful. King was in the second group, but he let on much less than most: it was in the nature of his role that he could rarely appear satisfied, nor could he ever let down his guard. In fact, one rarely saw him smile, at least in public, at least in front of white people. It was a source of frustration to some white photographers, who grumbled that King always looked the same.

King was still finding his way, defining his next act, when the Kennedy administration got under way. Its rhetoric was promising, even soaring—the "New Frontier" tapped into classic American notions of limitless horizons—and its instincts seemed sound—surely an improvement over what had come before. But he also knew that on racial questions the new team was shaky and unreliable. The Kennedys were not entirely convincing converts to the cause and were held hostage by segregationist southern politicians.

There'd be no sweeping legislation, at least for a time. Instead, the White House planned to issue executive orders, which a president was free to do on his own—like its pledge to outlaw discrimination in federally funded housing—and make lots of appointments, including a few important ones. They were a way to thank, and buoy, and buy off the black community. And there were symbols. On the afternoon of his inauguration, John Kennedy directed the integration of the lily-white Coast Guard contingent that had marched past him that morning. Thanks to the Kennedys, the centennial of the bombardment of Fort Sumter would not be celebrated at a segregated facility. Once the space program got under way, there were even to be black astronauts. (The most perilous part of their mission, comedian and activist Dick Gregory later said, would be driving through the South to Cape Canaveral.)

Doing the right thing on civil rights while maintaining the Solid South: it was a delicate mission, but one which the confident and naïve New Frontiersmen felt they could accomplish. In those heady early days, there was even talk that the civil rights division of Robert Kennedy's Justice Department would prove so effective that it would put the NAACP's litigation arm—or even itself—out of business.

Perhaps predictably, Robert Kennedy's announced first priority wasn't civil rights at all, but nabbing hoodlums. (*The Enemy Within*, a book he'd written about racketeering, was being made into a movie with a screenplay by Budd Schulberg, who'd also written the script for *On the Waterfront*.) It was only one respect in which Kennedy had near-Hollywood status; his first press conference attracted more reporters "than the Justice Department usually sees in a month," Anthony Lewis wrote in the *New York Times*. Kennedy seemed more focused on the interstate traffic in pinball machines than the interstate travel of black bus riders. "He saw civil rights in 1961 as an issue in the middle distance, morally invincible but filled for the moment with operational difficulty," Arthur Schlesinger later wrote. When Mary McGrory sized up his first six months on the job, the topic of civil rights barely arose.

The scant effort devoted to the issue would be directed toward voting rights. Such work was both politically palatable (making comparatively few waves) and practical: from the ballot, Kennedy believed, all other rights would flow. It was certainly less emotional than school desegregation, though the administration would help communities (Atlanta, Dallas, Memphis) doing it on their own. Before long, dozens of pins — in Alabama, Mississippi, Louisiana, and elsewhere — stuck out of a map Kennedy hung near his desk. Each represented a different voting rights lawsuit his office had brought, though always only after local authorities had failed to fix things voluntarily first.

Underlining his low-key approach, Kennedy spurned the man who would clearly have been King's first choice to head the Justice Department's civil rights division, Harris Wofford, in favor of Burke Marshall, a corporate lawyer (also white) who, though brilliant, meticulous, and unflappable, had no track record on race. "It sounds harsh to say it now, but we didn't want someone who would just cry for the Negro," Kennedy later explained. "We wanted someone who would do what had to be done in a proper, legal way, someone with judgment." For all his passion and expertise, Wofford lacked one key prerequisite: a commitment to do what Robert Kennedy wanted, which is what John Kennedy wanted, which was not necessarily what King or blacks collectively wanted.

Walking around the Justice Department, Robert Kennedy had the same kind of epiphany his brother had just experienced at the inaugural parade. "Where're the Negroes?" he asked. Horrified by the scant number of black lawyers at the place — by one count, 10 out of 950 — he made sure letters were sent to every law school dean in the country urging them to send them their most promising black students. (One, Thelton Henderson, was assigned to handle civil rights investigations in the South, though he had to stay on military bases when working there.)

The excitement, and the potential, and some of the reality of Robert Kennedy's arrival on the scene was best captured that May. He had been tapped to give the annual Law Day address at the University of Georgia, which had been painfully desegregated only a few months earlier. Speaking about race in the heart of Dixie was a classic move for Robert Kennedy, who, far more than his brother, relished personal challenges; while Kennedy's stance on civil rights was murky, his machismo was not. Before his arrival in Athens, Georgia, local police had arrested five people for painting "Kennedy Go Home" and other messages on the sidewalks. Top state officials managed to be somewhere else. (Governor Vandiver was at the Kentucky Derby.) The audience of sixteen hundred included the school's two pioneering black students, the future journalist Charlayne Hunter and Hamilton Holmes.

On how he planned to do his job, Kennedy was blunt. "You may ask: will we enforce the Civil Rights statutes? The answer is: yes, we will," he said. On his views of the *Brown* decision, which outlawed segregated public education, he was equally clear: he supported it. "But my belief doesn't matter—it is now the law," he added. "I say to you today that if the orders of the court are circumvented, the Department of Justice will act. We will not stand by and be aloof. We will move." It was a far cry from the silence or evasions of the Eisenhower era—or even the earliest days of the Kennedy presidential campaign. At the same time, it was an appeal to the law-and-order instincts of ostensibly patriotic southerners.

"For fifteen or twenty agonizingly long seconds there was silence," Kennedy's spokesman Edwin Guthman wrote in his memoirs. "Then applause spread through the hall. It continued for almost a minute, with many people standing as they clapped." A student reporter said the cheers were "as long and as loud" as what followed Georgia's victory over Georgia Tech. Praise quickly came from Jackie Robinson ("most encouraging"), the NAACP, and Eleanor Roosevelt ("It must have taken much courage"). Martin Luther King sent Bobby Kennedy a congratulatory telegram. Ralph McGill of the *Atlanta Constitution* wrote, "Never before, in all of its travails of by-gone years, has the South heard so honest and understandable a speech from any Cabinet member."

But the bar on such things was set very, very low. What was just as striking about the speech was how deferential, and gentle, and conciliatory, and cautious Kennedy had been. There were no references to the shameful racial record of Georgia; in fact, he praised the state for what it had already accomplished, however minimal that was, and acknowledged how difficult it must have been. He stressed that bigotry was a national, rather than a local, disease. He pledged that before the Kennedy administration ever resorted to military force to enforce court orders, as Eisenhower had done in Little Rock, it would turn to the courts; and before that, it would give southerners a chance to mend their ways themselves. Once again, he underlined his own ties to the region—southern employers, southern teachers, southern colleagues, southern classmates.

And he flattered southern sensibilities. Southerners, he said, "have a special respect for candor and plain talk. They certainly don't like hypocrisy." And on that, he suggested, they had a beef: northern muck-a-mucks who preached tolerance while leading segregated lives. (Though he didn't mention it that day, Kennedy would soon resign from the racially exclusionary Metropolitan Club in Washington.) Southerners must abandon white supremacy not necessarily because it was wrong, he implied, but because, in a time when the Soviets were rubbing America's nose in all of its racial problems, it was unpatriotic.

Once it was in place, the Kennedy administration kept King at a certain distance, cultivating his great rival—the more urbane, congenial, and manageable Roy Wilkins of the NAACP—instead. (To Robert Kennedy—and, even more, to his brother—King, who was sometimes shy around white people, would have seemed ill-at-ease, stuffy, and perhaps censorious by comparison. One of Kennedy's black advisers, Frank Reeves, suggested that the president meet separately with King because he favored discussions on a "high moral plane, without the intrusion of practical details.") When, in March 1961, King asked John Kennedy for a meeting, the president's chief of staff, Kenneth O'Donnell, put him off. (Before long *Jet*, which both kvelled over the Kennedys and monitored them closely for telltale signs of ingratitude, had deemed O'Donnell, Robert Kennedy's Harvard football teammate, the obstructionist-and-ingrate-in-chief. "The President—or at least his aides, particularly none-of-my-best-friends-are-colored Ken O'Donnell—have a short memory," it complained.)

Robert Kennedy *did* meet with King and other civil rights leaders that spring. And at least as Kennedy saw it, his increasingly familiar message—voter registration, yes; legislation, no, at least not yet—was not what King wanted to hear, or do. "I said that it wasn't as dramatic; and that perhaps there wasn't going to be as much publicity...but I thought that's where they should go," Kennedy recalled. "Martin Luther King and I didn't see eye to eye on some of these matters."

The two men would not remain so relatively detached for very long.

On April 26, James Farmer, the national director of the Congress of Racial Equality (CORE), a civil rights group with pacifist roots and principles, wrote to both John and Robert Kennedy about "Freedom Ride, 1961." In early May, he went on, some fifteen of its members—black and white, southern and northern, men and women—would board two buses in Washington and travel throughout the South, testing whether cities were honoring a recent Supreme Court ruling banning segregated train stations and bus terminals. That was the official goal. Unofficially, it was to goad southern bigots into doing something horrifying enough to shock and arouse the American conscience, something a racially mixed group of travelers taking seats in traditionally segregated buses, waiting rooms, and luncheonettes seemed pretty certain to do.

King and others had warned Robert Kennedy when they'd met that the Interstate Commerce Commission wasn't enforcing the ruling. But the attorney general and the president seemed unconcerned; neither answered Farmer's letter. Simeon Booker of *Jet* told Robert Kennedy he was going along with the group, and that there would probably be trouble. "I wish I could go with you," Kennedy, puzzlingly, replied. The first problems came in Rock Hill, North Carolina; the Freedom Rider targeted was twenty-one-year-old John Lewis, later head of the Student Nonviolent Coordinating Committee and, after that, a United States

The attack in May 1961 on a bus carrying Freedom Riders through Alabama was the first in a series, forcing a hesitant Robert Kennedy into action.

congressman. Attempting to enter the white waiting room, he was clubbed over the head and knocked to the ground. And things would only get worse. "You will never make it through Alabama," King (who, unlike some civil rights leaders, supported the Freedom Rides) whispered to Booker when the group reached Atlanta.

The next day, one of the Riders' two buses, this one belonging to Greyhound, was torched six miles outside of Anniston, Alabama; its passengers were very nearly trapped inside. When the other, a Trailways bus, reached the terminal in Anniston, a mob of Klansmen mauled those on board. When the Freedom Riders regrouped and headed for Birmingham, their attackers rode brazenly with them, minding them from the front seats. However ambivalent black attitudes toward Robert Kennedy may have been, to southern rednecks he already embodied the new and more tolerant regime in Washington whose emollient talk on race had fomented such protests. To his southern critics, he might as well have joined the Freedom Riders and was just as deserving of their blows. "Just tell Bobby, and we'll do him in, too," one of the attackers repeatedly taunted the bloodied victims at the back of the bus. When they arrived in Birmingham, the Freedom Riders were beaten again, not; the policemen of Eugene "Bull" Connor, Birmingham's notorious commissioner of public safety, conveniently showing up only fifteen or twenty minutes after the bus did. (It was Mother's Day, Connor explained; he was short-staffed.)

Robert Kennedy set up a command post in his office, trying to get the Freedom Riders to their destination and, thereby, off the road and out of harm's way and his hair. Wasn't there a way to get the bus to Montgomery? he asked George Cruit, the manager of the Greyhound terminal in Birmingham. Cruit's secretary transcribed the exchange. There wasn't, Cruit replied: fearing for their lives, his drivers wouldn't drive. How about colored drivers? How about school bus drivers? How about Cruit himself? None of those things would work.

"Well, Mr. Cruit, I think you should—had better be getting in touch with Mr. Greyhound or whoever Greyhound is," Kennedy went on. "I am...the Government...is going to be very much upset if this group does not get to continue their trip. Under the law they are entitled to transportation provided by Greyhound, and we are looking for you to get them on their way." The reference to "Mr. Greyhound" charmed some when it made the papers, but it was Kennedy's suggestion that the government had an emotional stake in the Freedom Rides that stuck. A dummy labeled "Robert Bobbie Sox Kennedy" was soon hung in effigy in Alabama, and Kennedy himself was saddled with the image of a co-conspirator. "It was published in the South...as proof of how ruthless Kennedy was," Burke Marshall later recalled. "I never recovered from it," added Kennedy. It was, he said, "just like waking the newspapermen up."

John Seigenthaler, who'd been dispatched from Washington, arranged to have the Freedom Riders flown to New Orleans. But another batch soon arrived in Alabama. With local and state authorities, including Governor John Patterson, refusing to protect them, they, too, were beaten — this time in Montgomery. And Seigenthaler, who had insisted that southerners who saluted the flag would never flout the law, landed in the hospital with a concussion.

The degree to which the Kennedys had underestimated the virulence and violence of southern race hatred sank in when one of their own — a white man at that — was victimized. It was the latest of Robert Kennedy's epiphanies. "He took it as if he had been down in Montgomery himself and been hit," the writer Peter Maas, a close Kennedy friend, later said. "He was in this thing for good then." Seeking to avoid using troops, Kennedy sent some hastily assembled federal marshals to restore order. Fifty of them escorted Martin Luther King when he flew in on the night of May 21 for a rally in support of the Freedom Riders at the First Baptist Church, where Ralph Abernathy was the pastor.

Fears quickly arose that the mob of around three thousand whites that gathered outside the crowded church would try to burn it down; in all likelihood, only the marshals and their tear gas kept it from happening. Having found shelter in the basement with Abernathy, John Lewis, and Rev. Wyatt Tee Walker, among others, King spoke repeatedly with Kennedy throughout the night. Strung together, in fact, it was probably their most protracted and intense conversation ever, with King alternately panicked, frustrated, and accusatory (shouting at Kennedy so loudly at one point that Kennedy had to hold the phone away from his ear) and Kennedy alternately reassuring, defensive, exasperated, and lighthearted — or at least trying to be. (So long as King was in church, "he might say a prayer for us," Kennedy told him at one point. "He didn't think that was very humorous," Kennedy later recalled.)

At one point, King berated Kennedy for letting the situation continue. "Now, reverend, don't tell me that," Kennedy replied. "You know just as well as I do that if it hadn't been for the United States marshals, you'd be as dead as Kelsey's nuts right now." It was an archaic expression about car parts and not, as Kennedy later surmised, something old and Irish and probably obscene. But the metaphor captured some of his attitude toward King: flippant, condescending, a bit resentful.

And, once the audacious Kennedy detected fear in King, a bit contemptuous, too. "The failure was more RFK's than King's—the goal of the civil rights leader at that moment was to get desperately needed help, not win machismo points with RFK," the Kennedy biographer Evan Thomas has written. King's gratitude and Kennedy's magnanimity were finite. The National Guard eventually restored order; King, and his flock, and Kennedy, all headed off belatedly to bed. "Good night—let's do this again some time," Kennedy joked to his beleaguered colleagues at the Justice Department. To King, it was just another brush with death. "You still thirty-two, Martin?" one of King's colleagues asked him a couple of days later. "Still thirty-two," King replied. "Thirty-two, hoping to make thirty-three."

Insisting that the Freedom Riders had made their point, that sooner or later some of them would get themselves killed, and that they were complicating things for President Kennedy abroad (he was about to meet the Soviet premier Nikita Khrushchev in Vienna), Robert Kennedy called for a "cooling off" period. "We have been cooling off for one hundred years," James Farmer retorted. "If we got any cooler, we'd be in a deep freeze." The Freedom Rides continued. (Murray Kempton was aboard a Trailways bus from Montgomery to Meridian when the Freedom Riders broke out into a calypso: "Come Mr. Kenn-ee-dee, take me out of my miseree.") But officials—largely, it seemed, Robert Kennedy and James Eastland, who spoke to one another thirty or forty times in couple of days—had worked out a deal that was face-saving for themselves and, arguably, life-saving for the riders: the buses were escorted to Mississippi, where the riders would be arrested and jailed for disturbing the peace. Unfair, yes, but to Kennedy, it beat beatings.

Here again, the two men were at odds: Robert Kennedy wanted the riders sprung; King wanted them in place, reproaching American democracy. ("Jail, not bail.") Their conversation on May 24, 1961, captures all at once the edginess and distance between them; their different points of view (soaring and philosophical vs. coldly pragmatic); the thin layer of civility in their conversations; the different powers—moral and official—that they held over one another; their strong wills, and poise, and toughness; the emerging respect between them both as adversaries and confederates.

> King: It's a matter of conscience and morality. They must use their lives and their bodies to right a wrong.

> Kennedy: That is not going to have the slightest effect on what the government is going to do in this field or any other. The fact that they stay in jail is not going to have the slightest effect on me.

> King: Perhaps it would help if students came down here by the hundreds—by the hundreds of thousands.

> Kennedy: The country belongs to you as much as to me. You can determine what's best just as well as I can, but don't make statements that sound like a threat. That's not the way to deal with us.

There was a brief silence.

> King: It's difficult to understand the position of oppressed people. Ours is a way out—creative, moral, and nonviolent. It is not tied to black supremacy or communism, but to the plight of the oppressed. It can save the soul of America. You must understand that we've made no gains without pressure and I hope that pressure will always be moral, legal, and peaceful.

> Kennedy: But the problem won't be settled in Jackson, Mississippi, but by strong federal action.

> King: I'm deeply appreciative of what the administration is doing. I see a ray of hope, but I am different than my father. I feel the need of being free now!

Kennedy: Well, it all depends on what you and the people in jail decide. If they want to get out, we can get them out.

King: They'll stay.

"It's a difficult thing to teach a President and his brother, who is a lawyer, about civil disobedience," King later wrote.

The attorney general's attitude infuriated James Hicks of the *Amsterdam News*. Kennedy, he wrote, "has snapped his finger to you and me and said: 'Okay—that's enough now! If you keep on fighting, you will embarrass ME!'" He continued:

> And when he said that both you and I at first reacted like we have reacted for 40 years—we stopped short like trained animals—because we simply have been brainwashed to react to 'good' white people like Pavlov's dog. But our kids just kept on fighting like Hell, because to them Robert Kennedy was simply another white man who pulls on his pants one leg at a time like everyone else. . . . So what happens? Our children are sitting in a Mississippi jail still fighting, by starving themselves inside the jail, and Bob Kennedy is standing on the steps of the White House demanding that we use our paternal love to persuade or force our children to give up on the fight so that he and his brother and our government won't be embarrassed.

But in the white press, Robert Kennedy got excellent reviews. "Late into the night he has been at his desk doing an unorthodox but thorough job," wrote Helen Thomas of United Press International. "Most of the work has been on the telephone. There have been calls to Alabama Gov. John Patterson and calls to the Rev. Martin Luther King—two major antagonists in the racial explosion. He used the same tone of voice with each man—patient, soothing, cajoling, but unrelenting. Sometimes he would chew gum. Sometimes he would put his feet on the desk and lean back in his swivel chair. Sometimes he would twist the holy medal around his neck." After watching him in action, wrote Louis

Cassels of the *New York World-Telegram and Sun*, "you don't feel like calling him Bobby anymore."

Kennedy had grown fed up with the Freedom Riders: he thought them unpatriotic and a little flaky. But here, too, his first and second impulses diverged: part of him realized they were right. According to King's most important adviser, Stanley Levison, it was Martin Luther King who urged Kennedy to lean on the Interstate Commerce Commission, which had jurisdiction over the matter, to issue regulations implementing the Supreme Court decision on segregated travel facilities. And when Kennedy said it couldn't be done, Levison recalled, King replied, "Well, I think if we keep the Freedom Rides going and your lawyers keep looking, they'll find the authority." By May 29, they had. The ICC order took effect on November 1. In bus and train stations throughout the South, the "White" and "Colored Only" signs came tumbling down.

In spite of the Freedom Ride victory, still unclear was whether the ICC order would be enforced, especially in the most resistant communities. That was what Jerome Smith and four other CORE volunteers set out to ascertain in November 1961 when they left New Orleans for one of the deepest pockets of white resistance, McComb, Mississippi. For Smith, such activities were nothing new: inspired by his merchant seaman father, as a ten-year-old he'd removed the screen separating the races on the local buses. An older black woman fended off the whites about to turn on him, pledging to take care of the uppity boy herself. She'd dragged him off the bus, put her arms around him, and told him, "Never stop." And he hadn't. In May of that year, Smith had been arrested in Jackson for attempting to integrate the local Trailways terminal; he'd only just been released from the infamous state penitentiary in Parchman. And before that, he had been jailed for trying to desegregate the lunch counters of Woolworth's and McCrory's in New Orleans. But for being incarcerated, Smith would have been on one of the inaugural Freedom Rides. The Justice Department knew of Smith's

work—he'd met once with Burke Marshall in Washington—and Marshall had given him the number of Robert Kennedy's office should he ever find himself in trouble.

The group's arrival in McComb was much anticipated: they did not operate by stealth. Robert Kennedy had already spoken about it to the mayor. Federal marshals had been brought in and were stationed across the state line in Louisiana awaiting orders. FBI agents (by one count, twelve of them), the press, and the Klan—everyone, it seemed, but the McComb police—were at the terminal when the bus pulled in. The group walked into the station and demanded service at the lunch counter while Smith made his way to the ticket window. There, a short, wiry white man of about thirty-five or so, jumped him and began beating him with brass knuckles. "The Negro doubled over and ducked his head under a rain of blows to the back of the neck, the shoulder and the stomach," one reporter related. "'I'll kill him! I'll kill him! I'll kill him!' yelled the white." Other men soon joined in the assault. Smith offered no resistance: it was a tenet of nonviolent protest. The attack might have been a fatal, Smith later said, had a man he'd spotted outside the station joined in the melee. But Smith had looked him in the eye and bidden him "good morning," and the man did not participate; it was a lesson—about the power of small interchanges to transform the human spirit—he'd learned from Martin Luther King, whom he'd met a couple times and read as well.

Battered and bloodied, the black protestors staggered out of the terminal and found their way to the black part of town. Only there could Smith find a doctor—a black doctor—to stitch up his lacerations. "Get Bobby Kennedy on the phone!" Smith shouted to one of his fellow Freedom Riders, Dorotha Smith. She looked at him, as she later put it, as if he'd taken too many blows the head, only to hear him bark out the number: RE 7-8200, extension 2154. "May

Stokely Carmichael, John Lewis, and Jerome Smith were among the Freedom Riders arrested on groundless charges and beaten by assailants brandishing bricks, knives, clubs, and pipes. The experience led many to question the efficacy of nonviolence.

I talk to Attorney General Bobby Kennedy?" she asked the man who'd answered. "This is he," Kennedy replied. Smith then talked briefly to Kennedy: his head injuries made speaking difficult. Kennedy asked what he could do to help. Treat the situation as he would if his own brother were one of the protesters, Smith told him. Kennedy offered to have the FBI drive the group back to New Orleans. Instead they went back to the terminal. Only the large crowd gathered outside kept them from going back in again, and probably getting themselves killed. The next day another delegation from New Orleans—minus Smith, who was too injured to go—officially desegregated the bus terminal.

Kennedy pledged a "complete" investigation from the FBI, but exonerated most of the people of McComb; only a few bad actors were to blame, he said. He congratulated the mayor for maintaining law and order on the second day, though several photographers and reporters were attacked. He did not follow up with Smith, who would be beset by his injuries—blurred vision, dizziness, headaches, and pain around his jaw and legs—ever afterward. No one was ever prosecuted for the beatings.

Kennedy later insisted that when it came to racial matters, he and his brother read from the same missal. "I don't think I ever had a conversation with my brother about whether we should or should not do a particular thing," he said. "It was all sort of so automatic and understood."

That wasn't how it looked. Perhaps because they were both so clearly alike and yet so recognizably different, people were forever parsing John and Robert Kennedy; few thought them perfectly in sync, even though, as the columnist Joseph Alsop saw it, that's precisely what they were. "Bobby never diverged for one instant from his brother's views, nor did he ever really consider anything except his brother's interest," he said. So what were the differences between the two on civil rights, and given Bobby Kennedy's monomaniacal devotion to John Kennedy, did they even matter?

Most observers, white and black, thought Robert Kennedy the more engaged, both for better and for worse. Segregationists considered Bobby the bad cop, egging John Kennedy on. Though the brothers were part of a common enterprise, Governor Patterson of Alabama never seems to have stopped liking John Kennedy. But Robert Kennedy he loathed. "In my judgment, Mr. Robert Kennedy either did not care or he did not have any understanding to amount to anything of our problems down here," he said. "It was 'you see it my way, or else.'" An official from the White Citizens' Council in Montgomery called on the president to fire the attorney general, who from its perspective was clearly freelancing. And of course, that had been John Kennedy's original intention for Bobby: as a buffer, shock absorber, decoy, and diversion—someone to leech off some of the venom.

Others took the opposite view: Bobby's mission was to protect his brother, which meant soft-peddling (or obstructing) civil rights. To these people, he was a drag on the more liberal, open-minded president, always weighing things, thinking pragmatically, placing political survival first. "The new Administration's central civil rights strategy—don't risk the loss of southern votes on other issues by pressing civil rights legislation—is the Attorney General's brainchild," Rowland Evans of the *Herald Tribune*, one of Robert Kennedy's closest friends in the press, wrote in January 1962. Civil rights workers like Jerome Smith were especially embittered, feeling that when they carried on precisely the work that Robert Kennedy's Justice Department claimed to support, they were left in the lurch. While FBI agents stood around, he complained, American citizens "were being beaten like dogs in the street." Kennedy's defense was invariably the same: the feds weren't the police. The police—the *local* police—were the police.

But to another group—Jackie Robinson among them—Robert Kennedy was John Kennedy's better angel. When the administration tried to curb the Freedom Rides, Robinson suggested it had only been because someone had "pulled the Attorney General's coat and told him to take the 'go slow' and the 'cool off' line." "I don't know whether it was Big Brother who did it," he wrote. "I sort of suspect that it was." A few months later, he called Robert Kennedy "a champion scrapper and a man of very deep convictions" and added, "I do not think our President is straight down the line on civil rights like Bob Kennedy."

John Lewis agreed: Robert Kennedy helped "educate" his more cautious brother and "bring him along." "He is, the signs show, more passionate and obsessed with the need to right the world's wrongs even than his brother is," Murray Kempton wrote. "The Administration figure to mastermind civil rights action is not a White House staffer—but Atty. Gen. Kennedy," Simeon Booker wrote in *Jet*. "He is considered the most accessible, active and gets a faster response. Thus, the Justice Dept. is [the] civil rights lane."

To those on the inside, things were complicated and evolving. Wofford later wrote that John Kennedy started out more enthusiastically, eager to use executive actions aggressively, while Robert Kennedy, more closely tied to southern politicians, would have resisted. But over time, he said, their roles reversed, with John Kennedy receding and Robert becoming ever more active and committed. "As he then developed, Bob Kennedy, in some sense, was the Puritan," he wrote. "For him, this became a black and white issue, a moral issue, and he responded immediately and strenuously on many issues in contrast to Kennedy, the President, who began to balance the thing much more." He continued:

> I think the greatest difference between the two that I saw was that Bob Kennedy, among other things, would ask in a very moral way, "Is this right or wrong?" You know, "Should we morally be doing it or should we not?" And then he would figure out whether he can do it. But I don't think [John] Kennedy would let himself say, "Morally, I ought to do this but politically I can't so I'm going to have to wait." . . . Most of [John Kennedy's] key decisions — anything really cutting in civil rights—were made alone by Bob Kennedy. . . . Bob's influence became good, better and better, day by day, in this whole field.

That was what Burke Marshall told the writer Victor Navasky. "The more he saw…the more he understood," he said of the attorney general. "The more you learned about how Negroes were treated in the South…the madder you became. You know he always talked about the hypocrisy. That's what got him. By the end of a year he was so mad about that kind of thing it overrode everything else." When Navasky asked Marshall to trace the arc of Kennedy's civil rights consciousness, "his right arm shot up to the sky." The contrast between the two brothers is starkest in Steven Levingston's 2017 book, *Kennedy and King*. Until the final few months of his presidency, he writes, John Kennedy was a nearly total passive bystander, all but abdicating to his younger brother. Just as he had "assigned his battles to his older brother, Joe" in prep school, Levingston claims, "in the White House, he let his little brother, Bobby, become the face of courage."

King's longtime lawyer, Clarence Jones, said he viewed the two Kennedys as a unit, largely interchangeable, with one devoted solely to serving the other. "He looked at the Kennedys—they weren't *bad* people; they were *nice* people. But they were first of all *political* people," he said. "They were people concerned with making the political expedient calculus, not the moral calculus. Bobby Kennedy was interested in protecting his brother."

"You can fault the Kennedys in many ways on civil rights, but there are three things for which you must give them credit: their talk, their appointments, and Bobby Kennedy," the head of the Americans for Democratic Action and one of the liberal stalwarts of mid-twentieth-century politics, Joseph Rauh, was to say. Those appointments included judgeships. By May 1961, *Jet* described the novel spectacle of black lawyers actually jockeying for positions in the federal judiciary. That September, Thurgood Marshall was named to the United States Court of Appeals. (Bobby Kennedy had reacted angrily a few months earlier when Marshall, the trailblazing NAACP litigator, had spurned his offer of a seat on a federal trial court. "That's the trouble with you people! You want too much too fast!" he'd exclaimed. Marshall found him like his old man: "cold, calculating.")

When a seat opened on the Supreme Court in 1962, Robert Kennedy had wanted to promote the only other black federal appellate judge, William Hastie. "It would just have a helluva impact around the world," Kennedy later said. On this, he agreed with King, who supported the choice. But when asked about it, Chief Justice Earl Warren and Justice William O. Douglas nixed the idea: Hastie was too conservative for their blood.

On the other side of the ledger, part of what King called the administration's "schizophrenic" stance on this issue, were the several segregationist judges the Kennedys were bound to name at the behest of southern senators. The most egregious—he once compared some blacks seeking to register to vote to "a bunch of chimpanzees"—was Harold Cox of Mississippi, the one-time college roommate of James Eastland. The appointments were embarrassing enough for Robert Kennedy to apologize for them in a letter to Eleanor Roosevelt. And they prompted outrage from King. Clarence Jones recalled a tense conversation between Bobby Kennedy and King after one of Kennedy's judicial selections blocked a demonstration. "The discussion got very heated, because Dr. King said, 'If your brother had not appointed all these segregationist judges, we wouldn't be in a situation like this,'" he recalled. (Jones depicted King's feelings about Robert Kennedy more bleakly than some others: King didn't dislike him, he said, because King didn't dislike *anybody*. "He believed every sinner can be redeemed," Jones said.

In October, King had his first formal meeting with President John F. Kennedy. (It came after an hour with Robert Kennedy, during which King learned that three key railroad lines had agreed to desegregate their services.) The meeting with the president was in the private quarters of the White House; the administration continued to keep its relationship with him under wraps.

The tour that followed included the Lincoln Bedroom, the perfect place for King to push one of his pet projects: the issuance of a second Emancipation Proclamation, one outlawing segregation in all forms, on the centennial of the first. Bobby had already dismissed the idea, saying it went far beyond what any president could do. But the more diplomatic John Kennedy asked King for more details. (Following up on the president's invitation, in May 1962, King submitted an elaborate, leather-bound legal brief on behalf of a second Emancipation Proclamation, complete with quotes from Woody Guthrie and Frederick Douglass and— copiously—John F. Kennedy himself. He also announced plans to collect five million signatures for a petition to be presented to the president. King even made moves to reserve the Lincoln Memorial for a New Year's Eve signing ceremony. His optimism was touching but unwarranted, and his submission went unacknowledged. After such a snub, King would surely have been miffed to learn that Kennedy had honored the Emancipation Proclamation privately, purchasing (for $9,500) a printed copy of it signed by Abraham Lincoln, and hanging it at Hickory Hill, his home outside Washington. (In 2010 that copy sold for nearly $4 million.)

It may have been on this visit—the timing is uncertain—that the White House elevator supposedly taking King up to Kennedy's private quarters made an unexpected detour to the basement, where King encountered Jacqueline Kennedy sporting blue jeans and a soot-stained face.

"Oh, Dr. King, you would be so thrilled if you could have just been with me in the basement this morning," the First Lady said. "I found a chair right out of the Andrew Jackson period—a beautiful chair."

"Yes, yes—is that so?" King very decorously replied.

"I've just got to tell Jack about that chair," she said once the elevator had made its way back upstairs, only promptly to excuse herself: "You probably have other things to talk to him about, don't you?"

The small talk helped relax King, Wofford recalled, which in turn relaxed the president. "There was always a strain in his dealing with King, who came on with a moral tone that was not Kennedy's style," Wofford later wrote. (Besides, King represented civil rights, which to the Kennedys "promised only headaches and political losses." King lamented to Wofford afterward that for all his political smarts and skills, John Kennedy lacked the "moral passion" for the job.)

In late October, film director Otto Preminger announced that King would soon be featured in a fictionalized version of Washington, appearing as one "Senator King" from Georgia in the film version of Allen Drury's best-selling novel *Advise and Consent.* Preminger insisted it wasn't a "publicity gimmick," but a "positive statement for this country here and abroad": "It should indicate that it is possible for a Negro to be elected to the United States Senate at any time, now or in the future," he said. For King's services, $5,000 would be donated to the SCLC. But it seemed that King had given neither his advice nor consent or else had sudden second thoughts. Levison quickly drafted a statement for him expressing fears that southerners "would have been inflamed" by such a portrayal, which in any case "could not be of any significance in advancing civil rights." The deal was quickly scotched.

What he didn't say was that there hadn't been a black senator from the South since Reconstruction, and wasn't about to be one now. The widely read liberal *New York Post* columnist James Wechsler did just that. "There is, of course, about as much prospect of Dr. King being elected to the Senate from Georgia, now or in any foreseeable future, as there is of my being summoned to manage the Yankees," he said.

In late November, as Robert Kennedy rounded out his first year in his post, Wechsler, who was to study him more minutely than anyone else, charting his evolution and divining his political prospects, visited him at the Justice Department. He was struck by Kennedy's enduring youthfulness—his tenure thus far "has exacted no visible toll"—and his informality: whatever else they were, these Kennedys weren't stuffed shirts. And his diffidence: "He is a gracious, shy, self-conscious man for whom private confrontation is less comfortable than it is for the President."

With Wechsler, too, Kennedy preached the gospel of voting rights. Wechsler, too, was shown that map of the South with all those pins in it. (Wechsler feared that Kennedy "perhaps underestimates the yearning of so many Negroes to affirm by acts of daring that now is the time to stand up to the racists, and to challenge the law's delay.") His greatest test, Wechsler predicted, would come less on civil rights, which were suddenly fashionable, and more on issues like wiretapping, where people were divided and Kennedy's prosecutorial background made him suspect. So he wondered, too, whether Kennedy would take on J. Edgar Hoover. (A year and a half later, he thought he had his answer. "Like all his predecessors, Bobby Kennedy clears his throat when the FBI director coughs," he wrote.)

Just where Bobby Kennedy would land in life was a mystery, for Wechsler, too, sensed in him an inner turbulence that would not be resolved anytime soon. "Beneath the surface there is a struggle for his political soul, which may be one of the large dramas of the coming years," Wechsler wrote after the meeting. "For one thing is clear; he has a long, lively political future ahead of him. After all, he will not be 50 until 1975." And that was a very long way off.

Most of the interactions between Kennedy and King took place on the phone following nonviolent actions that provoked violent reactions.

# FOUR
# THE UNKINDEST CUT

There was one more thing, apart from domineering fathers, that Martin Luther King, Jr., and Robert Kennedy shared: J. Edgar Hoover hated both of them. In fact, on his private "Public Enemies" list, they held two of the top three slots. (The third was a former FBI official with whom Hoover had feuded.) But since Kennedy was technically his boss, Hoover could hate King with greater abandon and impunity. He could also try to enlist Kennedy to hate King—or at least to distrust him and to monitor his every move. Ideally, he could even get them to destroy each other.

Hoover's hatred of Kennedy was straightforward: Kennedy was a usurper—someone who was monitoring him, inhibiting him, regulating him, pressuring him (to hire black agents and shift resources from warmed-over communist conspiracies to organized crime). He also resented Kennedy for failing to kowtow to him as generations of attorneys general without presidents for brothers had always done—and maybe, for fixing to get rid of him once that brother was reelected. (He also despised Kennedy's informal style, so alien to the G-man: working in shirtsleeves, his feet atop his desk.) Hoover was another one who found the key to Kennedy's personality in his size. "Sneaky little son of a bitch," he called him.

Hoover also had little use for blacks—he employed only a handful, all in menial positions, in part because, as he once explained, "everyone knows that Negroes' brains are twenty percent smaller than white people's." He had little use for King—"no good,"

Heeding King's demand to "give us the ballot," civil rights leaders organized a vast voter-registration drive throughout impoverished southern communities.

he'd called him—or civil rights. But initially, at least, he'd gone easy on him. True, an agent had been assigned to check King out and to "uncover all the derogatory information he could," and Hoover had also reminded all agents to keep on the lookout for any ties between the communists and the Southern Christian Leadership Conference. But nothing much seemed to have ensued; the bureau's pre–New Frontier file on Robert Kennedy, documenting his check-ered academic history and serial sycophancy with Hoover, was much thicker than its file from those same years on King. It was only with the Freedom Rides that Hoover's curiosity returned. Told that the FBI had never really investigated King, he wrote (in a memo in a thick pen and blocky script, as was his wont) "Why not?"

What Hoover learned when he did start to dig was far less about King than about Stanley Levison, the New York lawyer and businessman who had helped raise funds for the Montgomery Improvement Association in 1956 and stayed on to become King's most indispensable adviser, as well as his chief strategist, ghostwriter, fund-raiser, donor, financial counselor, book agent, cheerleader, muse, sage, and friend. "The white man closest to King," he once called himself—and no one could disagree. The "Assistant Chief," he was called among King associates, or so the FBI said.

As his FBI file revealed, Levison was not above some of the standard prejudices of his day, even with King. When, for instance, Levison's brother once said he "needs a Negro" (to fill a seat at a banquet for a progressive group) Levison asked whether it was for housework. On other occasions, Levison described King as "poorly read" and speculated that he "probably has not looked at a book in 20 years," ridiculed his writing, and described him as a "born sucker" who wouldn't listen to anyone. But what comes across throughout their interactions, meticulously documented by the FBI, was Levison's extraordinary devotion to King and, for the most part, the wisdom of his counsel. In his own far more benign way, he was Martin King's Robert Kennedy, and every bit as loyal. Just as Levison filled any number of roles for King, King supplied things precious to Levison, who had always had a strong

J. Edgar Hoover considered King and Kennedy two of his top "public enemies." RFK came to view Hoover as a menace to democracy, and although technically Hoover's boss, he was hamstrung by the FBI chief's voluminous secret files on him and his brother.

commitment to social justice: a mission and an outlet. He never took a dime from King and, indeed, supplied tens of thousands of them when the SCLC needed them. For all his good deeds, he got little publicly but flak; his phone calls were monitored far longer than King's. Theirs is surely one of the greatest cross-racial collaborations and friendships in the history of the civil rights movement, as King acknowledged in inscribing for him—with a nod to Lincoln—a copy of his first book, *Stride Toward Freedom*. "Let me assure you," he wrote, "that all of your kindnesses will remain in my thoughts so long as the cords [sic] of memory shall lengthen." "He was a saint," Andrew Young has said about him.

According to the FBI's informants, Levison had once been on the "executive committee" of the American Communist Party, and though his activities diminished, he continued to donate to it until late 1956 or early 1957. After that, the tie atrophied, probably for the same reasons—disillusionment with the Soviet Union and serial revelations of its atrocities—so many other American communists abandoned it. But Hoover fastened on Levison and ignored his diminishing party connections for at least two reasons. First, while even the right-wing Hearst papers acknowledged King himself was no communist—"*Dr. King Spurns Godless Red Appeal,*" one of its headlines screamed—there was always the chance that through Levison, American and Soviet communists were influencing him.

Levison's utter devotion to King made him more suspect: there *had* to be some angle. As David Garrow wrote in *The F.B.I. and Martin Luther King, Jr.*, the FBI was "hard-pressed to imagine that someone so important to the CP [Communist Party] as recently as the early 1950s would devote so much energy to Martin King solely out of the goodness of his heart." Second, at a time when American communism had grown laughable (the joke was that so many party members were actually FBI informants that Hoover could swing its elections), Levison represented the specter of traditional communism, on which Hoover's FBI had always fed. "He was very reluctant to give up the Communist menace," Peter Maas noted. "People don't like to throw away a good thing."

Hoover first learned of King's ties to Levison and told Robert Kennedy about them in early 1962. In one representative report the FBI sent him, from that May, he learned that according to one informer, a Communist party functionary said that "by reason of his association with the Martin Luther King movement," Levison was doing "the party's most important work" and that "the party has the Kennedys in its pocket" because the Kennedy Administration was politically dependent upon King. Kennedy had no reason to doubt Hoover nor any inclination to; as much as he denigrated him later on, calling him "dangerous" and "a psycho," Kennedy shared his anticommunist worldview and, when the occasion called for it, defended him vociferously. Those who accused Hoover of exaggerating the domestic Communist threat were "badly informed," he said in August 1962. "Leave the job to the experts," he advised. "Mr. Hoover is my expert." And he added: "I admired him and the FBI before I became Attorney General, but my admiration has increased tremendously after seeing his work close at hand." Though Hoover provided no corroboration—it might jeopardize sources, he said—Kennedy didn't press for any: Hoover's say-so and the seriousness of the allegations sufficed. So, at least for a time, Stanley Levison helped spare the FBI from Robert Kennedy's reforms. "He didn't suggest for one instant that he thought that there was any doubt about the information that he was receiving from the F.B.I.," the Washington columnist Joseph Alsop, with whom Kennedy had discussed Levison and King, later said. But Kennedy had a stake in King; were he discredited or smeared, someone worse might take his place. When he ordered an "extensive investigation" into King, he later explained, it was to "protect ourselves."

Around the same time, various Kennedy subordinates — Seigenthaler, Wofford, Burke Marshall—took turns urging King to cut ties with Levison. Incredulous and dependent—he had far more reason to trust Levison than the bureau, he said—King refused. In fact, King doubled down: at Levison's urging, he hired another staffer with past communist ties, Hunter Pitts "Jack" O'Dell.

In early March 1962, Kennedy, who actually attended a pair of meetings with Levison (sitting next to him at one), authorized the bureau to tap Levison's office phone. Later that year, the tap was extended to his home. Levison and King almost always talked of consequential things; there was little gossip. But now, whenever Hoover and his men overheard anything interesting, Robert Kennedy quickly knew. Ten days before a meeting with King and other civil rights leaders, for instance, Kennedy knew that one of King's deputies, the Reverend Wyatt Tee Walker, was urging him to go after the Kennedys more aggressively. "By being nice we haven't gotten anything," he'd said. He learned, too, how close King remained to Levison despite all the entreaties.


Published in March 1962, the second of King's annual reports on the state of civil rights in the U.S. used words like "impotence," "paralyzed," and "helpless" to describe the administration's performance. While its "vigorous young men" showed a certain "élan," he wrote, it had "waged an essentially cautious and defensive struggle," "aggressively driving only toward the limited goal of token integration."

But a meeting with Bobby Kennedy at the Justice Department in April, in which King and his colleagues detailed the perils of voter registration work in the South, was cordial and reassuring. The delegation included C. O. Simpkins, a dentist in Shreveport, Louisiana and SCLC board member whose home had been leveled two months previously by dynamite, apparently in reprisal for his voting rights work. (That came after months of harassment, in which a cross was burned on Simpkins's lawn and dead animals with bullets through their heads were thrown on his stoop.) Kennedy's concern was evident to Simpkins; most government officials "didn't give a damn," he later said. (There was one more thing he remembered about that day: King began his conversation with Kennedy by asking him about his convalescing father.) One of the few pictures of King and Kennedy together was taken on that occasion. It appeared only in the black press. As Seigenthaler remembered things, these early encounters with Kennedy were, for King, reconnaissance missions of a sort. "I had the feeling the first couple of times that, as much as anything else, Martin Luther King was looking for reassurance that this man was *really* as good in person as he seemed on paper," he said.

Shreveport was among the locales involved in a bizarre and sadistic initiative launched around the same time: the "reverse Freedom Rides." It was a program in which segregationist groups gave one-way bus tickets and pocket change to impoverished blacks, who were then dumped in more liberal cities, including New York, Los Angeles, and—in a move that was clearly no coincidence—Hyannis, Massachusetts. The program was the brainchild of Leander Perez, a Louisiana political boss who also headed a White Citizens' Council in New Orleans. "We want to see if northern politicians really love the Negro, or whether they love his vote," Amis Guthridge of the Capital Citizens' Council in Little Rock told the *Wall Street Journal.*

And the Kennedys were the most tempting targets. Roughly half of the two hundred or so blacks who participated in the program, several of them single mothers with large families, eventually showed up on Cape Cod. Ted Kennedy, then running for Senate, personally welcomed at least one of them. "I want you to know that in Massachusetts, you can travel on any bus or eat in any restaurant," he told him. King called the program "one of the most vicious developments ever to take place." The "haves" of the White Citizens' Councils, he charged, were taking advantage of black "have-nots." John Kennedy, too, weighed in. "A rather cheap exercise," he called it. The Kennedys soon asked James Eastland to get Perez to stop the whole ignoble enterprise, which he did. Three years later, only one of the black families imported to Hyannis was still there.

For many months in 1962, King was embroiled in the grinding protests against Jim Crow facilities and policies in Albany, Georgia. King may have "seen his power and prestige approach the dimensions of Booker T. Washington," as the *New York Times* claimed, but it was a debilitating experience—one in which he tangled with other black leaders and groups and local officials too savvy to play into his hands. There were more short jail stints, one of which forced him to miss an appearance on *Meet the Press*. Robert Kennedy monitored his incarcerations closely, and there were more calls to Coretta King, leading to charges that King was the most pampered prisoner ever.

There were additional confrontations with Kennedy—as King reminded him, the judge who enjoined a protest march there was a Kennedy appointee who, according to Andrew Young, had acted at Kennedy's behest—but while things grew heated, they were never irreparable: when it came right down to it, the two men needed one another too much. "Do you think Bobby Kennedy would prosecute me when he calls me at various places throughout the country for advice?" King once asked another black leader.

The Kennedy administration's largely hands-off approach in Albany and throughout the South, notwithstanding its interventions following mass arrests, beatings, bombings, and occasional murders, was much criticized. "The Kennedy Administration has talked of the New Frontier, but perhaps this frontier does not extend into the South or into the field of constitutional law," Howard Zinn wrote in the *Nation*. "Because of the limitations that the Administration has imposed upon itself, there is a vast no-man's-land for American Negroes into which they are invited by the Constitution, but where federal authority will not protect them." Murray Kempton asked what had happened to "that sense of indignation which has always been one of Robert Kennedy's most engaging personal qualities."

But while increasingly frustrated with the Kennedys, Kempton found the Kings a source of wonder. "She and he are essentially such reserved people, and to be conspicuous is such an embarrassment to them," he wrote. "It is one of the strangest twists of this strange country that Martin and Coretta King, of all people, should be become symbols of militant disturbance in the official South." Coretta King predicted to him that her husband's prominence would last only another five years, by which point the turbulence would have subsided. Ralph McGill pointed out how lucky the South was: were King equally charismatic but more radical, there'd be a "blood bath." "White southerners should thank the Dear Lord for sending them a Martin Luther King," he wrote. Few southerners felt similarly.

The protests in Albany ended inconclusively. For King, their most important ramifications came only several months later. "One of the great problems we face with the FBI in the South is that the agents are white southerners who have been influenced by the mores of the community," he offhandedly told a *New York Times* reporter in the robing room at Riverside Church in New York, where he'd just delivered a sermon. "To maintain their status, they have to be friendly with the local police and people who are promoting segregation." Whenever he saw FBI agents in Albany, he added, "they were with the local police force." It was with this off-handed comment that, the FBI later charged, King launched what it called "a campaign of slander and defamation' against the Bureau and its director.

His words quickly got back to J. Edgar Hoover. Maniacal about criticism (in part because he was almost entirely spared it, at least from anyone in officialdom or the press) and already hostile to King, Hoover was bound to react, especially since in this instance King, though quite right about FBI indifference generally, was mistaken on the facts: Four of the five agents in Albany were actually from St. Peter, Minnesota; Auburn, Indiana; Arlington, Massachusetts; and Kingston, New York, respectively. Things turned more sour when two of Hoover's top subordinates attempted to set King straight—and he failed to return their calls. (He was, one of them was told, "off in another building writing a book" and not to be disturbed. Then, when he hit the road, he said he'd call them when he could, but never did.) "It would appear obvious that Rev. King does not desire to be told the true facts," the head of the FBI's Crime Records Division, Cartha "Deke" DeLoach, wrote shortly afterward. "He obviously used deceit, lies and treachery as propaganda to further his own causes." The FBI promptly let Kennedy know of King's evasiveness.

The FBI's scrutiny of King intensified; at some point, he evolved from a mere useful idiot—King was, as one FBI document put it, "believed to be extremely naive in certain areas"—to a genuine Marxist-Leninist "from the top of his head to the tips of his toes." But, with the Kennedys around to protect King, Hoover's hands were tied. For the time being, he simply seethed.

The bureau, incidentally, also kept tabs on Robert Kennedy—if, for no other reason, to make sure that he, too, wasn't trashing it. Kennedy's television appearances were monitored; in August 1962, for instance, a special agent watched him chat with the country-and-western singer and television personality Tennessee Ernie Ford. (The two men talked of "family life, sports preferences, and vacation plans," he reported; there was "no discussion whatever of the Director or the FBI.") It wasn't clear how much longer

Kennedy would stay on as attorney general—already, there was talk of his becoming secretary of state—but Hoover, he predicted, would outlast several of the attorneys general who'd succeed him.

At regular intervals—in speeches, articles, and interviews—King complained about the Kennedy administration. Yes, the Kennedys had done some good things, he would invariably say, but "it does no good to apply Vaseline to a cancer." It hadn't kept its promises, like barring housing discrimination with the proverbial "stroke of a pen." (The phrase became a bitter joke, with activists inundating the White House with ballpoints and bottles of ink.) It hadn't enforced federal voting rights laws, which would prompt King and the Student Nonviolent Coordinating Committee to sue Robert Kennedy and J. Edgar Hoover in January 1963. Nor had it introduced any bills or offered moral leadership.

After operatic negotiations with Governor Ross Barnett and a day of rioting by white mobs that shocked the world and left two people dead, John and Robert Kennedy helped make James Meredith the University of Mississippi's first black student in September 1962. The *Jackson Daily News* taunted the attorney general with a newly modified fight song. "Ask us what we say, it's to hell with Bobby K.," it stated. Robert Kennedy had no time to be offended about the reaction to integrating Ole Miss; there were Soviet missiles in Cuba. And, incidentally, the Kennedy administration's handling of the ensuing missile crisis prompted King to write an effusive letter of praise to the president. By offering the Soviets a constructive way out of the impasse and allowing them to save face, he wrote, Kennedy had "utilized some of the elements of non-violent creativity in international conflict." Given Bobby's moderating influence in that debate, he was saluting not just one Kennedy, but two.

In November, John Kennedy finally signed a watered-down executive order on housing. It was the far less fateful of two strokes of the pen that day; with the other, Robert Kennedy authorized wiretaps on Stanley Levison's home phone. Now the FBI—and, effectively, Robert Kennedy himself—could overhear all of Levison's regular late-night conversations with King. Long afterward, Levison was oddly accepting of what the attorney general had done. To him, it was a fraternal gesture, one designed to protect them all. "I really understand his position," he told Arthur Schlesinger in one of the few interviews he ever gave or was ever asked to give, for apart from the FBI, few recognized how central he was. "You have to recall the time. We weren't too far away from the McCarthy period. They were so committed to our movement, their public support was so vast, they couldn't possibly risk what could have been a terrible political scandal. When I realized how hard Hoover was pressing them and how simultaneously they were giving Martin such essential support, I don't feel any enmity about their attitude toward me."

But others in the civil rights community were unhappy with the Kennedys' record in the area. One was Roger Wilkins, the nephew of Roy Wilkins and a lawyer who, earlier in the year, had taken a position with the Agency for International Development. He felt the Kennedy administration had failed to live up to its promises and, though he didn't yet know Robert Kennedy, he held him responsible. For all the talk about bringing blacks to the Justice Department, he noted, not one of the attorney general's key aides was black. "Pretty paternalistic, pretty small," he later called it. Assured by a Kennedy aide that he'd show it to the president, in November 1962, Wilkins wrote a memo laying out his complaints and recommendations, including legislation speeding up compliance with Supreme Court decisions, additional tools for the Justice Department, and a strong statement on civil rights in the forthcoming State of the Union address.

"It is difficult not to point out how painful it still is to be a Negro in America," he wrote. "And how much more painful this becomes when even their sympathetic fellow Americans seem unaware of this fact or indifferent to it. To me it is clear that Presidential indifference is the unkindest cut of all." It was, Wilkins said, the first Robert Kennedy ever knew about him, and it infuriated him—or at least ensured that Wilkins would never work in the Kennedy Justice Department. "Him? Oh, no!" Wilkins was told Kennedy remarked when someone recommended him for a job. "I think he's too brash. I think he needs more seasoning." (Nominated for a post in the Commerce Department three years later, Wilkins nonetheless asked Kennedy to introduce him at his confirmation hearing, and Kennedy agreed.)

New Year's Day 1963 at the Lincoln Memorial passed without any commemoration of the Emancipation Proclamation. Instead, King settled for a speech on the subject that the attorney general gave at the National Archives. (Arthur Schlesinger had written it for John Kennedy to deliver during a Christmas visit to Palm Beach—but mindful of celebrating emancipation from a segregated city, the president decided against giving it there. After hearing the attorney general at the Archives, Joseph Rauh passed Schlesinger a note. "Poor Lyndon," it said. Schlesinger asked Rauh what he meant. "Lyndon must know he is through," Rauh replied. "Bobby is going to be the next President.")

But in February the Kennedys emancipated the Great Emancipator from the Republicans, marking Lincoln's Birthday with a gala bash at the White House. Eight hundred blacks attended—eight hundred times as many, that is, as on that night sixty-two years earlier when, to the horror of much of white America, Booker T. Washington dined there with Theodore Roosevelt. The guest list was eclectic: Dick Gregory, Thurgood Marshall, Sammy Davis, Jr. (who, with his white wife there this time, was carefully hidden from the photographers), Ralph Ellison, even Langston Hughes, despite alleged communist ties that made Robert Kennedy uncomfortable. ("I said, 'I don't give a damn. We've got to have him.' And Bobby gave in," aide Louis Martin later said.) While Jacqueline Kennedy "wasn't too keen on this operation," according to Martin, her husband "had a ball." "Man, we had a fantastic turnout," he said. "As the boys say, the White House was Uncle Tom's Cabin for that night." "White House Sparkles with Tan Celebs," boasted the *Los Angeles Sentinel*. "Blacks don't give a damn about how somebody feels about them," Louis Martin later explained. "They want to be accepted socially." And, he continued, "If blacks are socially acceptable in the White House, where in the hell will they *not* be socially acceptable? This is it."

Feeling miffed and stiffed over his Emancipation Proclamation snub, King stayed away. The black press gave him cover, saying he was somewhere in South America. And not everyone at the party was seduced. An upbeat history of the American black community over the prior century called *Freedom to the Free* was presented to John Kennedy that night, then distributed to everyone else. "Don't give me that," one black guest told another when handed a copy. "I don't have my freedom." "You know, you're right," the man alongside him said.


By early 1963, King had stalled and—particularly to younger activists in the SNCC—seemed increasingly irrelevant. He needed to shake things up. That required a campaign of his own devising, and not one of someone else's design, in the most egregiously bigoted place possible, featuring the most heinous possible opponents. That was Birmingham, Alabama, which he called "by far the worst big city in race relations in the United States," largely because of its hot-headed commissioner of public safety, Eugene "Bull" Connor. It was a place likely to offend all fair-minded people and rouse to action even the reluctant Kennedys. But so dangerous would any campaign there be, King warned his associates, that some of them might not come out of it alive. He'd ask colleagues like Andrew Young what kind of eulogies they'd want. "Even though he was talking about me," Young later said, "I knew he was talking about himself."

Robert Kennedy was not just attorney general but becoming the administration's resident open mind. David Halberstam always remembered something that Michael Forrestal, a senior staffer on the National Security Council, once told him: that if you wanted to get a nonconforming idea into the White House, Bobby Kennedy was the best, or maybe the only, channel. And now, he was slowly coming around to King's point of view. "The Attorney General concedes that he came to the job with no emotional commitment on civil rights," Anthony Lewis wrote in the *Times* on April 7. "'I wasn't lying awake nights thinking about the Negro in this country.'" But he had learned, Lewis wrote, and changed. "'There are injustices,' he says, 'and they are flagrant. And I have the power and responsibility to do something about them. So I intend to do it. It's quite simple.'" "He does not say—as a restrained and pragmatic man he still resists saying—that his emotions have been stirred," Lewis went on. "But one suspects that there is now a commitment of the spirit on the race question." Still, Kennedy very characteristically asked King to wait: an election loomed in Birmingham, and Bull Connor might be forced out. King disregarded his request. As he often noted, the timing of these protests was *never* right. In early April, it got under way.

The goal of the Birmingham campaign was to desegregate department stores and lunch counters, increase black hiring there and in city government (including the police department), and create a biracial committee to expedite and manage integration. The protest began slowly, discouragingly: local blacks seemed apathetic, and the press, hostile. Once again, King was jailed for parading without a permit. And this time, Bobby Kennedy didn't get him sprung—"I'm not sure we can get into prison reform right at this moment," he said—thereby providing King the time to write his famous "Letter from a Birmingham Jail." When King wrote that "The Negro's great stumbling block…is not the White Citizen's Council-er or the Ku Klux Klanner, but the white moderate who is more devoted to 'order' than to justice," he might have had Kennedy partly in mind.

While the Birmingham protest languished, Kennedy himself returned to Montgomery to pay a "courtesy call" on Governor George Wallace, who was threatening to defy a court order and "stand in the schoolhouse door" in June to block the admission of two black students to the state university in Tuscaloosa. As a delegate at the 1956 Democratic Convention, Wallace had supported John Kennedy for vice president, and he raised money for him four years later. In between had come Robert Kennedy's triumphant speech to the local Chamber of Commerce. But by this point, the attorney general had become, as the *Alabama Journal* put it, "the worst enemy the South has had since Thad Stevens" (a reference to the radical antislavery congressman from Pennsylvania who had pushed Lincoln for an Emancipation Proclamation far more relentlessly than King had ever pushed Robert Kennedy). The *Birmingham Post-Herald*'s James Free foresaw a "drama-packed eyeball-to-eyeball confrontation" between the "two bantam-sized scrappers."

Montgomery greeted Robert Kennedy very differently this time around. No delegation of local businessmen awaited him at the airport. One state trooper refused to shake his hand, and another stuck a billy club in his gut. At a press conference, he was asked whether he belonged to the NAACP or the Communist Party. Picketers carried signs that said "Coon-kissing Kennedys" and "Alabama will resist with Vigah" and, tying racism, anti-communism, and antisemitism into one efficient little bundle, "Kosher Team Kennedy Kastro Khrushchev." It illustrated how Kennedy was taking it from all sides. "We were puzzled at the anti-Kennedy sentiment among Southern whites," one of King's deputies later said. "There was almost that much anti-Kennedy sentiment among Negroes in the movement."

At the capitol, just down the street from King's old pulpit at the Dexter Avenue Baptist Church, Kennedy was made to sidestep a wreath placed by a daughter of the Confederacy around the bronze star marking where Jefferson Davis had taken the oath of office. (The reception there was not entirely hostile: there were plenty of screaming teenage girls as well. "They're acting like Kennedy was a crooner," one policeman remarked.)

Kennedy walked into Wallace's office, where the governor pointed out the Confederate flag hanging behind his desk. After ritualized niceties, Kennedy broached the situation at the university. He stressed that the question wasn't one of segregation or integration, or even of states' rights—which he said he and his brother favored— but following a court order, something that Wallace, a former judge, surely understood. Without that, Kennedy said, there'd be chaos.

"Let me say this: we have more peace and law and order in Alabama in one minute than you have in an entire year in Washington, D.C.," Wallace replied. Besides, orders need not be obeyed when courts overstepped their bounds. In support of that proposition, Wallace cited an unlikely authority. "Well, Martin Luther King has said you have a right to disobey an unjust law," he said. "Now do you agree with Mr. King?"

"I think that he, like everybody else, Governor, should follow the orders of the court," Kennedy replied. "I think it applies to an ordinary citizen, I think it applies to a minister, and it applies to a governor of a state."

All this *was* a matter of politics, Wallace insisted. "I know with Mr. King, if there wasn't so many colored voters who bloc vote like they do in certain sections, why I doubt there would be so much interest evidenced in their so-called civil rights," he told Kennedy. Politically, he lectured, the Kennedys weren't doing themselves any good aligning with "Mr." King: the South would hold the balance of power in the next presidential election, and John Kennedy was undermining his own position there. "Every [voter] registration lawsuit that's filed does the Kennedy administration no good, all you're doing is making the white people solidify," he said.

Wallace went on to call King a "phony and a fraud." Instead of "marching and going to jail" and, he hinted, living high on the hog, he'd better serve his people by bringing jobs to Alabama in the way Wallace himself was doing. Kennedy, he said, should use his great influence with blacks—"the NAACP feels that you people are almost gods"—to stop integration forever, or "for the next ten years at least." And he should ask those black students to withdraw their applications to the state university and denounce King for advocating lawlessness instead of talking to him all the time on the telephone. Talking to Wallace was, Kennedy later remarked, like negotiating with a foreign government, but only once did he lose his cool. "Do you think it would be so horrifying to have a Negro attend the University of Alabama, governor?" he'd asked. Wallace didn't respond and Kennedy didn't press the point. The meeting was adjourned.

Afterward, Kennedy visited with Grover Hall, the highly literate and quirky editorial page editor of the *Montgomery Advertiser*. The next day, Hall offered his readers a few preliminary observations about the man:

"Kennedy is as strong as a percheron [a breed of field horse], but was nevertheless plainly used up by the time he got here."

"He is utterly humorless."

"Bobby is cold to everything save his own purposes, but to him his White House brother is a godhead."

"When agitated and off-guard, he reaches up and presses down upon the zoysia [a variety of creeping grass] on his head. The gesture proclaims a boyishness."


Everything changed in Birmingham with one tactical decision: to allow black youths to join the depleted and insufficiently fervent ranks of adult marchers, an idea first promoted by the SCLC's James Bevel. Schoolchildren as young as kindergarteners were recruited for the effort with flyers that beckoned "Fight for your freedom first then go to school." Everyone acknowledged Robert Kennedy's special bond with children, and not just because he eventually fathered eleven of them himself. Using them here, he cautioned, was "a dangerous business." Black children, King replied, "are hurt every day."

The "Children's Crusade," as *Newsweek* would dub it, brought endless waves of reinvigorated protests, and nightsticks, and arrests, and police dogs, and fire hoses forceful enough to strip bark (and clothing), and the instantly immortal photographs of black protesters besieged by German shepherds and columns of water that circulated worldwide. The most famous, of a dog lunging at a young black boy, appeared on May 3; John Kennedy said it made him sick, and he was far from the only person to have that reaction. "Approximately then some whites in the North, who had not previously cared one way or another, decided that this was too much," Mary McGrory wrote. One of those white

northerners was Robert Kennedy. "When you see southern sheriffs attack Negro children, you see the wrongness of it all," he subsequently told Richard Reeves of the *New York Times*.

On May 4, Burke Marshall arrived and began an intense round of meetings between black leaders and the "mules," or leading businessmen, of the city. As entrenched as it was, official segregation at least proved to be a surprisingly shaky edifice, mostly because it was bad for business—a fact the low-key, methodical Marshall pointed out. "The fire trucks are out, there are thousands of people in the streets," he told the moguls. "You have a choice. You can have this, or you can let Negroes eat at the lunch counters of department stores." Less than a week later, the parties had reached a tentative deal, one that would, among other things, end segregated lunch counters, fitting rooms, and drinking fountains within ninety days. That meant, reported Charles Portis (he later wrote *True Grit*) in the *New York Herald Tribune*, that Bull Connor "will at last be able to sit down in Loveman's Department Store and have a Coke with Dr. King." King, he wrote, "is a very somber man who almost never smiles, but yesterday he was beaming."

Never one to gloat or let anyone become too complacent or to cast judgments on one group while exempting another, Robert Kennedy noted at a press conference that while southern papers hadn't shown pictures of a dog attacking a black man, the northern papers had skipped photographs of a black man attacking a dog and a policeman with a knife and bottle. So people in the two places, he said, were "hardly talking about the same thing," and for things really to change, that had to change. "Over the period of the next decade and the next twelve months, really, all of us in all sections of the country have a hell of a lesson to learn on the importance of getting a dialogue going between the people of the North and South," he said.

The harsh realities of Public Safety Commissioner "Bull" Connor's attack on the peaceful protesters of the 1963 Birmingham campaign shocked the nation.

On May 14, with the truce in Birmingham holding, John Kennedy met at the White House with a group of newspaper editors from Alabama. One local editor implored the president to get Martin Luther King to leave town—something Kennedy said he was unable to do. But a couple of others conceded that Alabama needed to move forward on race relations and thanked Kennedy for helping it do so. Only once—when someone described King as a White House "pet"—did the president grow irritated. (He'd met the man only twice, he said, which wasn't quite right.) As the session ended, a majority of the newspapermen asked Kennedy for his autograph. "He did not bark, like Bobby," Grover Hall of the *Advertiser* wrote.

The group then headed en masse to the Justice Department to see Bobby, who praised King for helping to quiet things down in Birmingham. "You have to understand this about Martin Luther King," the attorney general told them. "If he loses his effort to keep the Negroes nonviolent, the result could be disastrous—not only in Birmingham but all over the country." It was King, he noted, who'd gone around to the pool halls of black Birmingham collecting knives, telling people to stay off the streets, to be nonviolent. "If King loses," he warned, "worse leaders are going to take his place. Look at the Black Muslims."

In the privacy of the White House a few days later, Robert Kennedy painted an unflattering picture of black Birmingham, one reflecting some of his old condescension. "Many in the Negro leadership didn't know what they were demonstrating about. They didn't know whether they were demonstrating to get rid of Bull Connor, or whether they were demonstrating about the stores, or whether they're demonstrating against the city government," he told other high officials, including the president. "None of the white community knew what they were demonstrating about, and none of the white community would get near the Negro community at that juncture because they felt that they were being disorderly and so nobody was talking to anybody."

In those same discussions, Kennedy warned of potential Birminghams everywhere, and not just in the South. "There must be a dozen places where we're having major problems today," he noted, citing how Chicago mayor Richard Daley had described surliness in the black community there. "The Negroes are all mad for no reason at all, and they want to fight," he continued. "[Daley] says you can't have a moderate Negro anymore." And, he noted, the moderates who were still around were fighting among themselves: "Roy Wilkins hates Martin Luther King."

The brutal reality of racial marginalization and the absence of legal tools to deal with it led the administration to a fateful decision: it would, at long last, introduce a civil rights bill, one that would, among other things, ban racial discrimination in public accommodations, education, employment, and housing. Robert Kennedy's press spokesman, Edwin Guthman, recalled how, en route to a conference in Asheville, North Carolina, on May 17, Kennedy and Burke Marshall sketched out its essential provisions.

The bill's chances, Kennedy knew, were bleak. But even if it failed, it would have succeeded: as important as enacting something was, as he later put it, it was equally important "to obtain the confidence of the Negro population in their government and in the white majority." In the meantime, he suggested a series of meetings with various groups—elected officials, theater owners, store owners, lawyers, ministers—to discuss and ease the tensions, to encourage voluntary measures until the law could be changed, and to build a consensus for such a measure.

The president agreed, though he specified that they see Martin Luther King last, after the southern officials and businessmen, and after the bill had gone up. "Otherwise, it will look like he got me to do it," John Kennedy explained. "The trouble with King is that everybody thinks he's our boy, anyway. So everything he does, everybody says we stuck him in there. We ought to have him well surrounded.... King is so hot these days that it's like Marx coming to the White House." Thanks to a primitive White House taping system, the sense that critics had always had of the Kennedy administration—that it had to soft-peddle, if not hide, its ties to Martin Luther King—is here magically and colorfully confirmed.

To King, Birmingham effectively bifurcated John Kennedy's presidency. Formerly, he was cautious and begrudging; now he was fully engaged, "ready really to throw off political considerations and see the real moral issues." "I think Birmingham did it," King later recalled. "Birmingham created such a crisis in race relations that it was an issue which could no longer be ignored." Only now could the president see "that segregation was morally wrong and...did something to the souls of both the segregator and the segregated."

It was a moment, like Lincoln's before the Emancipation Proclamation, when Kennedy realized he had to lead morally, rather than merely parrot the popular consensus. In the process, he won over King himself. Levison characterized the relationship between Bobby Kennedy and Martin Luther King as "rather formal." "They met mostly in meetings, except probably on those occasions when they discussed me," he told Schlesinger in 1976. "But Martin liked the Kennedys." And he instructed Levison to put a line in the book he was ghostwriting for him about the Birmingham crisis that, although he'd never cast a presidential ballot before, he planned to endorse John Kennedy for reelection in 1964.

The result, Levison later told Schlesinger, was a "de facto alliance" between the Kennedys and King and his movement. "They reacted positively and negatively so that any partisan can find ample quotes for his case," he said of John and Robert Kennedy on race. But "both brothers," he went on, "scandalously ignorant at the outset, pushed their way to a new perception that was more than the timeworn reformism. They were aware that the society needed major surgery to accomplish irreversible changes."

Perhaps an idealistic John Kennedy had at long last shaken off—or liberated—the more coldly pragmatic Robert. But it's far more likely that Robert Kennedy *changed him* (though only after first changing himself). Burke Marshall saw the results. "Every single person who spoke about it in the White House—every single one of them—was against President Kennedy's sending up that bill...against making [civil rights] a moral issue," Marshall later said. "The conclusive voice within the government at that time, there's no question about it at all, [was] that Robert Kennedy was the one. He urged it, he felt it, he understood it. And he prevailed." Only the president felt the same way, Marshall said, and "he got it from his brother."

"Even the president himself was not always rejoicing in the fact that we were doing it," Robert Kennedy later told Anthony Lewis, referring to the civil rights bill. "He would ask me every four days, 'Do you think we did the right thing by sending the legislation? Look at the trouble it's got us in.' But always in a semi-jocular way. It always seemed to me always quite clear that that's what we needed to do."

While in solitary confinement after violating an anti-protest injunction, King wrote his "Letter from Birmingham Jail" on April 16, 1963.

# FIVE

# THE MEETING

I got a home in-a dat rock, don't you see?
I got a home in-a dat rock, don't you see?
Between de earth an' sky, Thought I heard my savior cry:
You got a home in-a dat rock, don't you see?

Po' man Laz'rus, po' as I, don't you see?
Po' man Laz'rus, po' as I, don't you see?
Po' man Laz'rus, po' as I, When he died he foun' a home
    on high,
He had a home in-a dat rock, don't you see?

Rich man Dives, he lived so well, don't you see?
Rich man Dives, he lived so well, don't you see?
Rich man Dives, he lived so well, when he died he foun'
    a home in hell;
He had no home in-a dat rock, don't you see?

God gave Noah de rainbow sign, don't you see?
God gave Noah de rainbow sign, don't you see?
God gave Noah de rainbow sign, no mo' water but fiah
    nex' time
Better get a home in-a dat rock, Don't you see?

The words of the old Negro spiritual are one more thing that tied
Martin Luther King and Robert Kennedy together.

By 1962, frustration with the Kennedy administration had grown over the lack of
legislative action, and token gestures made toward remedying social inequality.

The biblical parable of Lazarus and Dives was one of King's favorites, the subject of an early sermon and a story he mentioned frequently. Dives, the rich man "dressed in purple and fine linen," ended up in hell not because he was wealthy, King said, but for thinking his wealth was part of the natural order of things and for turning his back on the poor. And Lazarus, the beggar covered in rags and sores, craving the scraps off Dives's table, didn't land in Abraham's bosom purely because he was poor, but because he was virtuous. King analogized the tale to America's racial problem: Dives was the white man suppressing his black brother because he conveniently considered segregation immutable, rather than something that man created and that man could also eliminate.

Robert Kennedy had no direct connection to the story of God and Noah in the final verse. But it lent James Baldwin the title of perhaps his most famous book, *The Fire Next Time*, a portion of which Kennedy read in the *New Yorker* in November 1962. The article hastened Robert Kennedy's crash course in American racial reality and, incidentally, eventually made him appreciate Martin Luther King all the more.

As dogmatic as Kennedy could be, he sensed what he didn't know and what he needed to know. He was curious and, within the limits of his beliefs, open-minded. He was fearless, willing to subject himself to other, sometimes hostile points of view, but he was also naive and self-righteous, convinced that his good intentions should insulate himself from criticism. Like King, he recognized that the next frontier in civil rights would be in the North, where everything was vaster and infinitely more complex. He needed a guide, and for that, he thought of Baldwin, whom he'd met at a White House dinner for Nobel laureates in April 1962. (Baldwin had voiced dissatisfaction with the FBI's performance in the South, a conversation Kennedy had promised to pick up at some point.) Seven months later came Baldwin's *New Yorker* article, "Letter from a Region in My Mind." It's easy to see what Kennedy liked about it.

There's Baldwin's brilliance, and his religiosity: he was a preacher's son, and though he'd left Christianity, he knew it had never fully left him, just as it was woven into Kennedy. And his honesty: only by a quirk of fate, he confessed, had he avoided crossing the thin line between law and lawlessness that ran through his childhood and which so many people he knew had traversed. And his bluntness: Baldwin didn't waste his time. (If Baldwin admired King because he didn't sound like your typical preacher, Kennedy may have admired Baldwin because he didn't sound as preachy as King.) And his wisdom: Baldwin reminded him of something people like him might not realize on their own: that blacks understood whites far better than the other way around, and for the same reason mothers understand their children—they have to. And his rage, with which Kennedy might have identified on some level. And his sense of injustice. "The brutality with which Negroes are treated in this country simply cannot be overstated," Baldwin had written. "For the horrors of the American Negro's life there has been almost no language."

There was also the contempt they shared for the sanctimoniousness and hypocrisy of liberals, though Baldwin lumped Kennedy in among them: when Kennedy predicted a black president within forty years, said Baldwin, he acted as if it was his gift to black America. And to suggest as he did that the Irish were a precedent— that if *we* now had a president, so, too, soon can you—was even worse. "Negroes were brought here in chains long before the Irish ever thought of leaving Ireland," Baldwin wrote.

Kennedy might have found Baldwin's pride and independence refreshing: unlike so many blacks he was dealing with, he was giving rather than taking, teaching rather than manipulating, asking mainly for honesty and understanding. If the handful of "relatively conscious" whites and blacks came together, Baldwin suggested, they could "end the racial nightmare" and "change the history of the world." But "if we do not now dare everything, the fulfillment of that prophesy, re-created from the Bible in song by a slave, is upon us: *God gave Noah the rainbow sign, No more water, the fire next time!*"

Kennedy might have had this kind of conversation in mind when, on May 22, 1963, while a tenuous peace was holding in

Birmingham, he invited Baldwin for breakfast at Hickory Hill. But he was taking a calculated risk: only ten days earlier, in a cable to Kennedy from Los Angeles, Baldwin had blamed J. Edgar Hoover, Senator Eastland, and President Kennedy himself—he had "not used the great prestige of his office as the moral forum which it can be"—for the turmoil in Birmingham. "You know, just insane!" was Baldwin's reaction to receiving the attorney general's invitation after issuing such a broadside. "But I thought I had to go, so I went." His plane was late, so they'd had only half an hour or so together. Still, he was impressed. "As a black citizen, it's really a cold day in August when one is overwhelmed by any politician," Baldwin later recalled. "But he seemed earnest and truthful. . . . Unlike most people in power, there was a way to talk to him, to reach him. Something might happen."

As they headed back to Washington with Burke Marshall (who had also attended the breakfast), Kennedy had an idea. He was going to be in New York the next day; could Baldwin get some of his "best people" together, and could they talk things over? "So I said OK, not quite realizing what I'd gotten myself into," Baldwin later recalled. "I got off the plane in New York, and I thought, 'I'm nuts. We're both crazy. But it certainly is something worth doing.' So I called up a few friends." He began with Harry Belafonte, then turned to the social psychologist Kenneth Clark, whose studies the Supreme Court had cited in *Brown v. Board of Education.*

"Kenneth, I've just come back from Virginia," Baldwin told him. Robert Kennedy had "wanted to get confirmation of my pessimism," and Baldwin had "laid it on the line" for him. Now he'd asked him to bring a group to his apartment on Central Park South. Actually, it was his father's apartment: the same place where John Kennedy had first met Martin Luther King.

"Oh, my God!" said Clark. "What do you expect me to do?"

"Just come and talk, because my feeling is that the guy really doesn't understand the seriousness of the problem," Baldwin replied.

Baldwin looked for people who could speak freely, who were unconstrained by institutional ties. So while someone slipped in from the Urban League, there'd be no one from the NAACP. He steered clear of people to whom Kennedy had already spoken, like Martin Luther King, though King's (and Baldwin's) lawyer, Clarence Jones, would be on hand. "I didn't want Martin there," he later said. Baldwin added some artists: Lena Horne, the jazz singer, and the playwright Lorraine Hansberry, who'd written *A Raisin in the Sun*. The *New York Times* was to call the group the "Angry Young Negroes." "Fairly rowdy, independent, tough-minded men and women" was how Baldwin himself characterized the group, which also included a few whites involved with the movement, like the actor Rip Torn. Kennedy had no advance word about Baldwin's choices.

Robert Kennedy had flown into New York the day before. That night, he'd attended a party at the Waldorf Astoria marking John Kennedy's forty-sixth birthday. (Without Marilyn Monroe on hand, it lacked the sizzle of the previous year's celebration.) The next morning, he'd met with three separate business groups representing variety stores, hotels, and restaurants, as well as retail merchants—all part of his campaign to encourage desegregation before it became compulsory. Some of the sessions had been held in public view at the White House; others were held surreptitiously somewhere else, so that the southern public wouldn't know that its merchants were meeting with the "Devil Incarnate," as Kennedy facetiously called himself. After all that arm-twisting—changing a way of life is not easy, even when you have the attorney general of the United States beseeching you to do so—the Baldwin meeting, set for four o'clock in the afternoon, would surely be a relief.

The guests began appearing, and from Kennedy's perspective, one problem became immediately apparent: apart from Kenneth Clark and Edwin Berry of the Urban League, no one could talk policy. Another bad sign was that the blacks all sat on one side of the room and the whites on the other, separate and unequal.

Kennedy began by laying out the administration's accomplishments. Skeptical to begin with, his audience was put off further by his tone. "This became Bobby's refrain: that he and his brother had done more for Negroes than any other administration, and *implying* that we should be grateful," Clark recalled. "He had called the meeting in hopes of persuading us that he and his brother were doing all that could be done," Lena Horne later wrote. "The funny thing was that no one there disputed that. It was just that it did not seem enough."

One additional person was on hand that day, to whom no one on either side of the room would have paid much mind: Jerome Smith, the twenty-four-year-old Freedom Rider who'd been so badly beaten in McComb, Mississippi, in the fall of 1961. He had not come close to recovering—"half-dead" was how Baldwin, who'd met and worked with him in the Deep South, described him that day—and in fact was in New York for treatment. He'd almost not appeared at Kennedy's apartment: by this point his faith in nonviolence had pretty much evaporated, and he suspected that rather than say anything enlightening, Kennedy would just "blow bubbles." (Still, walking into Joe Kennedy's place that afternoon, he'd felt a bit less alien than one might have expected; with its draperies and fancy appurtenances, it reminded him of the mansions along the bayou to which he'd once made deliveries for a drugstore back in New Orleans.)

Notwithstanding Kennedy's concern when he'd been beaten nearly two years earlier, for him, as for many activists down South, the attorney general was no friend of the movement. He'd encouraged their activism, particularly their efforts to register voters, then left them utterly unprotected. True, he'd sprung Martin Luther King from prison that time in Georgia, but Smith felt that was a matter of politics, not conviction. The moral force that had brought all those idealistic northern kids in Mississippi or Alabama was something quite foreign to Kennedy. And when Kennedy started speaking to the group, he only made things worse.

Smith sat on the floor—it was something you did in the movement—and listened disgustedly as Kennedy touted his accomplishments and warned that racial problems were harming American prestige abroad and the office of the presidency. He and Kennedy were "wrapped by different kinds of paper," he quickly realized. Kennedy talked

Back from a tour where he saw Medgar Evers, James Baldwin organized an informal meeting for Kennedy of black intellectuals in New York City.

"like a zombie," rattling off statistics, speaking utterly without empathy. "It was all about numbers," Smith recalled, "and that irritated me tremendously because of his power and the gift this country had given him. It made me feel like I needed to choke him or something." But his response, as always, would be non-violent: "we had to play the role of the lamb," he said. As Kennedy spoke, Smith began to have flashbacks about being beaten. "Everything, everything—it was all coming to me," he remembered. "I didn't see [Kennedy] erasing any of that. I didn't see him making it possible for another youngster not to experience that. I didn't see him putting himself up, like King. I just saw him as a person born with luck." Before long, he was moved to speak. He was sorry, he said, but as an American citizen, he couldn't be grateful to anyone. All he'd been asking for was the same rights as everyone else, and he'd gotten beaten up and imprisoned for it. Having to plead for such things, and now hearing all this polite talk, made him want to puke, he said. "You go down to my house and live," Smith told Kennedy. "You change places with me." He'd been taught to put up no resistance, and he never had, he continued, even when being pummeled by brass knuckles. But were anyone to come at *him* now with dogs or hoses, he'd pull out a gun, and when he pulled the trigger, you could kiss non-violence goodbye. Here were the Kennedys asking him to fight in Cuba to defend freedom when they couldn't even defend his at home. Kennedy should worry less about America's foreign enemies because the real dangers to the country were right here. He stared straight at Kennedy as he spoke, while Kennedy, he thought, tried to look away. "It was not personal at all," Baldwin recalled. "If you'd been in Birmingham and on those highways and in those jails waiting for the Justice Department or the FBI to act, you'd be nauseated, too."

Kennedy reacted to Smith's tirade characteristically, which is to say, viscerally, defensively. Rather than commiserate or comfort Smith, he glowered—"Bobby just got redder and redder and redder," Clark recalled—and when the young man said he would not fight for his country, Kennedy recoiled: it was damn near treason. "I don't see how any American could refuse to fight for our country," Kennedy said. At that, Hansberry recalled, "every Negro in the room said, '*Oh, you don't?*'" While Kennedy's brand of patriotism was "our country, right or wrong," Belafonte later said, Smith's was "our country be damned because it's wrong so often." "That really shook Bobby Kennedy to the core," he said. As if seeking reassurance, Kennedy looked toward all the others—"the reasonable, responsible, mature representatives of the black community," Baldwin later described them—and that, Baldwin said, "was a mistake": they all took Smith's side. "You've got a great many very accomplished people in this room, Mr. Attorney General," Hansberry told Kennedy, "but the only man you should be listening to is that man over there." "This boy just put it like it was," Horne wrote afterward. "He communicated the plain, basic suffering of being a Negro. The primeval memory of everyone in that room went to work after that.... He took us back to the common dirt of our existence and rubbed our noses in it." Kenneth Clark said he was shocked that Kennedy was shocked. And Baldwin was surprised that he was surprised, though he confessed that Kennedy must have felt blindsided.

"He was confronted, however untidy it may have been, by so many disparate types, yet united," he said. "What connected all of us to that student? No one had ever heard of him; he didn't sing or dance or act. Yet he became the focal point. I think that threw Kennedy. That boy, after all, in some sense, represented to everybody in that room our hope, our honor, our dignity. But above all, our hope."

As the conversation broadened, the gap only grew. When Kennedy tried talking about tangible things — statistics, legislation — he was rebuffed. "For him it was a political matter," said Baldwin. "It was a matter perhaps of even getting votes or finding out what's wrong in the Twelfth Ward and correcting it. But what was wrong in the Twelfth Ward in this case turned out to be something very sinister, very deep, that couldn't be solved in the usual way. Bobby didn't understand that." "None of us wanted to hear figures and percentages and all that stuff," Horne later wrote. "The point we were trying to put over was: 'Look. The Kennedys have a tremendous amount of credit with the American people,'" Clark later said. "'You and your brother must use this credit to lead the American people into an awareness and understanding of the nature of this problem.' He suggested that Jack Kennedy should make not only public announcements but a dramatic gesture, such as escorting a child into a desegregated school or go to the University of Alabama and declare, 'This is the law of the land.'"

That was precisely the kind of grand gesture Kennedy loathed. "Bobby kept saying, 'No. This would be senseless. This would be phony,'" Clark recalled. "We were saying: 'Not phony.' This was the abrasive clash here: our insisting that the crisis demanded extraordinary acts and Bobby retreating and saying no, and occasionally coming back and saying…well, implying…that we were ungrateful; that we were insatiable, et cetera."

The helmet of a U.S. marshal beaten during the integration of the University of Mississippi in 1962 served as a daily reminder of the work to be done.

When Kennedy claimed to have worked closely with King in Birmingham, and Marshall said that special Justice Department lawyers were protecting black activists in a way the FBI couldn't, the black guests laughed hysterically. "Even the laughter wasn't laughter," said Clark. "It was the laughter of desperation." (Wasn't *he* the boss of the FBI? Horne asked.) Kennedy even trotted out his prediction about the future black president. (Baldwin, very predictably, was ready for that one.) Participants later described Kennedy's "self-righteous arrogance" and charged that were it not for the upcoming election, he wouldn't even be in the same room with them.

Things turned, as Clark put it, "from a dialogue into a diatribe." Hansberry suggested southern blacks be given guns to shoot their tormentors. ("I didn't think that was a very satisfactory solution because ... there are more white people than Negroes, and although it might be bloody, I thought the white people would do better," Kennedy recalled.) "Mr. Attorney General, you can take all those pious statements and stuff them up your ass," Horne told him at one point.

Belafonte's attempts to cut the tension—recalling his happy visits to Hickory Hill—didn't help. "The most intense, traumatic meeting I've ever been at," Clark called it. Kennedy was "the white power structure in person, and so they attacked him," Burke Marshall said. Kennedy became increasingly silent, tense, immobile, resentful. No one had ever done more than he, right up to the moment he'd gotten there, spending the day hearing business types bitch about having to admit blacks into their lunchrooms and movie theaters. "Having put up with that sort of nonsense all morning, you know, it was just…it was difficult to be accused of not being even interested," Marshall later said. Nor were the people in the room much impressed when Kennedy said that some of them had sent him telegrams congratulating him over the job he was doing. His guests didn't know the law, nor the facts, nor what the administration was trying to do, Kennedy lamented to Schlesinger afterward. "You can't talk to them the way you can talk to Martin Luther King or Roy Wilkins. It was all emotion, hysteria."

"We never got through to him," Clark said afterward. "We might as well have been talking different languages." It dawned on Clark that "this man was an extraordinarily insensitive person, extraordinarily loyal to his brother; he personalized issues that did not seem to me to be understood by personalization." Making it much worse was the communal realization that for all his faults, the Kennedys were, in addition to being the only game in town, the best white America had to offer. "Nobody had anything against Bobby; it was nothing to do with that," Baldwin later said. "We all rather liked him, as far as that was concerned." But "if we couldn't make the Attorney General of the United States, who was a fairly young and intelligent man, understand the urgency of the black situation, there wasn't any hope at all!" By antagonizing him, in fact, they might have made things even worse.

Innumerable times, the meeting seemed about to break up. It finally did end about three hours after it began. The two men who tried bucking up Kennedy on the way out only aggravated him more. If Martin King really *had* appreciated his help in Birmingham, as Clarence Jones told him, why hadn't Jones said so to everyone? ("Hold on!" he'd replied. "I'm not carrying your water!" The antipathy between the two, stemming at least in part from this confrontation, may account for the apparent ease with which Kennedy authorized the FBI to bug Jones's phone shortly thereafter.) And if Belafonte truly believed Kennedy had done more for civil rights than anyone else, why hadn't *he* spoken up? (He couldn't have, Belafonte replied: it would have made him suspect, and limited his effectiveness, with the others.)

"The conflict was so intense, the anger was so great, he turned on me and Clarence and accused us of having betrayed him to a room full of people," Belafonte recalled. "We didn't talk for a long time after that." Bobby Kennedy was "in a crisis," he said: he needed the black community to accomplish his agenda, but could not find a way to connect to it. When Smith left, he refused to shake Kennedy's hand. "You don't put your hand in dirt," he explained. He walked back to Harlem through Central Park. "I had a cold feeling when I left there," he said. There was absolutely no doubt in the minds of everybody who was there that the Attorney General has no conception of the moral issues involved in the Negro's flight to gain equal footing in this," one of the women who participated said afterward. "It was a terrible meeting."

The speaker was almost certainly Hansberry, who was vocal—by name —in other stories. "He wanted a whole bunch of fancy Negroes to tell him he was great and that the Administration was doing a fine job," she said in one of them. "When we left the Kennedys' apartment I had a feeling of complete futility, and as we got on the elevator I wondered if there is any way to make the white people in this country understand," she said in another.

She lodged one more complaint about Bobby Kennedy—the same one Jackie Robinson had once had about Jack: never would he look her in the eye.

The next day—thanks, it seemed, to Baldwin—everyone got to reprise the experience on the front page of the *New York Times*. In the *World-Telegram and Sun* the session was described as a "gigantic flop." The rest of the press, white and black, soon weighed in. The Hearst papers called the meeting a second "disastrous sortie" for Kennedy, following his recent standoff with Governor Wallace in Montgomery. Jackie Robinson praised Kennedy for holding the meeting, but was puzzled that two men as smart as the Kennedys "find it so hard to understand our basic human yearnings." "We expect nothing more than those fine Irish-Catholics expected, who once were discriminated against and jim-crowed: fair play," he said.

To Peter Lisagor of the *Chicago Daily News*, the gathering proved how moderation was waning; the Kennedys "must now move, with undeliberate speed, to accelerate the pace of voluntary desegregation" before things got still worse. Fred Halsted of the left-wing *Militant* called the gathering the attorney general's own Bay of Pigs. "Robert Kennedy stands exposed for just what he is—an arrogant, imperialistic, ignorant, spoiled-rich, prejudiced white man," he wrote. *Jet* said Kennedy had "reached the 'wall' over which no white man seems able to step in understanding the Negro's aims and aspirations."

But Kennedy's interlocutors came in for some criticism in the black press. Turning to black intellectuals for answers, Whitney Young of the Urban League told the *Pittsburgh Courier*, was like asking Gregory Peck and Frank Sinatra about foreign policy. To William Shannon of the *New York Post*, the gathering didn't reflect a chasm at all, but simply two different but by no means irreconcilable approaches to life and politics. "Robert Kennedy is action-minded, but he lacks a touch of the poet," he said.

A Justice Department spokesman put out a defiant statement. "What did the Negroes up there expect to come of this meeting?" he said. "The Attorney General was just hoping to find some

Freedom Rider Jerome Smith (in overalls) challenged Kennedy at the Baldwin meeting for encouraging activism efforts in the South, but leaving volunteers unprotected from the brutal backlash.

answers to some very difficult questions. Nothing more." As for Kennedy himself, with Anthony Lewis of the *Times* available, he didn't have to say anything for attribution. "A source close to Mr. Kennedy conceded today that his meeting in New York Friday with Negro intellectuals had been unfortunate," Lewis wrote a few days afterward. "But the source contended that it was pointless to dramatize this one failure when Mr. Kennedy had held many unannounced meetings on the racial issue in the last two years." The "source" then added that "in retrospect, it would have been better not to have held the meeting."

On or before May 28, 1963, Kennedy contacted J. Edgar Hoover, evidently to discuss the Baldwin meeting. "The Attorney General had called and related a conversation he had had with James Baldwin, whom he considered a 'nut,'" was how a subordinate summarized the memorandum Hoover had written afterward. "The Attorney General advised that the whole conversation started by Baldwin making [*sic*] two determinations: (1)

Wouldn't think of fighting for the United States if the United States got into a war and (2) Thinking of getting guns and starting to shoot white people." That much seems to have been garbled in the transmission; Kennedy was surely referring to Jerome Smith, who'd said something more closely resembling those words. Similarly, when he described "Baldwin" as "an important figure in the Student Nonviolent Coordinating Committee," adding that Kennedy went on to say that blacks looked up to such people because they had "no outstanding leaders with the exception of Martin Luther King," it was probably Smith, and not Baldwin, he had in mind.

On Kennedy, Baldwin was publicly conciliatory. "No one can afford to look on it as a failure," he said of the meeting. "It has got to be looked at as the beginning of a dialogue. Like most Americans, Bobby Kennedy would really have no way of knowing what the extremity of the Negro's situation is." But Kennedy's romance with Baldwin had proved short-lived afterward. He took swipes at Baldwin's homosexuality and deposited the FBI's dossiers on Baldwin and the other participants on Burke Marshall's desk. "He is a nice fellow & you have swell friends," Kennedy wrote. After the meeting, "I think he was always a little mad at me, which is kind of sad, but understandable," said Baldwin. While they'd seen each other on occasion, they never spoke again.

The FBI was somehow blindsided by the gathering, but overheard and preserved some of the postmortems, which it eagerly passed along to Bobby Kennedy, riling him up anew. "[Clarence] Jones said that the Attorney General was under the sharpest attack that he had seen anyone undergo and that there was nothing that the Attorney General could say," one report stated. "Each time [Kennedy] said something it merely underlined the deep gulf. Levison said that the Attorney General really needed it."

"Jones agreed with Levison and said that the Attorney General had come there thinking that he knew everything and had not been prepared to change his mind," it went on. "According to Jones, the Attorney General took the simple approach stating that the current Administration had done more than anyone else in the area of civil rights. Levison replied, 'so he thinks he can get away with that, well he doesn't know what year this is. He doesn't know what Birmingham means.'" Levison suggested that King be briefed on the meeting before seeing the president. It didn't matter, Jones replied becasue Robert Kennedy was "running the civil rights movement." "The worst illustration of white arrogant liberalism," was how one participant described Kennedy. "This was a good description of the Attorney General," Levison replied.

A couple of days later, Levison had a second conversation about the meeting—this time with an "unknown male, possibly the FBI," speculated Jones again. "The unknown male told Levison that the Attorney General was really turned on his heels," stated the FBI report that followed. "Levison then commented that the Attorney General has been able to lick every competitor he has come up against, and has made this the passion of his life, but has run into the first force that he can't knock over."

For James Wechsler of the *New York Post*, the episode provided the latest chance to gauge who Robert Kennedy was and what he was becoming. Would he be embittered or enlightened by such a trial by fire? "His response on reflection could be a large clue to the size of the man," Wechsler wrote. Within a few days, Kennedy's views had eased, beginning with those on Jerome Smith. "I guess if I were in his shoes, if I had gone through what he's gone through, I might feel differently about this country," he conceded.

It was only in another chat with Anthony Lewis eighteen months after the fact—this time, his comments would be sealed for the next couple of decades—that Kennedy's unvarnished views of the meeting emerged. What also became clear is that Kennedy's reactions often went through *three* stages rather than two: first from the gut, then something more considered, then back to the gut again. One reason Kennedy was constantly seen to be evolving was that he was constantly regressing. These visceral views of his were not always pretty. The veneer of empathy was often very thin, and was quickly stripped away once he was challenged.

On display that afternoon in his father's apartment, he told Lewis, was the guilt of the privileged: Jerome Smith excepted, all those folks had it made. "So, the way to show that they hadn't forgotten where they came from was to berate me and berate the United States government," he explained. "None of them lived in Harlem," he went on. "I mean, they were wealthy Negroes. They were married to white people.... They all had money, except the one kid from SNCC [*sic*] who had been beaten up by the police, and he was sort of their hero." "I was foolish enough to sit down and talk to them and get involved with a lot of Negroes who don't speak for anybody and who used this meeting and used me," he continued. "It makes me cross at myself." But Simeon Booker, Bobby Kennedy's old friend from *Jet*, was impressed. A skilled politician wouldn't have exposed himself like that, but Bobby did," he wrote. "He went up there, and they cussed him out, and they told him he didn't know what the hell it was all about. I think it made him say, 'Well, we're not going in the right direction. There's some other things that we've got to explore and find.'"

Clark himself was heartened by a speech on race that Lyndon Johnson delivered a few days later in Gettysburg—one which, he thought, "contained almost every single suggestion we made to Bobby Kennedy at that horrible meeting." Unless Kennedy had a photographic memory, Clark theorized, he must have taped the proceedings, then passed along what he'd learned to the vice president, who'd taken it to heart. (Knowing little of the enmity between the two men, Clark could not have imagined how implausible that was.) But on Robert Kennedy's end, something had sunk in. "I knew that he had been seriously shook up from that meeting, and that he would never be the same again," said Belafonte. But "how that would resolve itself was not clear to me."

"Who sketches Robert F. Kennedy does so at his peril," the columnist Joseph Kraft, who grew close to Robert Kennedy, told Joseph Wershba of the *New York Post* almost a year after the Baldwin meeting. "The attorney general is a bundle of many dominant traits; and these are sometimes in tension, and at times finding new forms of expression. Inside as well as out, he is a man in motion." A White House aide put the matter a bit differently. "The one word I would apply to him with any confidence is 'educable,'" he said.

Interviewing Kennedy that day, Wershba was struck by another word to which Kennedy repeatedly returned when he discussed segregation. "The word was 'insult,'" Wershba wrote. "It is not a legal word. It was the word that James Baldwin and his friends had been trying to get over to the Attorney General. They may not have succeeded that day in May '63...but the Attorney General has a great capacity for learning."

Just three weeks after King was named *Time* magazine's Man of the Year, 116 demonstrators were arrested for picketing a segregated restaurant in Atlanta.

# SIX

# AS OLD AS THE SCRIPTURES

Martin Luther King savored, and exploited, the triumph of Birmingham. As part of a "victory tour" for the SCLC that also took him to Cleveland, Chicago, St. Louis, and Louisville, he held the Rally for Freedom on May 26 in Los Angeles—the printed program had a snarling police dog on the cover—with Joanne Woodward, Paul Newman, and José Ferrer, among other Hollywood luminaries, on hand. (Sammy Davis, Jr., donated a week's salary, or $20,000, from his upcoming engagement at the Sands Hotel in Las Vegas to the group.) A party at the Beverly Hills home of Burt Lancaster followed.

"We are through with gradualism and are through with tokenism and look-how-far-you've-come-ism," King told the guests. "I think we should be concerned with what-we-have-done-ism," Marlon Brando added afterward, pledging a day's pay to the cause. "'We Shall Overcome' rang out from the Lancaster home like 'Wings Over Jordan,'" *Jet* reported.

Sensing new opportunities and perils, an energized King pressed for legislation and a meeting with John Kennedy. "King stated that he would like to put so much pressure on the President that he would have to sign an executive order making segregation unconstitutional," J. Edgar Hoover reported to Robert Kennedy in late May after reviewing a conversation between King and Stanley Levison that the FBI had just monitored. King had never seen the Negro community as aroused, determined, or enthusiastic, he told

The slaying of Medgar Evers in 1963 was a chief flashpoint of the decade — and his funeral, the first in a series for prominent social justice advocates.

Levison a few days later. He now endorsed a mass "March on Washington," an idea A. Philip Randolph had first broached during World War II and had recently revisited. The same threat that had led Franklin Roosevelt to integrate the war industries might now frighten John F. Kennedy into action. Simply announcing such a march could be productive, Levison speculated. Even the faithful FBI employee transcribing their conversation could sense the euphoria: "They agree that all sorts of very exciting things are happening," she reported. Word soon emerged that the Kennedy administration would introduce civil rights legislation outlawing discrimination in public accommodations.

Events now unfolded with breathtaking speed. On June 6, King went on David Susskind's widely viewed and respected television program *Open End*. In the show, which famously went on as long as Susskind wanted it to, King had an hour and forty-three minutes to describe his grim assessment of race relations. He said that taking over from Eisenhower's, the Kennedy administration had substituted "an inadequate approach for a miserable one" and that "the plight of the vast majority of Negroes remains the same," and called on the president to cancel his upcoming European trip to push for new legislation. While Nehru condemned the caste system, he complained, "We very seldom if ever hear the president of the United States speaking to the nation on the moral issues of integration."

Near the end of the program, Susskind asked King if he thought it miraculous that he'd not been murdered. Many viewers might have found such a question startling or impertinent, though as Susskind may well have known, it was an issue King pondered continually, and he was ready for it. "I'm religious enough to say that this is the grace of God," he replied. The day after the interview aired, the *New York Times* splashed it across the front page, calling it King's "broadest attack to date" on the administration. It was viewed in a number of American cities, and both the BBC and Radio Free Europe rebroadcast it. History may well undoubtedly rank him one of the great men of America," *Variety* wrote presciently of King in a review of the show.

Five days later, Governor Wallace stood defiantly and, in the end, pointlessly, in the schoolhouse door in a futile attempt to keep the two black students out of the University of Alabama. Afterward, President Kennedy asked the major television networks to give him airtime at eight o'clock that evening to discuss the proposed new civil rights bill and to plead for racial understanding and conciliation. Given how momentous a speech it was, Kennedy handled it with astonishing cool; only minutes before, he had no text and was prepared to speak spontaneously—as Bobby Kennedy had urged him to do—if need be. Evidently, he was ready to say what he said. Perhaps he, too, was relieved at long last to be doing what was so clearly called for. "We are confronted primarily with a moral issue," he declared. "It is as old as the Scriptures and as clear as the American Constitution. The heart of the question is whether all Americans are to be afforded equal rights and equal opportunities, whether we are going to treat our fellow Americans as we want to be treated." To CORE's James Farmer it was "the strongest civil rights speech made by any president, Lincoln included." To those at a younger and more impressionable stage of life, for whom John F. Kennedy was their first real president, it was what stuck with them, and what made what would soon befall him so unbearable and enduring.

"It often helps me to be pushed," John Kennedy had once told King. Now King had pushed Bobby to push Jack, and the result was precisely the sort of speech King had long implored President Kennedy to give. Watching in Atlanta, he exulted. "That white man not only stepped up to the plate, he hit it over the fence!" he told a colleague. This was the moment when, as King later put it, the first John Kennedy receded and the second emerged. To Kenneth Clark, it suggested either that Robert Kennedy had been listening, and learning, that afternoon in New York City, or, more likely, that John Kennedy had learned something from his brother's ordeal. Hansberry, too, felt vindicated—that for all the rancor that day in New York, it turned out they had actually reached Bobby. "I think we penetrated," she said. "We are a hurt people and he got it."

John F. Kennedy's move from detachment to commitment on civil rights was startling; nothing in the historical record, or anything John Kennedy himself ever said, explains it. That's probably no accident: first, because it was largely Robert Kennedy's doing and, second, RFK, ever loyal and deferential to his brother, hid his tracks. In King's circle, meanwhile, there were more sober appraisals of Robert Kennedy. To one adviser, Vincent Harding, it was merely another example of the younger brother's keen sense of realpolitik or simple political survival—a savvy, last-ditch mending of the disintegrating social fabric or, as he put it more bluntly, a way "to get the niggers off the street." He compared Robert Kennedy—unflatteringly—to Abraham Lincoln as a good man whose first commitment was to the preservation of white America. "I don't buy the stories of how deeply he knew black people and blah blah blah," said Harding. "I don't think that's the case. I think he was in some ways brutally political, but was wise enough and sharp enough to see the ways in which black people had to be dealt with if the system was going to be carried on."

King, he said, felt this same ambivalence. "On the one hand, he really *hoped* that he could believe in people like Bobby," he said. "And on the other hand, a certain black wisdom told him that he had better not try to believe in them."

The legislation's prospects were poor. But to Robert Kennedy, guaranteeing southern blacks the right to sleep in motels rather than in their cars and to sit in hamburger joints rather than fetch their food around the back wasn't the only measure of success; there was also a message to be sent. "What in my judgment was even more important was to retain the confidence of the Negro population in their government and in the white majority," he said. "And I thought that there was a great danger of losing that, unless we took a very significant step, such as the passage of legislation. And although the legislation itself wouldn't affect the Negro in the North, I think that it was important to pass the legislation just to show the Negro in the North that the white population was going to do something about this problem."

June 11, 1963: The night Deputy Attorney General Nicholas Katzenbach confronted segregationist Governor George Wallace at the University of Alabama, John Kennedy called civil rights "a moral issue...as old as the Scriptures and as clear as the American Constitution."

How much more remained to be done was apparent in the early morning hours after the president's speech, when the NAACP's field secretary in Mississippi, Medgar Evers, was shot to death in front of his house in Jackson. Robert Kennedy quickly issued a statement, declaring that the FBI was already on the case. (Thirty-one years would pass before Byron De La Beckwith was convicted in the killing.) Robert Kennedy attended Evers's funeral in Washington and would grow close to his brother, Charles, especially once they shared the grim bond of losing their older brothers to assassination. But there was, arguably, some prior history, too. The previous year, the liberal Washington lawyer Joseph Rauh tried to alert Kennedy to repeated threats against Evers and his family, threats that neither the local police nor the FBI, Evers believed, took seriously. Kennedy recalled no such warnings, but James Wechsler of the *New York Post* had addressed the situation in his column, which would in all likelihood have been called to Kennedy's

attention. "No doubt Bobby Kennedy took the message seriously," wrote Wechsler after Evers's murder. He was surely being polite.

A few days after that shooting, demonstrators gathered outside the Justice Department in Washington. Among them was Jack Newfield of the *Village Voice*, whose wariness of Robert Kennedy dating back to the McCarthy era had only been fortified by what he saw as the administration's sluggishness on civil rights. Twice, he'd been jailed after demonstrations. "We liked Kennedy as little as the Southern governors did," he later wrote. After twenty minutes or so, Robert Kennedy, "slight" and "taut," emerged from the building and addressed the group. It was an absolutely extraordinary gesture, but won him few points from the protesters. "With pure fury," Newfield wrote, he stared at Kennedy's "crew cut face." "It was, I remember, a hard Irish face: alert, but without much character, a little like the faces that used to follow me home from Hebrew school, taunting, 'Christ killer.'"

Already annoyed by the placards—"Let Negroes Work in the Justice Department"; "Why an Almost Lily White Justice Department? It's Not Easter"—Kennedy tensed up further when someone shouted that he'd seen few blacks leaving the building. "His skin seemed to draw even tighter around his sharp features, and the hostility radiating from his blue eyes became even more intense," recalled Newfield. Of course, Kennedy had greatly diversified the Justice Department, but that wasn't the point he made. Instead, his reflexive reaction, as always, was defiance. "Individuals will be hired according to their ability, not their color," Kennedy shouted back through a bullhorn, which "made his voice sound both squeaky and strident."

It was "exactly the sort of impersonal, legalistic response, blind to the larger moral implications of our protest, that we felt made Kennedy such an inadequate Attorney General," Newfield wrote. "We booed him in a hoarse, throaty roar that ricocheted

RFK addressed CORE protesters outside the Department of Justice shortly after his brother's civil rights address.

off the white marble walls of the Department of Justice." Newfield soon came to hold a very different view of Kennedy with equal vehemence. But his (largely) New York (and more largely) Jewish hostility toward Kennedy—rooted in what was perceived to be his right-wing past and authoritarianism, his father's tolerance toward Adolf Hitler, and, perhaps for others besides Newfield, those long walks home from Hebrew school—was something that Bobby Kennedy, unlike the more congenial Jack, would never entirely overcome.

On June 22, three days after introducing the civil rights bill, both Kennedys met and spoke with black leaders at the White House. Their agenda that day was to get the group behind the proposed legislation and urge them to do nothing to undermine it, like staging an ill-timed and potentially off-putting march. "We want success in Congress, not just a big show at the Capitol," John Kennedy told them. "Some of these people are looking for an excuse to be against us, and I don't want to give any of them a chance to say, 'Yes, I'm for the bill, but I am damned if I will vote for it at the point of a gun.'"

"It may seem ill-timed," replied King. "Frankly, I have never engaged in any direct action movement which did not seem ill-timed. Some people thought Birmingham ill-timed." "Including the attorney general," the president interjected. Neither Kennedy was won over. They had now staked their political futures on civil rights—"I'm in it up to here," the president declared, pointing to somewhere between neck and forehead—and nothing could go wrong.

And, in that regard, despite repeated pleas from various administration officials, King *still* wouldn't drop Stanley Levison and Jack O'Dell as advisers. Instead, he tried rather half-heartedly to hide their continuing connection, fooling no one.

Robert Kennedy's views grew more distant from Hoover's by the day, but on questions of communism, they were largely on the same page. He took Hoover's warnings seriously; as exaggerated as they were—O'Dell was a peripheral figure and Levison's communist ties were extremely attenuated—they were one more reason he kept King at arm's length. "We never wanted to get very close to him, just because of these contacts and connections that he had, which we felt were damaging to the civil rights movement, and because we were so intimately involved in the struggle for civil rights, also damaged us," he later explained. "It damaged what we were trying to do."

Now, with a civil rights bill under consideration and a reelection campaign looming, the stakes had grown even higher. So King was triple-teamed that day at the White House, with first Burke Marshall, then Robert Kennedy (who checked with Hoover before doing so), and then John Kennedy pulling him aside and leaning on him to ditch Levison and O'Dell. The president's warning came during a stroll "*way* out in the Rose Garden," as Andrew Young put it,' that left King's associates, who already assumed that Hoover was listening in on them, marveling that he was evidently listening in on John F. Kennedy as well.

Both Levison and O'Dell were Marxists, the president told King; he had to let them go. Their fates were wed, said Kennedy: "If they shoot *you* down, they'll shoot us down, too." King was variously protective, resistant, incredulous, dismissive. He didn't believe the charges. He wanted proof. But he was also appreciative. During that same stroll, Kennedy told King, "I assume you know you're under very close surveillance." By making that disclosure, Andrew Young later said, the president had taken him into his confidence and tied their destinies together, something that was never to happen with the attorney general. That was why, Young went on, King "felt closer to John Kennedy in some ways than he did to Bobby."

Nothing having been resolved or promised, the two then rejoined the group. King and Robert Kennedy were photographed standing alongside one another that day—the only time that would ever happen. But while physically close, they appeared to be in separate worlds: Kennedy is smiling and appears perfectly at ease, while King looks off anxiously. He'd be on friendlier territory the next day in Detroit, speaking to a throng of 125,000 after a joyous Walk for Freedom. "I have a dream this afternoon," he told them repeatedly.

Robert Kennedy became the new civil rights bill's greatest champion before the various Senate committees considering it. "How can we say to a Negro in Jackson: 'When a war comes, you will be an American citizen, but in the meantime, you're a citizen of Mississippi and we can't help you?'" he told the Senate Commerce Committee. Before the Judiciary Committee, he fenced lightheartedly with the veteran segregationist Strom Thurmond, who asked whether a restaurant could still serve only red-haired secretaries if it wished. Only once, noted E. W. Kenworthy of the *New York Times*, did Kennedy's voice take on "an emotional timbre": when Thurmond—who, it was later revealed, had as a young man fathered a child with his family's sixteen-year-old black maid—asked him why the Supreme Court wouldn't throw out a ban on discrimination in public places now, as it had done in 1883. "Senator, I really think this country is moving along," Kennedy replied. "We are a different people." (Thurmond received Kennedy far more politely than a Harlem church had received King the day before, when five hundred people, primed by Malcolm X to "let Uncle Tom know that we are against him and do not believe what he preaches," hurled eggs at King as he spoke.)

During the same hearings, Mississippi governor Ross Barnett brandished the familiar picture from 1957 of King at that "communist training school," and George Wallace testified that King belonged to more communist organizations than anyone in the country. (He also attacked the administration for "fawning and pawing over" King and turning the White House into a "virtual switchboard" for him.) In fact, Kennedy countered, nothing suggested "that any of the top leadership of the major civil rights groups are communists, or communist-controlled." He cited the FBI as one of his sources and it was true: the bureau had never proved that King was "controlled" by anyone.

Nothing the FBI ever overheard in Levison's conversations with King suggested that Levison retained any connection to the Communist Party, let alone took orders from it or tried to bend King on its behalf. But Levison himself realized the liability he'd become; shortly after the White House meeting, he suggested to King that they part ways for the sake of the movement. "The movement needed the Kennedys too much," Levison later told Arthur Schlesinger. "I said it would not be in the interests of the movement to hold on to me if the Kennedys had doubts." King agreed, but only to a point: they would no longer talk directly. Henceforth, they would communicate through an intermediary: King's lawyer, Clarence Jones.

King's continued defiance prompted Robert Kennedy to take drastic action. On July 16, he proposed to the FBI that it tap both the home and office phones of both King and Jones. According to the head of the bureau's domestic intelligence operations, William Sullivan, Hoover had long wanted to tap King, but "Bobby Kennedy resisted, resisted, and resisted." But now it was Kennedy who wanted to do it and the FBI that counseled caution. Courtney Evans, Kennedy's liaison at the FBI, noted that since King was constantly traveling, eavesdropping on his home and office phones wouldn't yield much and—given the firestorm that would ensue if word of the taps ever leaked—probably wasn't worth the risk. Kennedy concurred; for the time being, only Jones would receive "technical coverage" (Hoover-ese for wiretapping).

But that was significant enough. With Levison—avuncular, cerebral, white—King's conversations were invariably high-minded and decorous. With Jones—who was black, roughly King's contemporary, and spoke more colloquially—they were more casual, candid, and raunchy—filled, as the King biographer Taylor Branch has put it, with "talk of sex" and "Negro vernacular." They would provide plenty of fodder to anyone out to destroy King. (An unanticipated bonus came when King and his family stayed with Jones for several days shortly after the tap was installed, enabling bureau moles to hear—just to cite one example—King joked with a friend about Bayard Rustin and his vices. He hoped Rustin "don't take a drink before the March," the friend remarked. "...And grab one little brother, 'cause he will grab one when he has a drink," King replied.)

Jones suspected his phone was tapped, mentioning it so often to King that he dismissed Jones as a "left-wing McCarthyite." "He would say that the FBI had more important things to do," Jones recalled. "And I would say, 'Really? There's nothing more important for them to do than to wiretap our conversations, Martin." And the bureau quickly passed along whatever it picked up to Robert Kennedy, who passed it on to John Kennedy. Of greatest prurient interest—and, of course, having nothing whatever to do with national security—were King's extramarital affairs.

Charges of womanizing had long dogged King, even in the black press. A "prominent minister in the Deep South, a man who has been making the headlines recently in his fight for civil rights, had better watch his step," the *Pittsburgh Courier* had whispered in 1957. It was a reason why King could not have gone to bat for Levison in 1963, Levison later told Schlesinger: the FBI just had too much dirt on him. King shared this trait with a Kennedy all right, Levison went on, though that Kennedy was John rather than Robert. "Both had powerful fathers who were men of notorious sexual prowess," he explained. "Perhaps both were unconsciously driven to prove that they were as much men as their fathers." He mentioned a conversation on the subject he'd just had with Roger Wilkins. "He made the point that in the black middle-class community wives always assume that their husbands are playing around," he went on. "The concept of *macho* is very big both in developing countries and among developing peoples in developed countries....Everyone has been trying to protect Coretta King, but she is mature and realistic and refuses to be upset. She said the other day, 'All I know is that Martin loved me and loved his family, and I don't care what else he did.'"

(Schlesinger dutifully tried to turn King's philandering into a virtue, depicting it as [a] proof of his passionate nature, [b] an attempt to outdo the virile Daddy King, [c] a way to combat a black man's feelings of subjugation, [d] a service that black preachers traditionally extended to female congregants, and [e] an expression of his religious faith. "Martin really believed in the gospel of love," someone told him.)

King's extramarital activities opened up a new front in the FBI's war against him—one more promising than its sputtering Red-baiting. It also provided a wedge for Hoover to drive between his two greatest enemies. Like Hoover, Robert Kennedy was a bit of a prude—the type who never cursed, or laughed at off-color jokes, or felt comfortable around gay people. ("There was something exotic about me that he couldn't entirely accept," his one-time neighbor, Truman Capote, once said of him.) Already uncomfortable around King—"rather formal" was how Levison described their relationship—any revelations about King's racy personal life would only disconcert him further. "Bob Kennedy just wasn't that kind of person," Burke Marshall later said. "He didn't understand that, you know, and he didn't like it. He wouldn't approve it." Within a few weeks, Hoover had gleaned enough dirt on King to compose a two-page memorandum, which made its way from Deputy Attorney General Nicholas Katzenbach to Robert Kennedy to John. "I thought you would be interested in the attached memorandum," he hand-wrote to his brother on August 20. It was not the only King-related piece of mail the president received around that time. Shortly after the death of two-day-old Patrick Bouvier Kennedy on August 9, King was among those sending his bereaved parents his condolences.


On August 28, with the Lincoln Memorial behind him, Martin Luther King stood before two hundred thousand people on the Washington Mall. Kennedy's minions had vetted the various speeches that day, and in the case of John Lewis, who was to deliver a fiery denunciation of the Kennedy administration's record on civil rights, neutered it.

King's speech was not vetted, nor did it need to be: as Levison noted, he'd given prototypes of it many times before. It began in rather pedestrian fashion, laden with the usual heavy-handed metaphors — beacons and flames, day and night, islands and oceans, dark valleys and sunlit paths, quicksand and rock, sweltering summers and invigorating autumns, warm thresholds and palaces. It gained some strength when he spoke of nonviolence and racial brotherhood, a message amplified by the magnificently mixed crowd arrayed in front of him, there for millions watching on television to behold. But it was only after Mahalia Jackson, who'd already sung two hymns, shouted out, "Tell them about the dream, Martin!" that the speech took off toward posterity. To another great orator, its greatness was also instantly apparent. "That guy is really good," John Kennedy said at the White House. "Oh, my God," Katzenbach told Robert Kennedy as they watched it together at the Justice Department. "He'll get that crowd revved up and then we're gonna really have a problem." "Come out quickly! Martin King is speaking!" someone shouted to the panel that Edward R. Murrow, then head of the United States Information Agency, had assembled to comment upon the march, and Marlon Brando, James Baldwin, and Sidney Poitier, among others, sat around a television and watched King tearfully. "What are you crying for, man?" Harry Belafonte berated them. "Why don't you smile and join the dream? You're listening to the first Negro President of the United States!'"

The *New York Post* offered reprints of the speech for a dime, and for less than a penny a pop for orders of five hundred or more. And King's lawyer, Clarence Jones went to court to enjoin three companies (one was Motown, another, Twentieth Century Fox) from selling bootlegged recordings of it.

Although the Kennedy brothers had reservations about the 1963 March on Washington, once plans were determined, Bobby did all he could to ensure its success. As did King, whose speech prompted John Kennedy to declare, "That guy is really good."

Right up until it happened, Bobby Kennedy's attitude toward the march had remained jaundiced. "So you're down here for that old black fairy's anti-Kennedy demonstration?" he had asked the diplomat Marietta Tree, referring to its principal organizer, Bayard Rustin. Then, when Tree had tried to talk about King, Kennedy attacked him. "He's not a serious person," he said. "If the country knew what we know about King's goings on, he'd be finished." Still, while the March on Washington appeared to be the indigenous work of civil rights activists, it was also in many ways a Robert Kennedy production. To avoid all possible snafus, Kennedy aides had worked full-time for weeks on the event, making sure that participants had portable toilets rather than trenches (as one Pentagon official suggested) at their disposal, had the proceedings ended before dark, that drinks be sold only in paper cups (so there'd be no bottles to hurl), that no police dogs were deployed (Birmingham had given them a bad name), that a switch be installed on the speakers platform to cut off all sound (should, say, some Black Muslims muscle their way in). "Bayard Rustin and A. Philip Randolph may have taken a good deal of credit, and they should. But the person that organized it, as a matter of fact, was the attorney general," Marshall said.

It's easy to forget how low white expectations of black America once were. In addition to fears of black violence were worries about black misbehavior. "What if they pee on the Washington Monument?" John F. Kennedy joked. "There is almost universal admission that this was an extraordinary exercise in organization and self-discipline," Wechsler wrote shortly afterward. "But there is the intimation that what made this so astonishing a display was that so many Negroes could congregate in a single place, along with some of their white brethren, without crudely disgracing themselves. The stereotype was that such a multitude would include a high percentage of rapists, thugs, dope-pushers and other varieties of vandals; hell would have to break loose in some form." Instead, thanks in part to Kennedy and his crew, everything had turned out just about perfectly. In what was one of Martin Luther King's crowning performances, Robert Kennedy had been a key choreographer.

Speaking to Arthur Schlesinger the next year, Jacqueline Kennedy recalled an odd event in the aftermath of the demonstration. "[Jack] told me of a tape the FBI had of Martin Luther King when he was here for the freedom march," Jacqueline Kennedy later told Schlesinger. "And [the president] said this with no bitterness or anything, how [King] was calling up all these girls, and arranging for a party of men and women, I mean, sort of an orgy in the hotel, and everything." Her husband hadn't editorialized about it, she said, but she did, contrasting the man in the recordings with the righteous figure who'd stood before the Lincoln Memorial only a few hours earlier. "I said, 'Oh, but Jack, that's so terrible. I mean, that man is, you know, such a phony then.'" But the FBI did not in fact begin bugging King's hotel rooms until the following January, and it seems more likely she was recalling a tape from then—featuring King, some SCLC colleagues, and two women from Philadelphia—selected from fifteen reels of recordings made at the Willard Hotel, that Hoover shared with Bobby Kennedy, and Bobby Kennedy then shared with her. In it, according to Taylor Branch, King can be heard shouting such things as "I'm fucking for God!" and "I'm not a Negro tonight!" "This will destroy the burr-head," a highly satisfied Hoover declared afterward when he got to listen to the proceedings.

To the FBI, King's very success in the March on Washington only proved how dangerous he was. "Personally, I believe in light of King's powerful demagogic speech yesterday he stands head and shoulders over all other Negro leaders put together when it comes to influencing great masses of Negroes," William Sullivan wrote to his colleagues. "We must mark him now, if we have not done so before, as the most dangerous Negro of the future in this Nation from the standpoint of communism, the Negro, and national security." To Sullivan, who'd fallen afoul of J. Edgar Hoover a few months earlier by pooh-poohing communist infiltration of the civil rights movement, demonizing King offered his only shot at rehabilitation. On September 6, he urged that Kennedy be asked to reconsider a tap on King's phone.

On September 15 in a crime that shocked the world, four young black girls were killed by an enormous explosion as they changed into their choir robes in the basement of the 16th Street Baptist Church in Birmingham. Once more, King pleaded with the Kennedy administration: unless it protected black lives, his calls for moderation would fail and "the worst racial holocaust this nation has ever seen" could follow. King's hold on the movement looked increasingly iffy. James Baldwin denounced him. The writer John O. Killen told a rally in New York that he could no longer be asked to "love" those who killed blacks. "It was clear to his audience that he was breaking with the doctrine of the Rev. Martin Luther King, Jr.," the *New York Times* reported. Bull Connor blamed the Supreme Court and "little Bobby Kennedy" for creating the climate for the bombing while suggesting that King's associates might have planted the bomb.

On October 7, Hoover formally asked Robert Kennedy for permission to wiretap King "at his current address or at any future address to which he may move," as well as the SCLC offices in Atlanta and New York. This time, Kennedy agreed. There are different explanations: Kennedy was irate at King for sticking by Levison. Kennedy feared that if he didn't, Hoover could help kill the civil rights bill, or spread word of John Kennedy's dalliances. Kennedy wanted to clear King, something he felt only tapping his phone — and thereby proving nothing nefarious was afoot — would do. The taps were authorized for only thirty days — enough time to see whether they were worth the risk. That meant Kennedy would revisit them in late November and early December. "I'm sure he intended to follow it very closely," said Ramsey Clark. But events intervened and, as Clark put it, "my guess is it was just blotted out of his memory."

Speaking to Anthony Lewis in 1964, Kennedy was more nonchalant about the decision than embarrassed or contrite. He described how, having heard in 1961 that King was "perhaps" tied up with some communists, he'd ordered an "intensive investigation" into him "to protect ourselves." "They" — presumably the FBI — made that intensive investigation, he went on, "and I gave them, also, permission to put a tap on his telephone." Lewis did not pursue the point, and there the matter rested. But it was one of the most fateful, telling moments in the King-Kennedy relationship — and, to Kennedy's critics, among its most damning. "One of the most ignominious acts in modern American history," the King scholar David Garrow has called it. A "low point," said Clarence Jones, who called the notion that Kennedy was actually looking out for King a "fairy tale." Kennedy was being Kennedy, he said, looking out only for the Kennedys. "My God, a man's privacy is almost sacred," Roger Wilkins later said. He called the wiretaps "just outrageous."

The taps interposed yet another barrier between Robert Kennedy and King: how does one act with someone one has spied upon, whose deepest secrets one already knows? "If Robert Kennedy could speak today, I think he would have said that was the worst thing he ever did," John Lewis later said. The question is whether the ever-evolving Kennedy lived long enough to reach that point, and whether, in the meantime, what the taps picked up drove an additional wedge between them.

"Robert Kennedy always had tremendous respect for King's symbolic importance not only in the black community but historically," Frank Mankiewicz said. "But I had the feeling...that he was somewhat less than happy about King's personal conduct and standing....He did make a face once every once in a while whenever called upon to defend King, which I must say he always did very eloquently." But Kennedy's longtime aide, Adam Walinsky, vehemently disagreed, insisting that some of Kennedy's older advisers were simply being overly protective. "Do you really think any Kennedy male was uneasy about somebody else getting laid?" he

On November 20, 1963, King was photographed by FBI surveillance in the company of key advisers Stanley Levison (left) and Clarence Jones (partially visible, right).

asked. "How could you have worried about that when you have Marilyn Monroe standing up there telling the world what was going on between her and President Kennedy?" Had King ever gotten caught, Walinsky added, Kennedy would have faulted him only for his sloppiness. Or, as another family member put it, "It just doesn't make sense to me. How could he have loved his father as much as he did if sexual behavior was important?"

The FBI construed its license to include not just King's homes, but also any place he stayed, so it began following him and tapping his phone wherever he went. And though Kennedy hadn't authorized it and the law in the area was fuzzy, the bureau assumed it was also free to sprinkle microphones everywhere as well, and then distribute what it learned to government officials and friendly journalists.

On the cold, rainy afternoon of November 20, 1963, two knots of men waited for Martin Luther King, who was between flights and en route to Chicago, at what would still be known—for a few weeks—as Idlewild Airport in New York. One consisted of Stanley Levison and Clarence Jones; the airport was one place where, they thought, they could talk to King without being overheard. Somewhere nearby was a second group, of FBI agents. Their mission was to photograph the three men together. Perhaps, a bureau official speculated, the picture would be introduced as evidence in a conspiracy trial against Martin Luther King.

That same afternoon, in Washington, fifteen or twenty of Robert Kennedy's closest associates gathered at the Justice Department to mark his thirty-eighth birthday. Kennedy seemed glum and depressed. Though he continued to inveigh, passionately and eloquently, against segregation, he was continually under attack, including from King, for watering down the civil rights bill. Meantime, in the white South, the Kennedys, *plural*, had become the enemy, just as Robert Kennedy had warned his brother when he was first offered the attorney general job. "Everything I did before, up to '61, '62 was focused on me, and *he* wasn't such a bad fellow," he said. "By 1963, it was focused on both of us." He had grown weary of the criticism. "You have probably done the most for Negroes, and you have probably been criticized the most by Negroes," Simeon Booker once told him in an interview. He asked him if he were discouraged. "I think I have to agree with Lincoln that if the end brings me out all right, what is said against me won't amount to anything," Kennedy replied. "But if the end brings me out wrong, ten angels swearing I was right won't make any difference."

Rumors persisted that Robert Kennedy would replace Dean Rusk at the State Department. (Richard Nixon had said he was well-suited for the post: "He is tough-minded and intelligent, and has the will to win.") Word was that Kennedy's secretary, Angela Novello, had been measuring the drapes in Rusk's Foggy Bottom office. She was mum on that, but the boxes from Tiffany's she handed out to everyone at the party that day seemed to say *something*: inside were cuff links with the department seal on one side and, on the other, "RFK," the initials of the recipient, and the years "1961–63." "We were all touched and, as the meaning sank in, shocked," Jack Rosenthal, then one of Kennedy's special assistants, later recalled.

As was his wont, Kennedy climbed up on the desk at his birthday party and began to speak. "In a whimsical sad vein, he reflected on what a lightning rod he had become for the president and perhaps what a burden" because of civil rights, Ramsey Clark recalled. Clark and a colleague noted Kennedy's melancholy as they left the party. Kennedy himself headed to the White House for a reception; his brother was leaving for Texas the next day to tend to an internecine squabble among Democrats there. "He seemed to think it was a useless trip, a strain on busy people," Clark remembered.

Racial issues followed John Kennedy to Dallas, and even to the Texas School Book Depository Building: had his motorcade not passed directly by the place at lunchtime, the superintendent there later said, half his white employees wouldn't have bothered watching it. "Except for my niggers, the boys are conservative, like me—like most Texans," he explained. As the procession passed by, Robert Kennedy was meeting with the United States attorney for Manhattan, Robert Morgenthau, at Hickory Hill. That's when Hoover called with the news.

Martin Luther King had Jones prepare an article for the *New York Herald Tribune*. It became his official line. "The late, great President John F. Kennedy," he came to call him. But at the time, on a more personal level, he had varied reactions to Kennedy's assassination, none of them exactly grief; there were times when the distance King very deliberately interposed between himself and all political figures had its advantages. "Oh, I hope that he will live, this is just terrible," he told his wife. "I think if he lives, if he pulls through this, it will help him to understand better what we go through." When word came that Kennedy had died—the assassin, Lee Harvey Oswald, would soon be apprehended—King went quiet, then said, "This is what is going to happen to me. This is such a sick society." Then, thinking very pragmatically, he called the killing "a blessing for civil rights." Had Kennedy lived, he reasoned, his civil rights bill would have floundered; his martyrdom would become a propellant. "So I do think we have some very hopeful days ahead," he said.

In the black community, James Farmer's reaction was far more typical. "I loved him," he said. "I was crushed for weeks. Just couldn't cope." He'd been in an elevator somewhere in the Midwest when he'd overheard two businessmen conversing. "Did you hear? They just killed Kennedy in Dallas," said one. "Yeah, they got the wrong fuckin' Kennedy," the other replied. "They should have gotten that little devil Bobby." "It was all I could do to keep from going after those guys physically," Farmer recalled.

It's unclear whether King attended Kennedy's funeral. He and his wife were invited, and Coretta King later wrote about being there. ("I watched Jackie Kennedy and felt a great sense of pain for the loss of her husband and the father of her children," she recalled. "As I kept thinking about Martin, I identified with her ordeal. Many people considered Martin's work to be more dangerous than that of the president. If they could kill a president, what did that say about Martin's chances for survival in America? In a strange way, Kennedy's funeral further prepared me to accept what I knew in my heart would be our own fate.") But as the FBI listened in (and, later, committed to paper), King told Clarence Jones he was hurt *not* to have been invited. Perhaps, in the famously disorganized SCLC offices, the invitation got lost, or perhaps the FBI eavesdropper made a mistake. There are, however, no photographs of King at the ceremony.

Earlier, Booker was startled by all the black faces in the line outside the Capitol as Kennedy lay in state. His piece in *Ebony*, entitled "How JFK Surpassed Abraham Lincoln," observed that more than any president before him, Kennedy had given new dignity to black Americans. Never, he went on, had President

Kennedy criticized a demonstration or Freedom Ride, though some in his administration had. It was Bobby's final gift to his brother: by playing the administration's bad cop, he'd given Jack a posthumous clean slate. And John Kennedy, in turn, would bestow a gift on Bobby: the love that black America lavished on him in death would live on, and come to suffuse Bobby Kennedy as well. Booker realized Robert Kennedy's new, unique power: assuming he stayed on in Washington, he wrote, he would be Lyndon Johnson's passport to the black community, the man who could convince them he wasn't a southern cracker. "RFK is the key," said Booker. "Where he walks Negroes will follow."

News of the assassination was also closely followed at the Missouri State Penitentiary in Jefferson City, where one inmate recalled his conversation with another. "That is one nigger-loving SOB that got shot," the second inmate remarked. Whenever the second man read anything about Martin Luther King, the first man said, he got agitated and started cursing King, and black people generally. He'd vowed to get King when he got out of prison. He'd elaborated on the idea to a third inmate, claiming that a "businessmen's association" had even offered him $100,000 to do the job. If there were still a bounty on King's head as there had been on Kennedy's, he said, he'd be the man to collect it. His name was James Earl Ray.

The president's funeral procession to St. Matthew's Cathedral, Washington, D.C., November 25, 1963. Jacqueline Kennedy remarked to her mother after the shooting: "He didn't even have the satisfaction of being killed for civil rights. It had to be some silly little communist." (overleaf)

# SEVEN

# THE LEAST WORST THING

For nearly four years, John F. Kennedy was the glue that had bound Robert Kennedy and Martin Luther King together. Yet another consequence of the assassination was that the two men would gradually uncouple. Over the remainder of their lives, they seem to have seen each other only a handful of times. Officially, they exchanged more than a few words only once—and even then, it was before the cameras, for public consumption. If they ever had any private conversations, either in person or over the phone after 1963, there is no record of them. On a couple of occasions, they wrote sincere but highly stilted letters of support to each other. But their interests came increasinly to overlap, and they keenly followed one another.

And in certain people's heads they became ever more intertwined. Some supporters, disproportionately black, saw them as twin tribunes for civil rights. When opposition to an unpopular war overseas brought them together, a few highly romantic sorts conjured up a presidential ticket of the two. So, too, were they joined in the minds of their enemies. On the eve of one of his greatest political triumphs, when he won the Democratic presidential nomination in the summer of 1964, Lyndon Johnson thought the two of them were ganging up on him. J. Edgar Hoover also felt tormented by them both. While dozens of would-be assassins focused on King alone, a few fantasized about picking off both. A man sitting on a barstool in early December 1963 told the truck driver sitting next to him, who told the FBI, how pleased he was

Portraits of slain voting rights activists James Chaney and Andrew Goodman flanked King as he spoke outside the 1964 Democratic National Convention in Atlantic City.

that the president had been shot and how, within the next thirty days, Robert Kennedy and King would both "get theirs."

In January 1964 Robert Kennedy invited King to participate in the oral history of the Kennedy administration that the family began assembling shortly after the assassination, one that would chronicle, extensively but selectively, the saga of the late president. The following month, Robert Kennedy himself sat for the first of what became eight days of interviews he gave to the project over the course of the year. One can easily imagine how therapeutic and cathartic this was for Kennedy, knowing they would not be read for many years. (They were opened only in 1988, though many key passages remain closed to this day.) He thus was free to unload on everyone, including King. Kennedy acknowledged rather begrudgingly, even condescendingly, that King's leadership was "quite effective"—"It was constructive, I think"—but on the matter of King's well-being and very survival, the attorney general was curiously nonchalant. "Martin Luther King was concerned about whether he was going to live and his people were going to live," he said of the siege of the Montgomery church in May 1961. "And I was concerned about whether the place was going to be burned down." "He was exercised, anyway, about whether he was going to live, I guess," he added. As was often the case with him, one couldn't be sure whether such flippancy was genuine or a cover-up for caring.

The last of Kennedy's interviews was conducted by Anthony Lewis, his good friend at the *New York Times*, and despite Lewis's repeated goading, Kennedy was at pains to stress that his views on race never changed, and to point out that King and other blacks neither deserved, nor received, any preferential treatment from him. Again and again, Lewis pushed Kennedy to concede that black suffering was in a class by itself; again and again, Kennedy pushed back, almost *too* vehemently. It might have offended his sense of fairness or reflected a self-deprecating reluctance to appear heroic. More likely, it stemmed from a reluctance to be pigeon-holed or stereotyped, especially as a liberal. His early conservatism never entirely burned off, and part of what remained was a disdain for liberals, whom he continued to consider unmanly, superficial, hypocritical, and smug. For all their conspicuous piety, he thought, they were intolerant and ineffectual. "They think if your intentions are fine you are relieved of the responsibilities of action," he once said. Keeping his distance from them was a source of perverse pride to him. ("We'll make sure that this entire conversation is kept out of New York politics for the next 150 years," Lewis laughed.)

King's oral history, by contrast, was perfunctory — twenty-seven pages over one day — cautious and uninformative: though promised the same confidentiality, King remained wary. (Even in private, the black man was on his best behavior. Besides, who knew whether the Kennedys would sneak peeks?) He stuck to those same mild scolds — though "intellectually and emotionally committed" to civil rights, John Kennedy had settled for a "sort of crystallized tokenism" — he'd repeatedly made in public. Historians would find nothing revealing, or nothing much at all, about Robert Kennedy in King's recollections. Certainly, King saw nothing like the leading role in civil rights others attributed to him, depicting him more as John Kennedy's ventriloquist than his conscience. "I felt that he was doing exactly what the president wanted him to do and had instructed him to do," he said. "Whenever I talked with the attorney general, I always felt that I was talking with the president." On June 5, Robert Kennedy pressed King to complete the history and to be "full and frank" in his comments. In fact, whether because King felt he had already said his piece or because the Kennedys didn't push him very hard or both, King had already finished.

For months after November 22, 1963, Robert Kennedy had gone into what James Wechsler of the *Post* called a "tragic trance." A trainer without his horse was how Murray Kempton had described him. He'd stayed on as attorney general — he wanted to see the Civil Rights Act passed — but Kennedy, his black tie affixed by one of the PT-109 tie clasps his brother's presidential campaign had mass-produced to commemorate John Kennedy's wartime heroism in the Pacific, was a specter around the Department of Justice, performing his chores listlessly, rarely attending cabinet meetings, bridling under the authority of a man he reviled and champing at the bit to leave. Around this time the political cartoonist Jules Feiffer saw him at a White House reception. "He looked like a ghost," he recalled. "He was haunted. He looked emaciated. He looked awful — a wraith. And my heart went out to him. He looked at death's door."

In his better moments, it had been Kennedy who cheered up the downhearted. There was that time at Hickory Hill when he'd swooped up a despondent Judy Garland and brought her back to life on the dance floor. But no one had been able to do that for him, though Simeon Booker had tried. When, several weeks after the assassination, Kennedy invited him to his office, Booker found him at his huge desk, head in hands. Then, when Kennedy looked up, it was evident he'd been crying. "Come on, now," Booker told him. "You've got to forget the past. Hell, you're Irish and supposed to be tough. I'm Negro, and you think you can push me around." The words jolted the attorney general, and he smiled, saying, "Booker, you always know how to knock somebody off balance."

(But Booker figured he owed it to him. In twenty years of covering Washington, he later said, he'd never met a public figure as friendly and respectful. "I found few of the VIPs even considerate of the black press, few willing to accept me as a working newspaperman," he wrote. In an era in which, for black reporters, every encounter could bring some slight, Bobby was the first member of the Kennedy cabinet to invite him to briefings, to his home — and for a swim. If Kennedy himself hadn't realized how extraordinary such hospitality was, Booker did, and reminded him of it when, at the end of an evening, Kennedy stood on the porch of Hickory Hill to bid Booker good-bye. "You'd better duck inside before real estate values decrease," Booker joked.)

As bad as the loss of a beloved brother had been, Kennedy had also had to deal with the instantaneous evaporation of his power. "Nobody wants to talk to me anymore," he lamented to an aide named Walter Sheridan, and it was understandable: "He had gone from the second-most-powerful person in the country to a lame-duck attorney general," Sheridan recalled. The tone of J. Edgar Hoover's voice with him literally changed overnight, from when he'd telephoned Kennedy with the bulletin from Dallas on November 22 to when, on November 23, he once more had a friend in the White House. (For twenty years, Hoover had lived across the street from the new president, and took a certain pride in having watched the Johnson girls learn to walk.)

Kennedy's despair was starker still because, arguably, he did not know who he was: so completely had he sublimated himself to his brother that he'd never defined himself, nor charted out his life. "The most intense of the Kennedys seems the most casual," Kempton wrote in 1962. "His brother Edward, who probably wants a Senate seat the way other young men want a Jaguar, set beside Robert, almost burns in the night." To him, Robert Kennedy was "the Kennedy without personal ambition."

Kennedy coped. He read Greek literature and the French existentialists and Shakespeare with an avidity that startled his friends. "I thought to myself, 'My God, what things to be reading this late in life!'" Joseph Kraft later wrote: Robert Kennedy had started to grow at the very point where most people stop. To get out of town and give himself something to do, in early 1964 Kennedy went on a diplomatic mission to Indonesia and Malaysia. When King and other civil rights leaders met with President Johnson in mid-January, Kennedy was in the demilitarized zone between the two Koreas. He found his greatest solace with children, both his own—there were now nine, two short of completion—and Jack's. Three months after his brother was shot, he brought John, Jr., to the FBI's indoor rifle range, where, under a special agent's watchful eye, the boy got to try a real revolver, then collect the paper target. Given the family history, it seemed an odd form of entertainment or convalescence, but Kennedy enjoyed it enough to take his own kids there, too. (Showing him his model airplanes and promising to send him one that very afternoon, Hoover communicated far more easily with John-John than with the boy's uncle.)

While Robert Kennedy remained in a fog, Martin Luther King became *Time*'s Man of the Year for 1963. Though the magazine put him on the cover and called him the "unchallenged voice of the Negro people," King was unhappy with its portrait. It's instructive sometimes to study the pre-hagiographic histories of saints. In his generally admiring June 1963 profile for the *Saturday Evening Post*, for instance, Reese Cleghorn described King's poor administrative skills, premeditated and strategic laughter, and rivalries with other black leaders, and played into some stereotypes: King, he wrote, "can match Perry Como in languid laziness of appearance." For its part, *Time* now suggested that King put on airs, was physically "unimposing" and had "little sense of humor," wasn't hip (he'd never heard of the football player Y. A. Tittle or the musician George Shearing), dressed with "funereal conservatism," and favored "downright embarrassing" extended metaphors (e.g., segregation was "the adultery of an illicit intercourse between injustice and immorality" that "cannot be cured by the Vaseline of gradualism"). Levison, too, considered it a "hatchet job," though it might prove helpful, he thought, by getting some of King's backers good and angry. At least it sidestepped the whole issue of communist influences.

Perhaps King's circle would have been comforted to know that Hoover was unhappy over the story as well. "They had to dig deep in the garbage to come up with this one," he wrote of the award. But now, with JFK gone, RFK largely AWOL, his old friend LBJ now at the White House, and his position secured (though he had just turned sixty-nine, Johnson told him he could stay on as long as he was president), Hoover could go after King full throttle. The physical assassination of one man effectively unleashed the character assassination of another.

On December 23, 1963, the FBI brass held a nine-hour meeting on "neutralizing King as an effective Negro leader." Participants hashed out twenty-one separate proposals featuring ministers, "disgruntled" acquaintances, "aggressive" newsmen, his housekeeper, his wife, or "a good-looking female plant" to be placed in his office. The focus had evolved from King's communist ties to his character; the objective was to "take him off his pedestal" and expose him for the "fraud, demagogue and scoundrel" he really was. The plan's architect, FBI head of intelligence operations William Sullivan, conceded that toppling King could throw blacks into the embrace of Black Muslims or even bona fide communists, but vowed that the FBI would fashion and anoint a King substitute—"a truly brilliant, honorable and loyal Negro who would steer the 18 million Negroes away from communism"—to take his place.

In addition to the ongoing wiretapping of King and several of his associates, microphones were installed in at least fifteen hotels King stayed in over the next twenty-two months, beginning with the Willard Hotel, where King lodged while in town in January 1964 to hear oral arguments at the Supreme Court in *New York Times v. Sullivan*, a libel case arising originally out of a perjury charge against King. (This particular Sullivan was the public safety commissioner of Montgomery, not the FBI official.) FBI officials sent the highlights to the White House. But concerned over his ties to King—and that he might spill the beans to him—the bureau debated whether to share them with the attorney general. Hoover quickly nixed the idea. "No. A copy need *not* be given the A.G.," he wrote, though, judging from Jacqueline Kennedy's conversation with Arthur Schlesinger, one soon was.

But Hoover (who described King as "a 'tom cat' with obsessive degenerate sexual urges") did agree that material picked up during King's trips to the West Coast and Hawaii a few weeks later would be shared with Kennedy, just to remind him of the kind of man King was. In March 1964 Kennedy was given an eight-page "top secret" memorandum with a summary of the recordings. One conversation must have been especially difficult for Kennedy to read. In it, several people joked about John Kennedy's funeral: how Cardinal Richard Cushing, the veteran Kennedy family cleric who had presided, had supposedly gotten drunk on the ceremonial wine; how the pallbearers had almost dropped the coffin; and how, when she'd bent over to kiss it, Jacqueline Kennedy had aimed at a particularly suggestive spot. " 'That's what she's going to miss the most," King is said to have said. Intent upon removing "all doubt from the Attorney General's mind as to the type of person King is," the materials were sent to Bobby Kennedy. It's hard to imagine that what the FBI characterized as "King's vilification of the late President and his wife' did not influence Robert Kennedy's attitude toward Martin Luther King.

While Kennedy's feelings about King's indiscretions are uncertain, what *is* clear is that by failing to keep tabs on—and to stop—what the FBI was up to in his final year at the Justice Department, Kennedy inadvertently aided Hoover's campaign. When the Senate committee headed by Frank Church of Idaho concluded in 1976 that "high officials of the Executive Branch must share responsibility for the FBI's effort against Dr. King," it clearly had Kennedy among others—and perhaps more than the others—in mind.

What Kennedy *did* worry about were King's continuing associations with Stanley Levison and Jack O'Dell, especially after he'd assured the Congress—while pressing for his brother's civil rights bill—that King's communist ties were negligible. A proposed story in early 1964 by Reese Cleghorn, again for the *Saturday Evening Post* and documenting communist infiltration of the SCLC and SNCC, sent Kennedy and his aides into a tizzy. Burke Marshall and Justice Department spokesman Edwin Guthman met hastily with FBI officials and distanced themselves from King—"Guthman quickly added that he and the Attorney General, of course, knew that King was no good," stated a recapitulation of their meeting by "Deke" DeLoach—and sent the department's file on King to Lyndon Johnson's personal assistant, Walter Jenkins.

To the FBI, Kennedy's motivation was clear. Lyndon Johnson had yet to pick his running mate, and Robert Kennedy coveted the job. Any revelations about King "could certainly injure the Attorney General's political chances in the future," wrote DeLoach. He revisited the subject in a second memo two weeks later. "Jenkins, of course, is well aware of the fact that the AG has shielded King for a long time and that the AG was particularly vulnerable because of defenses he had made to a committee of the Senate in behalf of King," he wrote. "Jenkins believes that the Attorney General, who desperately wants to be Vice President, is now going on record with the President with the fact that although he has, for political purposes, defended King, he wants the President to realize that he, the Attorney General, is well aware of King's communistic background."

One way or another, King continued to be a headache for Kennedy. The issue surfaced again in April 1964 in a column by the highly influential Washington columnist and on-again, off-again Kennedy confidant Joseph Alsop. "An unhappy secret is worrying official Washington," he wrote. "The secret is that despite the American Communist Party's feebleness and disarray, its agents are beginning to infiltrate certain sectors of the Negro civil rights movement." While SNCC and CORE were implicated, Alsop went on, "the subject of the real head-shaking is the Rev. Martin Luther King." Clarence Jones surmised that Kennedy had planted the story in yet another attempt to get King to drop Levison. "It is almost as if someone in the Justice Department or in the Administration had said 'now we are very concerned; this is the reason we are concerned; and we would like to have this conveyed to him,'" Jones remarked.

King was far too dependent on Levison to drop him, but he conceded a certain weariness over the whole communist issue. By vouching for him before the Senate, he said, Kennedy had given the issue of his affiliations "a decent burial," he thought. Otherwise, his problems were mounting, in ways that might not have been perceptible to the (white) editors of *Time* or, soon, the (white) jurors behind the Nobel Peace Prize. The SCLC was perpetually broke and it was losing ground among younger activists to SNCC. Levison complained to Jones about King's "failure to have any definite plans on anything" and "his complete lack of leadership ability"; Jones suggested the two of them go to Atlanta to "shake King up." The SCLC and its leader would become "second rate," warned Levison, unless "we can get to King." But as King faded, Kennedy slowly began to reemerge.

Kennedy liked the host of *The Tonight Show*, Jack Paar, and in happier times had appeared on the program periodically. In fact, way back in 1958, Paar wrote that young Robert Kennedy would one day be president of the United States. And on March 13, Kennedy went on again, for the first time since the assassination. ("He said, 'I've got to come out of this,'" Paar noted afterward. "'I've got to appear somewhere. I got to start acting a normal life again.'") In April, McGeorge Bundy reported to Johnson that Kennedy was in "much the best state of mind" he'd been in since November 22, and urged Johnson to speak with him in the next couple of weeks about civil rights.

Around this time, the *New York Post* launched a six-part series called "Bobby Kennedy Today." *Post* reporter Joseph Wershba depicted the state to which he had been reduced—"His weight, always close to the bone anyway, had gone down frighteningly. His jaws had a sunken, hangdog look. His collars swam about his neck. His wide shirt cuffs gave his hands and wrists a skeletal appearance. His eyes had a glazed look. Often, gazing distantly, he had to wrench himself back into this world"—and signs of a revival, like a scene one day outside his office at the Justice Department. "Perched on his shoulders was a 3-year old boy who draped his legs around the Attorney General's neck, rumpled his hair and let out brief shouts of triumph at being higher than anyone else," Wershba wrote. As Kennedy turned, twisted, kneed, and hugged John F. Kennedy, Jr., "he seemed to be saying, I'll be your father for now; I'm going to put spine into you as he would, had he lived; and if I hug you too tight, forgive me....I'm trying to get some of him back through you."

"Robert Francis Kennedy, Attorney General of the United States, was coming back to life," Wershba concluded.

As catastrophic as his brother's death was for Kennedy, it liberated him still more. Because he'd experienced life at its most random and cruel and irrational, because he feared he had already peaked, because his heart wasn't really in anything, because he carried the banner of someone even more popular in death than he'd been in life, and because he looked and sounded so much like him, Kennedy had a long leash; any criticism he might encounter was child's play after what he'd already endured. He was free to be whatever he wanted, whenever he figured out that. Arthur Krock of the *New York Times* had seen it all before: just as Jack was riddled with doubts until Joe, Jr., had died, only with Jack's death could Bobby come into his own. That his father was out of commission from a stroke also helped.

Even though he had already planned to leave the Justice Department, Jack's death, oddly enough, was prolonging Robert Kennedy's tenure: he pledged to Johnson that he'd stay through the election in November. But what came next? He could go back to Massachusetts and teach. Or head the Department of State or Defense if asked. He could become an ambassador somewhere like the Soviet Union or even Vietnam. (He offered as much to Johnson, but tempting as that might have been for LBJ to deposit him in Saigon—in one deft move he could simultaneously remove Kennedy from the scene, shut him up, and tie him to his policies—the new president demurred: Kennedy might be killed there, and then Johnson would have *that* on his conscience.)

Kennedy, the short-lived journalist, thought of buying a newspaper somewhere—maybe the perpetually struggling *New York Post*—or running a foundation. His first thought had never been elected office because, well, it had never been: he hadn't imagined himself in that role. "As long as it's on me and not on my brother, that's the way I want it," he liked to say during the White House years. "I'm not going to ever run for anything." But others fantasized: Walter Lippmann recommended a bid against Governor Nelson Rockefeller of New York, apparently not aware that, having failed to live in New York for five years nor voting there, he couldn't, constitutionally. Kennedy adviser Richard Goodwin suggested Adlai Stevenson leave his post at the United Nations to run for the Senate and Kennedy take his place. That was the option that Schlesinger, yearning for a Kennedy restoration and always exploring the angles, favored. "It would keep Bobby in the administration but away from Washington; it would enable him quietly to establish a political base in New York; and it would help kill the public impression of him as the ruthless prosecutor," he wrote.

In late spring 1964, as the Civil Rights Act slowly surmounted southern opposition—Levison's brother urged Levison to stop King from going on a hunger strike to press for its enactment, warning that King "most likely will starve to death" if he did—both Kennedy and King went out into the field. In his first trip south since the assassination, Kennedy was rapturously received at West Georgia College, near Atlanta, which was naming a chapel after John Kennedy. There, even before King had done it, he connected the issues of civil rights and the Vietnam War: six blacks had been killed recently in the war, he noted, but if the widow of any of them had come up from the South for his burial in Arlington, she'd not have known where she could stay, or eat, or even wash up en route. "How would any of us like it if we were in that situation?" he asked. "This is a continuous insult," Kennedy said. "That part of the legislation is long overdue. Yet some states won't deal with it. Mississippi and Alabama are not going to do it. Therefore [blacks] are entitled to have the federal government do it." "At this point," wrote John Herbers of the *New York Times*, "the audience broke into loud applause that lasted almost a minute." Kennedy was "almost mobbed" when he left.

King, meanwhile, brought his protests to St. Augustine, Florida; the oldest city in the country remained firmly in Jim

Crow's grip as it marked its four hundredth anniversary. Here, too, he faced death threats: on May 29 the house in which King was to stay was sprayed by gunfire. King pleaded, to no avail, with Kennedy's Justice Department for protection. Around the same time, the FBI intensified its surveillance of King, homing in, for instance, on the Atlanta "Hide-Away" where he purportedly had his assignations. (One agent proposed monitoring the rear entrance to the place "possibly with a Zoomar lens during daylight hours and with field glasses.")

On June 10 King's march in St. Augustine was attacked by a white mob. Kennedy, meantime, celebrated the imminent passage of the Civil Rights Act of 1964. "Hello, hero," Johnson greeted him as he walked into the Oval Office. Three weeks later, for their first reunion since seeing one another in the White House Rose Garden the previous June, King and Kennedy were on hand for the bill's historic signing, seated far apart in the large room. For the often-solemn King, it was a joyous occasion, and he smiled as he shook Johnson's hand and collected his souvenir pen. Kennedy, by contrast, was conspicuously sullen and disengaged. "I watched the Attorney General's impassive face and the very measured clapping of his hands which would not have disturbed a gnat sleeping calmly in his palm," Lady Bird Johnson later wrote. (It was nothing personal: Kennedy always "claps like Caspar Milquetoast," the *Baltimore Sun* observed on another occasion.) King felt sorry for him. "Our enthusiasm—that of Dr. King and myself—was sort of dampened by the sadness that we saw in Bobby's eyes and the coldness with which the President obviously treated him," the SCLC's Washington representative, Walter Fauntroy, was to write.

Perhaps with that in mind, King sent Kennedy a "Dear Bob" note two days later. "Your able, courageous and effective work in guiding the Civil Rights Act of 1964 through both Houses of Congress has earned for you an even warmer spot in the hearts of freedom loving people the world over," he wrote. Kennedy wasn't moved, at least to judge from his very clinical conversation

King took the desegregation fight to St. Augustine, Florida, in 1964, and was
arrested and jailed with others for demanding service at a whites-only restaurant.

with Lyndon Johnson a couple of weeks later. King was speaking
in Greenwood, Mississippi, Kennedy explained over the phone,
and might need some protection from the FBI. "It's a ticklish
problem...because if he gets killed...it creates all kind of
problems," Kennedy said. "Not just him being dead, but a lot
of other kind of problems." A White House stenographer noted
that Kennedy "chuckled slightly" as he said so.

During the drafting of the party platform for the Democratic
National Convention that August, both men testified, though
Kennedy proved the vastly greater draw. They also appeared at the
convention itself, though not without raising fears in some quarters.
In King's case, it was among his aides, who worried how he would
either control or keep his distance from more radical black activists
pressing to seat a largely black slate from the "Mississippi Freedom
Democratic Party" alongside the regular, all-white state delegation.

For his part, Johnson worried that Kennedy's presence might help him seize the vice presidential nomination by acclamation. Or that Kennedy and King acting in league might disrupt things on behalf of the black Mississippians. (Johnson had the FBI monitor the two electronically, then tell him whatever it learned. But any contact between them was minimal.)

Despite his electrifying appearance at the convention—the applause when he was introduced lasted twenty-two minutes—Kennedy faced an uncertain future. One reporter, Robert Donovan of the *Los Angeles Times*, composed his political epitaph. In passing him over for the vice presidency, he wrote, Johnson had "finally closed out the Kennedy era, the New Frontier, the fabulous period of sisters, brothers, cousins, romping children, Harvard professors, twisting in the East Room and ponies and dogs with names like Macaroni and Charlie." Were another Kennedy to reach the White House, he predicted, it would be Teddy.

Talk of Robert Kennedy running for the Senate in New York had first surfaced in the spring of 1964. Kennedy adviser Kenneth O'Donnell quickly dismissed the idea: though Kennedy had lived in New York as a child, he was too conspicuously a carpetbagger; the move would breathe new life into those charges of ruthlessness. Others coveted the seat. Liberals, reformers, and Jews (often, all three combined in the same person) would be wary. Kennedy didn't even *like* New York City; his favorite part of town, he once said, was the Central Park Zoo. Then, in June, Ted Kennedy very nearly died in a plane crash. ("Is it true you are ruthless?" he asked his brother after coming to.) On August 22, 1964—"still a wounded animal, half a zombie," as reporter Jack Newfield later put it—he announced his candidacy against the liberal republican incumbent, Kenneth Keating. For him, it was "essentially as a kind of *pis aller*—the least worst thing to do," as Joseph Alsop later put it.

One Democratic activist, Ronnie Eldridge, recalled Kennedy's appearance before a group of reform Democrats on the eve of his nomination. "Almost everybody was sitting there, waiting for this ruthless, aggressive man to come in, and they were filled with resentment," she remembered. "And the doorbell rang....And, I'll never forget, this scared little guy came in. And he really just looked so out of it all, and he looked slightly schizophrenic....I mean, he was just not with it: very shy, his eyes down on the floor all the time, and it just took everybody by such surprise because they were really there to eat him up, and there really wasn't anything, you know, *to* eat up. And it was very sad."

There were the inevitable jokes. Art Buchwald imagined Kennedy and his advisers huddled around a large map of New York City, with his brother-in-law, Stephen Smith, running the tutorial.

"Now, Bobby," he says using a pointer, "this is the Hudson River over here and this is the East River."

"Say, that would make Manhattan an island, then, wouldn't it?" Mr. Kennedy says. Some jokes Kennedy all but told on himself, like the way in which—after neglecting to insert a token—he'd nearly emasculated himself on a subway turnstile.

And there were harsh editorials, especially in the *New York Times*, reprising all of the old liberal shibboleths about the man and further fueling Kennedy's lifelong conviction that the *Times* was anti-Catholic. Was the Empire State really "so poverty-stricken," it asked, that it had to import someone from somewhere else? "New York is not an underdeveloped territory, waiting to be civilized through a Kennedy colonization," echoed the *Herald Tribune*. A group of apostate Democrats, including such progressive stalwarts as I. F. Stone, Paul Newman, Nat Hentoff, and—still smarting from their encounter barely a year earlier—James Baldwin, called themselves Democrats for Keating in support of the incumbent senator.

"The words that recurred were 'ruthless,' 'arrogant,' 'cold,' 'power-hungry,'" James Wechsler later wrote. "And now New York was to be the helpless victim of his insatiable lusts." Never, one of Kennedy's former spokesmen, Wes Barthelmes, was to observe, could Kennedy convince certain people that he was "anything but a smart-aleck, rich man on the political make." It was, he theorized, partly a "knee-jerk" reaction of "Liberal Jew reporters" associating him with his father. The task of combating his image as "a Little League ogre" was, as *Esquire* put it, "not unlike that of getting tuna fish moving after a botulism scare." Lurking over everything was his image as an outsider. Campaigning at the Fulton Fish Market, Kennedy was comforted to learn that the mackerel there also came from Massachusetts.

Before colleagues and five thousand local children, most of them black, who'd come to thank him for his work on Washington's public schools, he departed from the Justice Department on September 3 to devote himself full-time to the campaign. "Kennedy may not be the best Attorney General this nation has had in a generation, but...he is awfully close to it," James Clayton, who covered the place for the *Washington Post*, wrote. Hoover awarded him an FBI agent's gold badge, though it was really Hoover who deserved the prize, for outlasting yet another Attorney General. (He boasted afterward of resisting Kennedy's pressure to water down standards to hire more black agents.) Kennedy gave his indomitable and steady deputy, Burke Marshall, an inscribed picture of himself. "To Burke, who knew how to 'tame the savageness of man and make gentle the life of the world,'" he wrote on it. He used the same phrase, borrowed from the ancient Greeks, in a farewell speech to his subordinates. In one final act, Kennedy made sure to gather up the FBI's scurrilous reports on Martin Luther King, and send them back to the bureau. Then he hit the campaign trail—for the first time on his own.

Early poll numbers showed him slipping in the race, and maybe even losing it. Some found something frightening, almost demagogic, in the frenzy of the crowds he attracted. Others didn't like his almost morbidly incessant references to his brother, and his apparent assumption that that—and not engaging Keating on the issues—was enough. Upon hearing how Kennedy, on a campaign swing upstate, was retracing his brother's itinerary from 1960, his most mysterious and hard-boiled political operative,

Paul Corbin, let Kennedy have it. "Get out of this mysticism! Get out of your daze!" he shouted. "Get hold of yourself. Goddamn, Bob, be yourself. You're real. Your brother's dead."

A week into October, Keating was, in fact, beating him. Were a Republican less extreme than Barry Goldwater topping the ticket, Kennedy would almost surely lose. Was it possible, Schlesinger asked him at one point, that he was the same man who'd run his brother's allegedly superb effort of 1960? "Well, that wasn't so hot, either," Kennedy admitted. So he retooled. And however ambivalent he'd been about the job—the second-most-powerful position in the United States is a tough act to follow—the struggle to become New York's junior senator proved therapeutic. "Whatever the political medicine-men say about Kennedy's Senate race, it is surely what the doctor should have ordered," wrote Wechsler. "He has shed that distant look of inconsolable grief and lost bearings; there is visible animation of battle and the feeling that he is on his own, and one is quickly persuaded that he welcomes the trial."

King, too, was in motion—heading to Rome for an audience with the pope. As was its wont, the FBI had done its best to sabotage the meeting, sharing King's dossier with Cardinal Francis Spellman of New York in early September, then enlisting him to bad-mouth King to the Holy See. It hadn't worked—"Astounding," Hoover complained—and on September 18, a few days after speaking at an arts festival in Berlin dedicated to John F. Kennedy, King and the pontiff met for half an hour. Hoover fumed. "I am amazed that the Pope gave an audience to such a degenerate," he wrote. Worse, he soon learned, King was a front-runner for the Nobel Peace Prize. "King could well qualify for the 'top alley cat' prize!" he commented. Evidently, the FBI had no more clout in Oslo than in Vatican City, for on October 14, King officially won the award.

The FBI listened in as Martin Luther and Coretta Scott King discussed how few high officials had congratulated him: Johnson, for one, said nothing. With their enhanced political power, Coretta King observed, perhaps blacks shouldn't allow

When he left the Justice Department, more than five thousand D.C. children, most of them black, came out to thank Kennedy for his work in the local public schools.

the president to get away with such a snub. But they had no such beef with Robert Kennedy, who called the honor "richly deserved." "The quest for brotherhood is strengthened by this great honor and the greatest of American ideals is given new international recognition," he said. King had, arguably, peaked: he'd find adulation in Oslo, but only divisions when he returned. Robert Kennedy, meanwhile, was slowly emerging from his tragic trance to find himself freer than he'd ever been. And climbing his way back to the top.

# EIGHT

# HOW LONG?
# NOT LONG!

On the front page of the *New York Times* of October 15, 1964, above the fold, was a picture of Martin Luther King, the newest winner of the Nobel Peace Prize—and the youngest. Awakened by his wife with the good news, he said he thought he was having another dream. It *did* seem odd where King had been photographed for the story: in a hospital bed. The paper offered alternate explanations for that: King had checked in either for a routine physical examination or simply for a rest. Both seemed strange for a seemingly healthy man of thirty-five.

With the 1964 Civil Rights Act ending segregation in public accommodations and the battle having moved on to broader issues, King was asked whether he still mattered. It was a fair question, given that Nobel prizes often come late in people's careers, awarded more for lifetime achievement than for future possibilities. King sort of ducked the question. "History has thrust me into this position," he replied. "It would be both immoral and a sign of ingratitude if I did not face my moral responsibility to do what I can in this struggle."

King also stressed that he planned to give "every penny" of his winnings to the movement. That resolve demonstrated his commitment to the cause and his spirit of self-denial—the same spirit that later made him squirm in his relatively large new house in Atlanta, and depict it as smaller than it really was. It also showed how well-behaved and abstemious a black man, no matter how eminent, even one ministering to the poor and steeped in Gandhian self-denial, still felt he had to be.

King received the 1964 Nobel Peace Prize in Oslo; he was the youngest-ever recipient of the award, and only the second African American winner.

Inside the paper were some reactions to the award. "They're scraping the bottom of the barrel when they pick him," said Bull Connor. To Leander Perez, the Louisiana political boss who'd helped bankroll the Reverse Freedom Rides, it "only shows the communist influence nationally and internationally. Shame on somebody." "King lives like a king on money he has fleeced from his people and is known to consort with communists and perverts," declared Al Lingo, Alabama's director of public safety. Hoover said nothing publicly but commented in an FBI memo. King was the "last one in the world who should ever have received" it, he wrote. But there was also lots of praise, beyond that from Robert Kennedy, including from Cardinal Cushing and Ralph Bunche.

There was word of Kennedy's doings, too, in that day's *Times* — specifically, about a party held on his behalf on the Upper West Side of Manhattan, hosted by William and Jean Stein vanden Heuvel in their apartment at the Dakota. Kennedy himself wasn't there, but Gay Talese, then a young reporter for the *New York Times*, was. On hand for the event was a dazzling swath of New York's liberal intelligentsia: Leonard Bernstein, Gloria Vanderbilt, Jason Robards, Jr., Lauren Bacall, John Kenneth Galbraith, Paddy Chayefsky, Lillian Hellman, George Plimpton, and Jules Feiffer, just for starters. The goal that night was to win over such people for Kennedy in his close race against Keating. These guests too, remembered the sins of Robert Kennedy and his old man. And the avuncular Keating had a respectable liberal record.

The evening marked a restoration of Camelot, with a rare, brief, and highly strategic appearance from the queen of the realm, Jacqueline Kennedy herself. One of the main speakers — sharing his duties with the Harvard economist John Kenneth Galbraith — was the New Frontier's house intellectual, Arthur Schlesinger, Jr., who, speaking "as a historian," was there to certify that Robert Kennedy was his martyred brother's rightful heir, and Keating merely "a nice, white-haired man."

With Lyndon Johnson's victory over conservative Republican Barry Goldwater in less than a month a foregone conclusion, the

New York race generated national attention and enormous local passion. Talese described how one guest (he didn't say who, though it is said to have been George Plimpton) sent another (the playwright Arthur Kopit) sprawling over a sofa, drink and all, after he'd repeatedly touted Keating. But the Kennedy forces claimed at least one convert that night: Bernstein. "Before the party, he was uncertain about supporting Mr. Kennedy, but on his way out he told his hostess, 'I'm exhausted from my conversion,' but that his vote could be counted upon," wrote Talese.

"If it is Goldwater in '64, it will be hot water in '65, bread and water in '66, and no water at all in '67," King had quipped that August but the presidential race *was* a snooze; the marquee contest was in New York, and for all the misgivings about him in certain quarters, Kennedy had quickly become its star. "Usually they pay little attention to what he says," wrote Homer Bigart in the *New York Times*. "They have come out to see him and, if possible, touch him. He can evoke shrieks of pleasure from women and girls, who predominate in the crowds, simply by running his hands through his tousled hair." (Comparisons to the Beatles, who'd arrived earlier in the year, were both inevitable and commonplace: the cartoonist Bill Mauldin showed a longhaired Kennedy surrounded by the same swooning groupies. "With a guitar, there'd be no stopping him," the caption went.) A crush of people formed around Kennedy at Grand Central Terminal during his first day on the hustings, very nearly trampling a woman. "I think somebody's going to be killed," Kennedy warned as he surveyed the scene.

The frenzy extended into traditionally Republican upstate. A "political hurricane," Relman Morin of the Associated Press called the Kennedy campaign. The crowds were huge, and enthusiastic, and patient: four thousand people in Glens Falls waited until one in the morning to greet him. (If he won, Kennedy promised, he'd return at a more civilized hour.) Kennedy perfected a way to stand atop a moving car without toppling or being pulled over, a ploy he'd picked up during a recent trip to Poland: one aide grabbed him by his belt, while another held his legs. "It was like the 1960 campaign all over again, but with one difference," Morin observed. "John F. Kennedy was almost invariably gay and high-spirited between spots, whereas vestiges of the stricken, haunted expression still come over Robert Kennedy's face and he stares out the window in long silences." The release of the Warren Commission report on September 28 only intensified his melancholy. "I feel sorry for Keating," said Mayor John Lindsay of New York. "He's running against a ghost."

But that same ghost proved a crutch, keeping Kennedy from finding his own voice. It could also be a bit creepy, stopping people, James Reston wrote, "as if they had suddenly seen an apparition." Any comparison to the martyred president was, almost by definition, unflattering: Bobby's voice, posture, declamation, and manner were, respectively, more thin, more hunched over, more halting, and less assured than his brother's. Wrapping oneself tightly in his mantle, invoking his name constantly—"President Kennedy this" and "President Kennedy that"—could generate hostility and resentment in some as easily as it did sympathy, nostalgia, and protectiveness in others. It could also be considered morbid, presumptuous, even exploitative.

"It is always this way with Robert Kennedy," Jimmy Breslin wrote. "They are not touching Robert Kennedy, candidate for office. They are touching his brother, or they are touching another Robert Kennedy, the one who walked in the streets behind his brother's body and walked so straight and with this terrible discipline that you never can forget. He wants his own life now, but they confused him with his brother, as he always will be confused with his brother." Confused, but not preferred. "Look, I like Jack as much as anybody, but Bobby is not Jack," the editor of New York's weekly Irish-American *Advocate*, James Nicholas O'Connor, told Talese. It endorsed Keating.

Kennedy's problems as a public speaker persisted. "It was just something to behold," one of his most steadfast advance men, James

Tolan, later said. "I mean, he was really introverted, shy, stammering, never looking at people in the eye, always looking down, and just totally ill-at-ease before groups of people." His formulaic speeches—"one-line openers making fun of himself or his family; an outline of the subject; facts; a program of action; an appeal for reason with appropriate quotes from Jefferson, Camus, Aeschylus, George Bernard Shaw, Oliver Wendell Holmes, Tennyson, or John Kennedy," as Guthman summarized them—could be risible.

In only one community was Kennedy truly secure: black New York. The Kennedy-Keating race presented a situation that would soon be quite inconceivable in American politics: one in which the black vote remained very much in play, with the two major parties actually attempting to top each other's civil rights activism. Beyond building up their own candidate's record, the Keating forces listed Kennedy's sins: appointing racist judges, delaying civil rights legislation, leaving his Justice Department job before the new civil rights law could be enforced and tested in the courts. To prove Kennedy's cluelessness on race matters in the North, even the star-crossed Baldwin meeting was fair game.

Medgar Evers's surviving brother, Charles Evers, embraced Kennedy at the annual convention of the New York NAACP in Buffalo in early October, just as Kennedy had once embraced him. "Bobby Kennedy means more to us in Mississippi than any white man I know, including yourself, Senator," he told Keating, who was present. When Kennedy's turn came, he was interrupted by applause almost forty times. "He ain't no JFK, but he's still a piece of Kennedy, and I love him," said one of the four thousand people to greet him on another occasion outside Harlem's Hotel Theresa. A week later, Kennedy led a crowd of Brooklyn blacks through three verses of "We Shall Overcome." Blacks (Count Basie, Cab Calloway, Miles Davis, Lionel Hampton, and Gordon Parks among them) were amply represented in the group of 245 writers, artists, composers, and performers who took out a full-page ad for Kennedy in late October; Davis hosted a champagne reception for him at his home.

Pockets of resistance in the black community remained. The *Pittsburgh Courier* reported that "underworld elements in New York" were "squirming" over having prosecutorial Bobby Kennedy around. A still skeptical Jackie Robinson reminded readers of the *Amsterdam News* how Kennedy had urged blacks to "go slow" after the Freedom Rides, and how the FBI's record on race-related killings and church bombings "did not measurably improve under Bob Kennedy." Robinson was tough. Kennedy, he wrote, "has been awfully silent on such vital matters since the death of his brother and we have been at a loss to know why." He, too, was for Keating.

So was Lorraine Hansberry, who still hadn't forgiven Kennedy for the Baldwin debacle. Only two things, she said, would inspire her to leave the hospital, where she was being treated for cancer: the opening of her latest play, *The Sign in Sidney Brustein's Window*, and the chance to vote against Bobby Kennedy. (When her show foundered, its backers asked then-senator-elect Kennedy to vouch for it in a way that could be advertised in the *New York Times*, and despite all the bad blood, he did.)

As time passed and the race tightened, Kennedy fine-tuned his message and demeanor. "No longer does his campaign have the flavor of a personal-appearance tour by a movie star," wrote R. W. Apple, Jr., in the *Times*. He stopped dropping his brother's name so often, tied himself to the more popular Johnson's coattails, and warmed himself up. Convinced he was at his most appealing in seemingly tough question-and-answer sessions, his admen filmed an appearance before the Columbia-Barnard Democratic Club, then broke it into commercials of a half hour, five minutes, and one minute. (Unbeknownst to viewers, much of the "spontaneous" event was scripted, with questions passed out to selected plants beforehand.) Throughout, he tried to shed his time-honored tag. "Kennedy Fighting 'Ruthless' Image," David Halberstam announced in the *Times* a week before the vote.

He won, though Johnson's margin at the top of the ticket was, astonishingly, four times as big. At the victory celebration, people predicted another transformation. "Bobby is his own guy now," an onlooker told journalist Mary McGrory. "He's not his father's son anymore, or his brother's brother—he's himself." At four that morning, Kennedy returned to the Fulton Fish Market, where the mackerel were no longer the only Massachusetts import. "It smells better here than it did two months ago," he said. "The workers cheered and jostled him," a reporter noted, "and one of them yelled, 'For God's sake, don't kill him now, we need him.'" Then, keeping his promise, he flew up to Glens Falls. Along the way, he was asked whether he was glad it was all over. He said he was. "Now," he added, "I can go back to being ruthless."

Ever since Martin Luther King had dumped on the FBI in November 1962, claiming offhandedly in the robing room at Riverside Church that the southern-born agents working in Albany, Georgia, had teamed up with local officials to impede civil rights investigations there, J. Edgar Hoover had bided his time, awaiting the proper moment to respond. There was always some cause for delay, like Kennedy's assassination, or King's audience with the pope. But shortly after Bobby Kennedy's election, he was ready.

Hoover rarely gave press conferences. But on November 18— four days after Coretta King presented *Montgomery on the March,* a program of song and narration at New York's Town Hall—Hoover put on a very different kind of performance before a group of women journalists at his office in Washington. Leading the group was Sarah McClendon, a fixture in the Washington press corps who reported for a number of small-town newspapers. McClendon's club had carved out a place for itself in old-time, chauvinistic Washington, giving "lady reporters" occasional, precious access to important officials. For his part, Hoover figured they'd be soft touches, or at least softer than the men. ("With men journalists, the questions are loaded and the reporters are trying to trip you up," he explained.) It didn't much matter, because Hoover did most of the talking anyway.

Hoover—"known hereabouts as an eligible bachelor," as one of those in attendance later wrote—escorted the seventeen women into his office, offered them coffee to "calm everyone's nerves," and then began to speak. He'd allotted them an hour but continued for nearly three. "On and on he spoke, and on and on we wrote," Mary Graff of the *Chicago Tribune* (Mary Pakenham at the time) later recalled. He had many targets that day: the newly released Warren Commission report (which had faulted the FBI for not warning the Secret Service about Lee Harvey Oswald), southern sheriffs, and Robert Kennedy's Justice Department, whose "harsh approach," he said, had made matters worse in Mississippi. But he was hardest on King, and his claim about the biases of those southern-born agents. In fact, Hoover pointed out, 70 percent of his force was from the North, including four of the five assigned to Albany. King, he said, was "the most notorious liar in the country."

Three separate times during the session, Deke DeLoach passed Hoover notes urging him to put that comment off the record. But Hoover didn't, and the world quickly knew about it, perhaps even before King did: he was on vacation in Bimini, working on his Nobel Prize acceptance speech, and the telephone lines there shut down at 6 p.m. The statesmanlike response he soon fashioned should have won him a second Nobel Peace Prize. "I cannot conceive of Mr. Hoover making a statement like this without being under extreme pressure," it declared. "He has apparently faltered under the awesome burden, complexities and responsibilities of his office." He had "nothing but sympathy," he added, "for this man who has served his country so well." (Even a wordsmith like William F. Buckley admired King's tone. "Utter suavity" he called it.) Said privately but omitted from King's official statement, but heard nonetheless by the FBI: King declaring that Hoover was "old and broken down" and "getting senile."

As for Kennedy, Anthony Lewis recalled that while Hoover's attack caused him "great distress," he had the same reaction—of "amused amazement"—he had over anything to do with the FBI head, including his brazen insubordination with him. "Hoover had made this utterly unwarranted and ludicrous attack on Dr. King," he recalled. "And Bobby's reaction was, 'Isn't it awful? But isn't it part of life?' 'Isn't it terrible that I can't do anything about that?'...It was just a sense of the wrongness of things that this kind of thing could happen; but there it was! He really couldn't change it." It was a measure of black impotence that civil rights leaders couldn't call for Hoover's removal for fear it would only backfire. Hoover told Betty Beale of the *Washington Evening Star* that of the forty telegrams he received, all but two or three were favorable.

Hoover's FBI quickly intensified its war against King. On November 21 it sent a tape comprising assorted grunts, groans, and moans picked up in King's various hotel rooms to his wife. With it came a primitive anonymous note, ostensibly from a disenchanted black follower. FBI officials had evidently read in King profiles of his boyhood attempts at suicide—jumping out a second-story window, for instance, when his beloved grandmother died. Now they hoped to induce something more successful.

"King, look into your heart," it stated. "You know you are a complete fraud and a great liability to us Negroes....You are a colossal fraud and an evil, vicious one at that." There was, it continued, "but one way out for you. You better take it before your filthy, abnormal fraudulent self is bared to the nation." It gave him thirty-four days to do so. The package got buried in a pile of mail, and the deadline had passed before Coretta King got around to opening it. The FBI also dusted off and revised the report on King it had sent out the previous year, and which Kennedy had ordered withdrawn, providing copies to the White House, members of Johnson's cabinet, assorted other dignitaries, and members of the press.

And, a few days after meeting with the women, Hoover launched another broadside, complaining of "sexual degenerates' in pressure groups. That alarmed Roy Wilkins, who recognized it was King to whom Hoover was referring, and that in going after him, Hoover could bring down the whole civil right movement.

He quickly asked for, and got, a meeting with DeLoach. "Wilkins told me that he personally does not mind seeing King ruined," DeLoach reported, and had then pleaded for time in which he and other black leaders could find some way of sidelining King—say by making him either the president of some small college, or as a pastor somewhere. According to FBI papers, other black leaders—including Bunche and James Farmer—made similar pleas to the Bureau. Roy Abernathy, meanwhile argued that it was the FBI to destroy King, "some demagogue like Malcolm X would move in and take over the civil rights movement."

King pondered his response to Hoover. Once again spurning those who would have him take Hoover on, he decided to "extend the hand of peace," as he put it. On December 1, accompanied by Abernathy and Young, he did more than that; if they are to be believed, DeLoach's minutes of the meeting showed just how much King debased himself before Hoover. The meeting at Hoover's office began with Abernathy slathering the FBI director with praise, declaring what a great privilege it was for members of the "Negro race" to meet with so distinguished a man, who'd done so much for his country and for them. Then King assured Hoover that any criticism of the FBI attributed to him was "either a misquote or an outright misrepresentation." He added that he "personally appreciated the great work" the FBI had done, especially in Mississippi, then expressed concern about communism—which he recognized as "a crippling totalitarian disease"—in the civil rights movement.

Conducted on those terms, it was small wonder that the hourlong meeting was perfectly civil—"quite amicable," as King put it afterward. DeLoach said it was "more or less of a love feast," while Young called it "a mutual admiration society." The FBI director, Young recalled, seemed almost defensive, about the scarcity of black agents, for instance, and the difficulty of finding the bodies

King's December 1, 1964, meeting with J. Edgar Hoover alerted him to the fact that he'd been subjected to intensive and long-term surveillance, including wiretapping.

EDGAR HOOVER
DIRECTOR
DERAL BUREAU
OF
NVESTIGATION
ENTRANCE

of three slain civil rights workers—Andrew Goodman, Michael Schwerner, and James Chaney—who'd just been murdered in Mississippi. Afterward, as the FBI listened in, King was more honest, complaining that "the old man talks too damned much," a claim that DeLoach's minutes bear out: most of the paragraphs begin with "The Director told," "The Director made it clear," "The Director explained," "The Director spoke," "The Director praised," or some such phrase.

Two days after King met with Hoover, Anthony Lewis was back interviewing Kennedy for his oral history. He asked Kennedy for his understanding of what had happened at the tête-à-tête. The Kennedy family subsequently redacted the most sensitive portions of Kennedy's reply, but not before Schlesinger had looked at it for his forthcoming book on John Kennedy and copied some of it in his notes. So portions of what Kennedy said are available only in Schlesinger's shorthand.

> I wasn't present at the meeting.... Martin Luther King was in a very vulnerable position, first, because of his association with members of the Communist Party, about whom he had been warned.... 2ndly, he has a v active sexual life; & his activities in this field were not confined to just one person at a time. He participated in v active orgies, of wh a no of people who were involvd w him afterwards gave detailed interviews w the FBI, as to what occurred & what role he played, what role his companions played. Then, on other occasns, there were recorders in the rm where all of what tk place was all recorded, incl his own activities & his requests to all of those who partipated w him. I guess they were whites & Ns... in rather large nos.... It's been recorded over a period of yrs....
>
> [W]hen he came in to see Hoover, from what I under-stand from what Hoover's account of it that he's given to the FBI offices around the country, is that he [Hoover]

told him that he [King] was a Marxist, and he told him that he was involved in sexual orgies, and that Abernathy said that you can't say that to him, and that [Hoover said] he wasn't going to take any lip or any opposition from anybody like that who's had this kind of background in these kinds of activities. And evidently Abernathy spoke up, and [Hoover] said 'You were involved, too,' and gave him the time and the place, and went into considerable detail and gave him a lecture for an hour about the fact that [King] should, he was not in a position to be finding fault with the Federal Bureau of Investigation based on his record. I believe that was the reason why Martin Luther King was so mild when he left the meeting, and eventually made a, some kind of commun...had some kind of a communication or made a telephone call in which he expressed great concern and great amazement that Hoover had so much information regarding his activities.

Asked about the meeting more than fifty years later, Andrew Young still maintained it included none of the rancor that Hoover evidently described to underlings, and that those underlings shared with Kennedy, and that Kennedy shared with Lewis. "When we left, we were surprised that Hoover had been totally apologetic," Young said. "He didn't mention anything about Martin's personal life or even communists. He never charged us with anything, never addressed anything controversial, so much so that as soon as we left, Martin asked me to call back and try to get another appointment for us to talk with him about these charges." If, as seems likely, Hoover was putting out disinformation, it was surely because roughing up King comported far better with his no-nonsense image around the FBI than the idea that he'd treated him civilly.

King evidently felt he'd defused things sufficiently to collect his Nobel Peace Prize in peace. He was in good spirits en route, predicting on British television that the United States could have a black president in twenty-five years, fifteen years more optimistic than Kennedy's timetable. His stop in London included a visit to a chichi restaurant that in turn produced a scabrous story in a right-wing Italian scandal magazine called *Lo Specchio* that in turn interested the FBI.

Titled "A Rest Stop in the 'Dolce Vita' on the Road to the Nobel Prize," it described how, after ogling the glamorous white women, King's party (which it likened to cannibals) spent a small fortune on grub that it wolfed down like animals, and only a day after King had called for moderation and piety from the pulpit of St. Paul's Cathedral. Few Americans ever learned about the piece. But FBI linguists faithfully translated it and had it sent around for anyone interested, as a bureau memo put it, in King's "true background." Later, the FBI listened in as Rustin described how the Oslo police caught a prostitute coming out of the room of King's brother and "naked girls running up and down the corridors of the hotel," and passed along Rustin's observations to the White House.

As the new year began, King's valedictory lap was complete, and once more he faced his familiar conundrum: what next? Kennedy had no such problem. On January 4, 1965, he was sworn in to the United States Senate. Two nights later, he spoke at the National Women's Press Club. "First of all, I want to say how delighted I am to be here representing the great state of…ah…ah…," he said, ostentatiously fumbling through his notes. (Here and in other instances, the comedian Alan King had helped him.)

Kennedy settled into New York. By June he had bought a five-room, $68,000 co-op at 860 United Nations Plaza, and before long was eligible to vote in the state. He came to like the city's rhythms and anonymity. "Everybody is in such a hurry that I can walk from here to there without being stopped every five minutes," he explained. He liked upstate New York even more; the people there, he explained, weren't all politicians. But he never much liked the Senate, which he dismissed as "five or six old men sitting around." That he came to appreciate it more than he expected attested only to how low his expectations had been. He made few friends there and spent his happiest times elsewhere. It was what he would do until whatever he did next.

Two precocious young men—the highly opinionated Adam Walinsky and the more low-key Peter Edelman—became his most crucial aides, muses, prods. They came to define how different Robert Kennedy's staff was from John's, a distinction Jacqueline Kennedy noticed. Bobby's people, she told Frank Mankiewicz, were the more impressive, smarter, and more interesting to talk to. What accounted for that difference, Mankiewicz later explained, was the difference between Jackie and Ethel—their very different interests and the homes they created. When Robert Kennedy got home, he'd find Andy Williams or John Glenn; when John Kennedy did, he'd find genuine intellectuals. "Robert Kennedy tended, I guess, to get his serious, heavy, intellectual stimulation at work and relax at home," said Mankiewicz, "and John Kennedy probably had it the other way."

Kennedy was treated differently than your average freshman senator, and one veteran complained to a subcommittee chairman about it. "Oh, no," the chairman remonstrated. "I treat him the same way I'd treat any future president." But he began slowly, ducking the developing quagmire in Vietnam and taking a mini-sabbatical from civil rights (and, perhaps, from Martin Luther King). Much of his first year was devoted to shoring up his ties to his new "home" state.

King made much greater news in the deeply segregated town of Selma, Alabama, to which he journeyed two days before Kennedy was sworn in. Selma was King's latest, perfect specimen town, this time to highlight the need for legislation to protect voting rights. Just as Birmingham embodied segregated public accommodations, Selma reflected black political powerlessness: only 256 of the 15,000 blacks of voting age there were registered. Weeks of protests—King was arrested on the same day Kennedy gave his maiden Senate speech—culminated in the "Bloody Sunday" of March 7, when peaceful protestors bound for Montgomery,

including John Lewis, were mauled by police in riot gear, some on horseback, while seeking to cross the bridge leading out of town. Here, too, films of the melee shocked the world.

Robert Kennedy was among those horrified by the attack. The crackdown was "deplorable" and "a wanton abuse of police power...bordering on hooliganism," he said, and he urged that the perpetrators be held accountable. And within a week, Lyndon Johnson, who'd just told King that he hadn't the votes for the federal Voting Rights Act, especially so soon after the civil rights bill, went on television, and with King and millions of others watching, declared, "We *shall* overcome."

On March 21, just as Kennedy was about to scale the newly named, 13,900-foot Mt. Kennedy in the Yukon, King and his minions set out on a very different but more dramatic journey. "Walk together, children, don't you get weary, and it will lead you to the promised land," King counseled his army before leading them, this time successfully, across the Edmund Pettus Bridge. Three nights later, at the gates of the state capital, on a stage fashioned from rows of wooden coffins, Harry Belafonte, Leonard Bernstein, Tony Bennett, James Baldwin, Sammy Davis, Jr., and Peter, Paul, and Mary, among many others, entertained the marchers who'd endured the fifty-four-mile route. The next morning, the procession entered Montgomery. "You're only likely to see three great parades in a lifetime, and this is one of them," Deputy Assistant Attorney General John Doar, monitoring things for Robert Kennedy's old office, told a student. King made his way up the steps of the state capitol, where Kennedy had met with Governor Wallace only a year and a half earlier. Then, with Wallace peeking periodically through the Venetian blinds in his office, King pronounced segregation "on its deathbed"; the only remaining questions, he said, were how long it would take to die and how costly would be the funeral. "How long? Not long!" King repeatedly declared in his famous peroration. "I used to think that the 1963 march on Washington was the greatest thing we in the civil rights movement ever did," said Bayard Rustin, who had organized it. "I was mistaken. I am convinced what we are witnessing today is the most significant event in civil rights history."

Carol Burnett, Carol Channing, Barbra Streisand, Ethel Merman, Jack Benny, and Walter Matthau were but a few of the stars who performed on April 4 in a fund-raiser called *Broadway Answers Selma* (Martin Sheen was the co-originator of the evening), but according to the *New York World-Telegram and Sun*, the evening's most "deafening" ovation went to Martin Luther King. Three days later, Stanley Levison reflected on King's achievement. Though smaller in scope, he wrote, "Selma was bigger than Birmingham," because "for the first time whites and Negroes from all over the nation joined the struggle in a pilgrimage to the Deep South." "A true cross-section of America," as he described it, had been mobilized. King, therefore, had become "one of the most powerful figures in the country—a leader now not merely of Negroes, but of millions of whites in motion." King's movement was "the great moral force in the country today," and King himself had "more purity than any American has attained in decades."

Even without understanding the true ferocity of Hoover's ongoing vendetta, Stanley Levison nonetheless sounded some cautionary notes to his friend: King must not overstep his bounds; his movement was "basically a coalition for moderate change, for gradual improvements which are to be attained without excessive upheavals." It was militant "only against shocking violence and gross injustice. It is not for deep radical change." He might have added that King's mandate concerned civil rights and not larger economic policies—let alone political ones; let alone foreign policy; let alone wars overseas; let alone Vietnam.

Recognizing, perhaps, that King's time of greatest eminence and power also posed his moments of greatest peril, the *New York Times* updated its King obituary. "To many millions of American Negroes, the Rev. Dr. Martin Luther King, Jr., was the prophet of their crusade for racial equality," wrote the veteran reporter Murray Schumach. "He was their voice of anguish, their eloquence in humiliation, their battle cry for human dignity."

Reflecting the doggedness of those arrayed against him, four times along the road to Montgomery marchers passed one of the hundreds of billboards being erected nationally showing King at his "Communist Training School." But while the South grappled with a new era, to the north, America's cities—alien and even hostile territory to King—were smoldering. And overarching everything was Vietnam. A day after the bloodshed on the Edmund Pettus Bridge, thirty-five hundred Marines, the country's first combat troops, landed in Da Nang, signaling that carnage would soon come in Vietnam on a vastly larger scale. Soon, King would have to confront both issues. The question was how long King could maintain his lofty perch, or even his balance. How long? Not long!

The impact of the Selma march prompted the swift introduction of the Voting Rights Act. In a live televised address Lyndon Johnson demanded that "there must be no delay, or no hesitation, or no compromise with our purpose," closing the speech with the words "we *shall* overcome."

# NINE

# RIPPLE OF HOPE

From early on, and without ever having to check into the Hanoi Hilton, both Robert Kennedy and Martin Luther King became prisoners of the Vietnam War. Both men knew they had to address the problem, but for them, too, it proved a quagmire.

Though he'd not been involved in war-related decisions as intimately as he had been during the Cuba Missile Crisis, Robert Kennedy had been as committed a Cold Warrior as his brother, and like him and so many others, had seen Vietnam as a place to take a stand against communism. "The United States will remain here until we win," he said during a tour in 1962. But he acknowledged that it would be a new kind of war, "fought not by massive divisions but secretly by terror, assassination, ambush, and infiltration." The Kennedys were seduced by such "counterinsurgency," which was—like them, they were convinced—simultaneously smart and tough. This was, after all, the era of the Green Berets.

"Bobby liked the cult of the tough," recalled David Halberstam. "He himself had really barely gone into World War II, and he admired people who had great war records and had been in combat." It was, Halberstam added, "really a sort of romantic period, with a certain naiveté to it, and the whole notion of counter-insurgency—these brilliant, young, great physical specimens in their green berets, swinging through the trees, arm over arm, and speaking six languages, including Chinese and Russian, who had PhD's in history and literature and ate snake meat at night"—Robert Kennedy had bought into all that.

As New York's senator, Kennedy prioritized the challenges of urban poverty, focusing his attention on neighborhoods like Bedford-Stuyvesant, Brooklyn.

As late as 1964, when he left the Justice Department, he remained on board: communism needed to be stopped, he said, "and we mean to see this through to the finish." So turning against it meant not only acknowledging he was wrong but sullying the memory of his sainted brother, to say nothing of taking on Lyndon Johnson, who would hardly be the only person to insist Kennedy had no business criticizing a policy he helped devise and had championed, especially for his own selfish political ends. Before Kennedy appeared on *Face the Nation* in March 1966, Schlesinger and Kennedy aide Fred Dutton prepared him to be asked about what his brother would have done in Vietnam. " 'Well, I don't know what would be best: to say that [JFK] didn't spend much time thinking about it, or to say that he did and messed it up,' " Schlesinger reported him to have said. "Then, in a sudden, surprising gesture, he turned to the sky, thrust out his hand and said, 'Which, brother, which?' "

King faced different but no less serious constraints. Like any black leader, he was on a short leash: stray too far from the American mainstream, question America's underlying decency, do anything to suggest that blacks were unpatriotic, and you both riled up the bigots and lost your allies, white and black; challenge any Democratic administration, including the current one, and you bit the hand that fed you. White opposition to the war was treasonous; black opposition was all that plus ungrateful and uppity. In January 1965, King adopted the party line, connecting its ostensibly lofty ends to his own. "In Vietnam we are engaged in a death struggle to protect freedom in Southeast Asia," he wrote. "Now let us see to it that we preserve democracy in Alabama and Mississippi."

But King developed doubts. In March 1965, he called for a negotiated settlement. "The war in Vietnam is accomplishing nothing," he said. In April, he again connected Vietnam to civil rights, citing the existential threat posed by a wider nuclear war: "It is very nice to drink milk at an unsegregated lunch counter—but not when there's Strontium 90 in it," he said. During one vacation in Jamaica, Andrew Young recalled, King brought with him a suitcase of books on Vietnam to better understand the history of the place. And from that his skepticism only deepened.

As he reiterated his opposition to the Vietnam War in the coming months, more conservative civil rights leaders, concerned about rocking boats, grew alarmed. As long as blacks remained third-rate citizens, Roy Wilkins warned, whatever they thought about Southeast Asia didn't matter. "We think we have enough Vietnam in Alabama to occupy our attention," he said. The White House, too, began to worry. In July, it asked the FBI to investigate King's evolving stance on Vietnam and whether it dovetailed with the Communist Party's. (Eager to ingratiate itself with Johnson and to discredit King, the FBI immediately linked the two.) But King, the Nobel Peace Prize winner, envisioned a more ambitious role: to interject himself into the peace process. In August, he and seven other Nobel Prize winners sent joint letters to Johnson, Ho Chi Minh, and the leaders of the Vietcong, the Soviet Union, and China, urging them to all come together to settle the thing.

A step behind King and still more tentatively, Kennedy also began speaking up. He could see that at the very least, the war was diverting attention, if not resources, from the problems of America's inner cities, problems he was coming to address as a rookie United States senator, beginning with those in the nation's capital. One way or another, America had to get out of Vietnam. "You can talk about Selma, you can talk about Saigon," he said at a town meeting on Washington's public schools in March, "but you should be talking about the District of Columbia." In April, he spoke to Johnson about a pause in the bombing. In May, he criticized the bombing and the corruption of South Vietnam's leaders and said the problems there were political and diplomatic rather than purely military. But while King sidestepped the issue of withdrawal, Kennedy positively urged against it; it would repudiate three administrations and weaken Asian democracy.

In April, Harry Belafonte came to Atlanta to mediate a dispute between King and James Forman of SNCC, who had just told a shocked church gathering in Montgomery that "if we can't sit at the table, let's knock the fucking legs off it!" In his traditional arena, King continued to struggle with younger and more extreme activists who considered his approach to civil rights as, in the words of one critic, "too nonviolent."

Meanwhile, when King attempted to inch his campaign northward, he encountered hostility from established black leaders, who were none too eager to cede their turf. In New York, he got a hostile reception from Congressman Adam Clayton Powell. "All observers said that Mr. Powell had indicated that Harlem did not need any more 'leadership' and that Dr. King had agreed with him," one contemporary account related. The flamboyant and territorial Powell told King to kindly head somewhere else lacking such "leadership"—like Chicago, Cleveland, Newark, or Washington. The head of the Philadelphia NAACP dismissed King as the "unwitting tool" of "appeasers, social climbers, and the egghead white power structure." Resentful local leaders weren't the only problems posed by King's shift north; as Levison pointed out, white donors preferred problems that were far from their own front doors.

He was more welcome in Washington, at least for the signing of the Voting Rights Act on August 6. The segregationist senator Strom Thurmond inadvertently paid King the highest possible compliment when he grumbled that King and Johnson should cosign the new bill. A "solemn-faced" Robert Kennedy, too, was there; determined not to slight him as some thought he had done when the Civil Rights Bill was signed, Johnson scanned the room for him, then walked over and handed him one of the souvenir pens, as he had already done for King. Previously, King had written Kennedy to thank him for the unsuccessful attempt he'd made with his brother, Senator Edward Kennedy, to include a ban on poll taxes in state elections as part of the bill. "You and your brother scored a great victory in terms of principles," he'd written. "Like your late brother and our beloved President, you stand as the conscience of the nation on the issue of civil rights."

Two thousand miles from the segregated counties of Alabama, the Watts riots
began as a minor scuffle after the arrest of a black motorist in Los Angeles.

But if King and Kennedy spoke to each other the day of the bill
signing, no one noted it for posterity.

Though its monitoring of King tapered off—after the Justice
Department tightened its rules, the taps on King's phones were
removed—enough of his associates remained under surveillance
for the FBI to keep close tabs on him. Thus, when acting Attorney
General Nicholas Katzenbach needed to track down King on the
eve of the roll call for the Voting Rights Act, he knew whom to
call: in little more than an hour, the FBI informed him that King
was in Suite 9-B of the Sheraton-Cleveland Hotel. (Katzenbach
hadn't asked what he was doing or with whom, but the bureau
could probably have told him that, too.) From its large supply of
volunteer vigilantes, the FBI was forever fielding outlandish tips
about King: that he was carrying out something called "Operation

Paralysis," designed to bring the country to a halt; or that (according to signed documents from a Norwegian sailor) while in Oslo, he had paid $500 to have breakfast in bed served to him by a white waitress in a bikini; or that he'd just placed an order for twelve thousand Remington automatic rifles.

The FBI documented King's alleged breakdowns, the varying physical and psychological diagnoses of his associates, and their proposed remedies, such as a year of reflection in Switzerland. It monitored the ever-precarious finances of the SCLC and King himself—learning, for instance, that in February 1965 he didn't have the $5,000 required for a trip to Nassau or Bimini. (King's incontrovertible poverty did not discourage the bureau from believing that he stashed his cash in foreign accounts, and trying to track it down.) It did its best to keep King and his operation broke—for example, leaning on the Ford Motor Company to lean on the Ford Foundation not to donate anything. (Unfortunately, according to one FBI memo, foundation president McGeorge Bundy had other thoughts: that a large grant to King would "impress Senator Robert F. Kennedy.") The Bureau also documented the SCLC's attempts to climb out of its hole, sometimes through benefit concerts. "[Clarence] Jones announced that arrangements had been made with a current popular entertainment group known as the Supremes," went one memo from February 1966.

The FBI had to periodically mollify frustrated politicians. "As a Member of Congress, I can learn where every nuclear submarine is located, its rocket load, its accuracy, its destructive capability...but...I cannot find out what this Government knows about Martin Luther King," Representative Bill Dickinson of Alabama complained. It got to editorialize on King's allegedly deficient parenting skills: "The amount of time KING spends with his children is practically negligible," one agent reported. And it chronicled the endless series of threats to King's life and its own utter lack of concern about them. As Hoover regularly reminded everyone, the Kennedys included, his agents were investigators, not wet nurses.

Finally, there were Hoover's ex cathedra pronouncements, scribbled thickly on the bottoms and sides of the memos he'd receive. In these bite-sized Delphic declarations, which his anxious, obsequious subordinates well knew to read and heed, the director got to do many things. He'd express revulsion over some honor King had received ("This is disgusting," he wrote after some benighted Franciscans awarded him a medal "for truly Christ-like efforts in behalf of peace among all men"); gripe about King-coddling by various attorneys general ("King has been pampered by Dept. to point he is indifferent to possibility of any action being taken against him") and King puff pieces in the newspapers ("Even this obvious 'white wash' doesn't clean him up"); and dismiss King's complaints about the bureau, like its paucity of black agents ("This loud mouth degenerate had better take care of his own business"). When King told Hugh Downs of the *Today* show that "sex was basically sacred," Hoover's poison pen was poised. ("This is positively nauseating coming from a degenerate like King," he wrote. Hoover was pleased when the FBI sabotaged King's effort to hit up Jimmy Hoffa for a contribution to the SCLC ("Excellent") and frustrated when, after looking into King's tax returns, the IRS declined to take action. ("What a farce!") Such treatment wasn't reserved for King. Once, a Philadelphia paper warned of Hoover's untrammeled authority. "Sounds like Bobby has planted this story," he scribbled.

The North came to Martin Luther King on August 11, after a white policeman killed a black motorist in the Watts section of Los Angeles. King was en route to Puerto Rico as the rioting there, which ultimately killed thirty-four people, began. Both Levison and Rustin urged him not to go; he'd be seen as an Uncle Tom, Rustin warned. He went nonetheless. There, too, he met resistance. "Some Negroes angrily resent the visit, charging that Mr. King will simply distract leaders from the tough immediate work that must be done," wrote Peter Bart in the *New York Times*. When King toured the riot zone he was "absolutely undone" by what he saw, Rustin recalled. On August 19, King had a stormy meeting with the pugnacious mayor of Los Angeles, Sam Yorty, and William Parker, its chief of police. Yorty, too, told him he should have stayed away. "Get out of here, Dr. King! We don't want you!" someone shouted at him when he visited the Watts community center. "I would say to my brother: we are all Negroes, and we all go up together or we go down together," King told the man as he was ushered out. "All over the U.S., the Negro must join hands and..."

"And burn!" someone interjected.

"...and work together in a creative way."

Asked what blacks could do about police brutality, someone else shouted: "Burn, baby, burn!" Soon, though, according to *Jet*, "the jeering had stopped, and the cynics were drowned out by applause and cheers" for King. The factionalism in the black community, and the divisions over King himself, were there for all to see. That night, King spoke to President Johnson by telephone. Though the topic was ostensibly Watts, it veered to Vietnam. "They've all got the impression too that you're against me in Vietnam," Johnson said, referring to other civil rights leaders. "I want peace as much as you do, and more so." Again as with Hooer, King said he'd been misinterpreted, and that he, like the president, opposed unilateral withdrawal. Though they ended on a conciliatory note—Johnson told King to telephone whenever he had the money for a pay call and to call collect when he didn't—Johnson and his staff knocked King afterward for his disloyalty.

King's growing embroilment in Vietnam brought charges of treason, appeasement, meddling (perhaps illegally) in American foreign policy, and vanity raining down on him. It also upset contributors. "When we went into this Vietnam thing, we decided that he who controls the purse strings doesn't control our philosophy," he said. But he nonetheless soon staged a hasty retreat: he didn't have the stamina to fight two battles at once and had gotten too far ahead of the public, he told his advisers in September. "My star is waning," he lamented. He resolved to steer clear of the issue but, characteristically, wrestled over the decision and reproached himself for it afterward. "My name then wouldn't have been written in any book called *Profiles in Courage*," he later said.

As Robert Kennedy emerged from his melancholy and set his priorities, his orbit and King's began once more to overlap. And it was no longer a shotgun marriage: Kennedy post-assassination clearly empathized more with black America than he had before, and the reason was simple. "He had one great fact in common with every man in the room," Murray Kempton wrote of a meeting Kennedy had in Harlem. "He had a face which has known great trouble and has endured." The objectives of the two men, and even their language, converged. "I've worked to get these people the right to eat hamburgers, and now I've got to do something...to help them get the money to buy [them]," King had told Rustin in Watts. "You could pass a law to permit a Negro to eat at Howard Johnson's restaurant or stay at the Hilton Hotel," Kennedy said. "But you can't pass a law that gives him enough money to permit him to eat at that restaurant or stay at that hotel."

The racial and cultural divide remained wide for Kennedy, but he was unfazed. James Farmer remembered riding with him in Harlem once and coming across some kids playing baseball. "They recognized Kennedy, and one of them yelled, 'Hey, Bobby! Gimme five!' " he said. "Kennedy looked and said, 'What does "Gimme Five" mean, Jim?' I guess he thought he wanted five dollars. 'No, that's an expression of affection. It means "Give me five fingers. Shake hands." ' He said, 'Oh, I see.' Then somebody else yelled when they recognized him. They said, 'Hey, Bobby, we want Kennedy for president.' Bobby thought that was very funny. He laughed." Only a few years earlier, he'd nervously asked an adviser what to say to a black audience. Now, as the columnist Joseph Kraft put it, he'd become the "first American politico of any importance who had learned how to talk to blacks." Just as important—or perhaps more so—he learned to listen.

His interest and King's further merged in a remarkable address Kennedy gave in the midst of the Watts riots in Spring Valley, New York, to the Independent Order of Odd Fellows. On display that night in Rockland County were what would become the hallmarks of Kennedy's speeches, especially on race: originality, bluntness, evenhandedness. They were philosophical hybrids, impossible to situate on a conventional left/right, liberal/conservative spectrum. They were color blind. They neither exonerated nor patronized. They were provocative. There was invariably something in them to make people squirm. They broke new ground. They took on conventional wisdom and untouchable personalities. No one got off the hook, including himself (or his church, or his country) or even Martin Luther King.

The violence in America's cities, Kennedy said that night, was "no isolated phenomenon, no unlucky chance," but entirely foreseeable: "All these places—Harlem, Watts, South Side—are riots waiting to happen," steeped as they were in the heartbreak of blacks who'd come north for better lives only to have their hopes dashed. The calls for law and order were futile and unfair: "The law to us is a friend, which preserves our property and our personal safety. But for the Negro, law means something different....Law has been his oppressor and his enemy." The difficulties down South were almost quaint compared to the intractable problems in education, housing, and employment in the North, problems for which everyone, white and black, was picking up the tab in welfare costs, lost revenues, policing: "Our slums are too expensive; we cannot afford them." Many were to blame in Los Angeles, included even the local Catholic Church (a "reactionary force") and the black community itself. "The army of the resentful and desperate is larger in the North than in the South, but it is an army without generals—without captains—almost without sergeants," he said. The black middle class had "failed to extend their hand and help to their fellows on the rungs below," opening the gates to demagogues. Black leaders needed to up their game, broaden their ranks, and maybe change their doctrines; the problems "affect too many people too directly for involvement to be restricted to those with the patience, the discipline, and the inclination to practice nonviolence." Sit-ins couldn't cure illiteracy; marches didn't create jobs. Despair didn't license lawlessness: "Many of the rioters are simply hoodlums, with nothing more in mind than booty and the thrill of defying the law." But the major black organizations had failed, or at the very least, ducked. It was "disappointing and dangerous," he said, "that Negro leaders of stature have devoted their major efforts to the South—which is important, but is only one part of a larger problem." It was a theme Kennedy himself had sounded before. "Why do they go to Selma?" he once asked the writer Richard Rovere. "Why not to 125th Street?"

Kennedy's accusation soon reached King and, according to Andrew Young, stung him. "I said, 'Look, Martin, here we are with about a half-million-dollar budget and maybe a hundred staff members and this rich boy who has the resources of the entire federal government at his disposal is telling us we haven't done enough?' But Martin took it very seriously.... Bobby Kennedy's words ate at him." "We as Negro leaders—and I include myself here—have failed to take the civil rights movement to the masses of the people," King said in Los Angeles the day after Kennedy's remarks. And before leaving town, he'd acknowledged "a growing disillusionment and resentment [in Watts] toward the Negro middle class and the leadership it has produced."

Two months later, Kennedy was asked at the University of Southern California whether he approved of a student group's plan to send blood to North Vietnam. "I'm willing to give blood to anyone who needs it," he said. It was "a humanitarian reaction," Peter Edelman later said, but Kennedy was quickly charged with treason—and linked to King. Such gifts, the *Chicago Tribune* complained, only enabled the enemy to "shoot at more Americans." Kennedy's comments, the paper went on, were "a further extension of the Rev. Martin Luther King's dictum that it is perfectly permissible for anyone to decide for himself what laws are unjust and to go ahead and break them."

Kennedy enjoyed a larger margin for error than most politicians and an infinitely larger one than King. William F. Buckley marveled that he'd somehow get away with this one. But Kennedy, too, quickly retreated; not only were his comments on Vietnam hurting him politically, he told Jack Newfield, but they were counterproductive—maybe even lethal. "I'm afraid that by speaking out, I just make Lyndon do the opposite," he said. "He hates me so much that if I asked for snow, he would make rain."

As bad as it looked to his left-wing critics—"While Others Dodge the Draft, Bobby Dodges the War," I. F. Stone wrote of him—Kennedy continued to insist he more or less backed Johnson's policies. Coaxing Kennedy more firmly into the antiwar camp became the mission of the political activist Allard Lowenstein. As he saw it, Vietnam became a kind of solvent for Kennedy, eating away at his conventional views on many issues, including civil rights. "I would talk to him a good deal about Martin Luther King and about why it was important to get blacks" in his camp, said Lowenstein. "I mean, he was still very, very much at the fringe of understanding a lot of the black stuff when I first began talking with him, which is '66." For all Kennedy's hesitancy, antiwar forces still sensed he was one of them and maybe still their best hope. "We won't end the war," one protestor told Kempton in late November 1965. "Bobby Kennedy or someone like that will have to end it."

In December, when the administration let it be known that domestic programs would have to be trimmed to fund the war, King and Kennedy protested almost in unison. "Tragic and terrible," King called the turn of events. "A terrible mistake," said Kennedy. Once more, just as with the protests of the Mississippi Freedom Democratic Party at the Democratic Convention in Atlantic City, Lyndon Johnson spotted an entente between the two men. Three or four intellectuals had started all this antiwar talk, he complained. "Then Bobby began taking it up as his cause, and

King arrived in Watts in July 1965 as the community still smoldered. There he declared that "the violence was environmental and not racial."

with Martin Luther King on his payroll, he went around stirring up the Negroes."

Late that fall, shortly before leaving for three weeks in South America, Kennedy asked Edelman to draft a speech on civil rights that he could deliver on his return. Edelman, along with Burke Marshall, wrote something enumerating important but smaller-gauge items remaining on the southern civil rights agenda: protecting civil rights workers, for instance, and addressing police misconduct and jury exclusion. Kennedy wanted something broader, on the northern-type issues raised by the Watts riots. The project would soon expand into a trilogy of speeches by Edelman and Walinsky that Kennedy would give in the new year. Kennedy celebrated his fortieth birthday while on his trip and, upon his return, would mark his first year in the Senate.

During that time, James Wechsler noted, he'd confounded, then won over, many of his former critics. He quoted one of them, whom he identified only as a "local liberal woman activist." "I really hated him during that campaign," she recalled. "Now I write him letters once a week telling him he's the man who can save the world."

Martin Luther King would have been satisfied saving a piece of Chicago—the piece where one million blacks, more than in all of Mississippi, now resided. It was there he would launch his maiden northern campaign in January 1966. He'd picked it because of all northern cities, Chicago was the most organized and most storied—the promised land for so many southern blacks. Its long-lost allure gave it another, less happy credential: its slums were most prototypical. King declared war on them, charting out an elaborate progression from organizing to training to boycotts to mass actions. He moved into his own ghetto apartment (though not before the anxious slumlord imported a team of painters, plasterers, plumbers, and electricians to fix up the place for him).

From the beginning, though, advisers foresaw disaster; the city was too vast, the problems too deep, the power structures, both white and black, too entrenched. Squaring off against the machine of Mayor Richard J. Daley, Rustin predicted, King would be "wiped out." And sure enough, the disdain of city hall, and of white businesses, and apathetic local residents, and black politicians—along with the cold weather and racism more virulent, King later said, than anything he and his entourage had ever faced in Alabama or Mississippi—soon had King's colleagues feeling homesick for the South. "This is no hick town," noted Ralph Metcalfe, the former Olympian and now a local alderman, who charged that King had an "ulterior motive." "I have never seen anything so hostile and hateful as I've seen here today," King said after being hit by a rock while marching through an all-white neighborhood on August 5. "Only white people were under the illusion that the South was different," James Baldwin had observed. King later accused city officials of reneging on a hard-won agreement to open up housing in Chicago, and by early 1967 he'd moved out and moved on to other issues.

Kennedy also tackled the inner city, but more slowly and deliberately, delivering three speeches on urban affairs in New York on consecutive nights in January 1966. Their premise was that the slums were too vast and deeply rooted to eradicate quickly and must be reinvigorated in the meantime. He laid out a list of tenets: that "welfare" programs (in quotation marks in his printed text) were invasive, degrading, and counterproductive; that good jobs were the key to urban revival; that slum residents — the dropouts, the unemployed, welfare recipients — weren't liabilities at all but valuable, untapped resources; that private groups — labor unions, universities — and businesses were crucial to any solutions; that urban problems *were* soluble, but residents had to take the lead in solving them.

Kennedy toured one of New York's most notorious slums, the Bedford-Stuyvesant section of in Brooklyn, two weeks later. Residents accustomed to fly-by visits from white politicians greeted him with weariness bordering on hostility. Kennedy reacted much as he had to James Baldwin and company three years earlier: put out. Here, too, his first impulse was to play the abused benefactor. "I don't have to take that shit," he said. "I could be smoking a cigar in Palm Beach." But Kennedy soon directed his energies more constructively, devising the sort of partnership for Bed-Stuy he'd prescribed on the dais. Though of course he never put it that way, the program was a repudiation of, or alternative to, Martin Luther King's. "He had no commitment to the civil rights revolution and downgraded integration as a social priority," said Jack Newfield. "Bobby was for black power. He was for job creation and recognized how bad the old welfare system was." He further impressed the sociologist Kenneth Clark, whom he'd last seen alongside Baldwin, and who committed himself to work on the project with Adam Walinsky. "You know, it is possible for human beings to grow," Clark said to himself.

By now, both King and Kennedy were voicing steady opposition to the war in Vietnam—though Kennedy occasionally found himself backpedaling when criticism flared. King called it "bad for our nation and the world" and suggested that draftees opposed to it be allowed to do civil rights service instead. A month later, Kennedy called for offering the Viet Cong a share of power in South Vietnam. King at least was impressed: more than a solution to one conflict, he wrote Kennedy, the senator had offered "a political philosophy for an era," one of coexistence with antagonists, even repugnant ones. "Former President Kennedy, your great brother, carried us far in new directions with his concept of a world of diversity; your position advances us to the next step which requires us to reach the political maturity to recognize and relate to all elements produced by the contemporary colonial revolutions," he wrote in March.

The Johnson administration was furious; it quoted no less an authority than John F. Kennedy himself on the folly of coalitions with communists; "Ho Chi Kennedy," the *Chicago Tribune* called Bobby. But King's letter prompted a reply from Kennedy, creating the most substantive written exchange ever between the two men. "If we succeed in this effort," Kennedy replied, referring to a possible coalition government in South Vietnam, "much of the credit will be due to you and your colleagues in the civil rights movement. You have taught us a great deal about reconciling opposed interests within our own country; your statement of 1960, that you were concerned not with the 'New Jerusalem,' but with 'the New Atlanta, the New Birmingham, the New South,' was in my judgment a landmark in American history—a commitment to solve our problems not by escaping to the North, or the West, but by facing our conflicts and resolving them where we stood." King's call to tackle problems where they existed, rather than favor pie-in-the-sky solutions elsewhere, aligned neatly with Kennedy's plan for Bed-Stuy and similar ghetto communities. He directed King's attention to his

In the years following JFK's assassination, Robert Kennedy and Martin Luther King rarely spoke; Andrew Young proved to be a critical link between them.

trilogy of speeches on the cities. "With the perspective of your work in Chicago, I would be pleased to hear your reactions," he wrote. But the correspondence appears to have stopped there.

In March Kennedy visited Ole Miss and the University of Alabama, the two schools he desegregated only a few years earlier. A state legislator in Mississippi likened his visit to a murderer returning to the scene of his crime. But five thousand people greeted him in Oxford with what Roy Reed of the *New York Times* called "brimming cordiality." And when, in the question session that followed his speech, he described how Governor Ross Barnett had asked him during the integration of Ole Miss to have U.S. marshals point their guns at him so he could stage a show of defiance, he had them laughing. "When J. Edgar Hoover stated that Martin Luther King was the biggest liar in America, the only mistake he made was not including Bobby Kennedy," said the by-then-former governor, who called Kennedy "a hypocritical left-wing beatnik without a beard." Tuscaloosa was equally hospitable, but Kennedy was savvy enough to know that goodwill can be cosmetic and that human nature was more immutable than all his newly sprouted fans on these southern campuses suggested. "You can't be sure how they'll react once they leave the university and settle down in their old communities," he told Wechsler.

The reception he got from Cesar Chavez, the head of the United Farm Workers union, whom he met that month in hearings before the Senate's Migratory Labor Subcommittee, was warmer still. The two bonded instantly—"they just could communicate through their pores," was how Fred Dutton put it—in a way that Chavez had never had even with his brother. The Mexican Americans had respected and admired John Kennedy, Chavez later said, "but with Bobby it was like an entirely different thing.... It was like he was ours." Native Americans felt the same way. To the writer and activist Vine Deloria, Jr., the usual rap on Kennedy was a plus: Kennedy was "as great a hero as the most famous Indian war chiefs precisely because of his ruthlessness," he wrote. "Indians saw him as a warrior, the white Crazy Horse." The writer

Andrew Kopkind marveled at Kennedy's androgynous political identity. "He is an elusive phenomenon, even more than the other Kennedys," he wrote in the *New Republic*. "He is not a liberal or a conservative or a hawk or a dove or a machine politician or an independent. The favorite journalistic game these days is to examine his motives. Is he making a calculated, almost diabolical drive for the Presidency? Is he on some joy ride in politics, doing and saying the first thing that pops into his head?"

What *was* clear was his uniqueness, and appeal, and potential. "He generates the only genuine emotion in American political life today," said Kopkind. "He offers the hope of restoration to the Kennedy mourners. He still provides the novelty of discovery to the liberals who once deplored him. He can make people laugh when he speaks and make them cry just by appearing." Kempton had called Kennedy "both more radical and more conventional" than his older brother. But the liberal wariness persisted. When Kempton even hinted that Kennedy had changed — yet again — he'd be deluged with angry mail telling him he'd been duped.

Kennedy won over former skeptics like Jack Newfield of the *Village Voice*, who believed that he'd evolved from a stolid, unregenerate McCarthyite into someone who was empathetic, skeptical, and straight – not your prototypical "plastic politician." "He had natural reactions, he would get angry at you, he would tell you you were full of shit," he said. "I didn't feel he was trying to con me." He also liked his positions, which were, in a word, post-liberal. "He knew that the labor unions were conservative and fat and not worth anything anymore; he knew that the whole rhetoric of the Cold War and anti-communism was obsolete; he was in tune to what the people in the ghettos want." People often talked about the tell-all blue eyes Kennedy had inherited from his father. To Newfield (whose own wary eyes had clearly grown starry), even those had somehow changed. "His blue eyes were now sad rather than cold, haunted rather than hostile," he wrote.

On June 4, Robert Kennedy, accompanied only by his wife, his secretary, and Adam Walinsky, flew into Johannesburg, South Africa, in what would be yet another transformational episode in his life. Viewed from several thousand miles away, the developing philosophical and political congruence between Kennedy and King may have been easier to spot: nearly a year earlier, progressive white students in South Africa had asked each of them to come and speak there. King, who'd previously denounced the country's white supremacist regime, hadn't a prayer of getting in. To the apartheid regime, he was what segregationist governors like Ross Barnett and George Wallace, along with all those billboards along southern highways, said he was: a communist. Kennedy's odds were far better because his credentials in that department were that much more unassailable. "I very much look forward to [the South African Broadcast Corporation's] attempt to prove that Senator Kennedy is also a communist," Ian Robertson of the National Union of South African Students, which had invited the two of them, declared.

"After due consideration," the South African government had predictably refused King's request for a visa. And if it had been smart, the reactionary publisher of the *Manchester* [New Hampshire] *Union-Leader*, William Loeb, had warned, it would have turned down Robert Kennedy flat as well. "Bobby Kennedy is the most vicious and most dangerous leader in the United States today," Loeb wrote. "It would make no more sense to us for South Africa to admit Bobby Kennedy... than it would to take a viper into one's bed." But Kennedy got his visa, though none of the forty American journalists who applied to cover the trip would be allowed to tag along. South Africa would not allow Kennedy's visit "to be transformed into a publicity stunt... as a build-up for a future presidential election," the Department of Information explained.

When he arrived in Johannesburg, Kennedy gave a short speech in the "non-white" section of the airport terminal. He'd come to listen to South Africans of all opinions, and he said, and, again invoking that anonymous sage from ancient Greece, "to tame

Along the Meredith March Against Fear in June 1966, Ralph Abernathy found one more thing to protest: the ever-present smear campaign against King.

the savageness of man and make gentle the life of this world." Two days later, on the student group's Day of Affirmation of Academic and Human Freedom, he flew to Cape Town. Passing over Robben Island, where Nelson Mandela was imprisoned, Kennedy's plane dipped its wings in tribute.

Fifteen thousand white students greeted him at the University of Cape Town. Like many of his greatest speeches, his address there was the product of many hands: Walinsky, Lowenstein, Richard Goodwin, Kennedy himself. Reluctant as ever to lecture or hector, Kennedy once more began preemptively, acknowledging his country had racial problems of its own. In fact, he devoted more time to the situation in the United States than to South Africa; when he finally mentioned apartheid by name, it was juxtaposed against discrimination in New York. To this audience at least, he could describe the agonies of his Irish-American ancestors without winces. He even gave himself a rare pat on the back, claiming that more had been done for blacks in the United States over the previous five years than in the previous century. Though problems remained, he said, America now had a black astronaut in training and a black solicitor general, and another black man—Dr. Martin Luther King—had just won the Nobel Peace Prize. He did not mention a prior black Nobel laureate: Mandela's predecessor as head of the African National Congress, Albert Luthuli, who by government edict languished virtually incommunicado in internal exile.

Kennedy was a respectful guest. He stuck to generalities. He offered neither prescriptions nor timetables. But his words were powerful. "Each time a man stands up for an ideal or acts to improve the lot of others or strikes out against injustice, he sends forth a tiny ripple of hope, and crossing each other from a million different centers of energy and daring, those ripples build a current that can sweep down the mightiest walls of oppression and resistance," he said. The next day, the *Cape Times* reprinted the entire speech. "Ripple of hope"—the phrase was Goodwin's—were the words that lingered. They would reappear one day around Robert Kennedy's grave.

Kennedy spoke to two audiences of Afrikaner students ("What the hell would you do if you found out that God was black?" he asked one of them); sang "We Shall Overcome" with a group of blacks encountered on the street; toured the teeming black township of Soweto; and met with Luthuli. King and Luthuli had denounced apartheid together and drawn strength and inspiration from each other; Luthuli had called King "my hero" and King had praised Luthuli in his Nobel acceptance speech. While it's unclear whether, as has been suggested, Kennedy passed along to Luthuli a note from King he'd smuggled into the country, his visit must have pleased King immensely. Using a record player he'd brought him as a gift, Kennedy and Luthuli listened to some of John F. Kennedy's speeches, including his civil rights address of June 11,

1963. He also met with Ian Robertson, the student who'd invited him to South Africa and who, like Luthuli, was quarantined. (Told by Robertson that his room was very likely bugged, Kennedy jumped in the air a couple of times, taking care to land hard on both feet. Sudden movements, he explained, threw off electronic devices for several minutes. Robertson asked how he knew such things. "I was attorney general, wasn't I?" Kennedy replied.) At the University of Witwatersrand, he confronted charges that blacks were too barbarous to rule, noting that *they* hadn't invented poison gas or the atomic bomb or the death camps of Europe.

The South African novelist Alan Paton called Kennedy's visit "a fresh wind from the wider world." The Afrikaner newspaper *Der Transvaler* extended its "deepest sympathy" to the American people" should Robert Kennedy ever become president. But at a press conference at John F. Kennedy International Airport upon his return to New York, he said he had no plans to run for anything. Nor, he promised Walinsky, who was eager to launch the economic redevelopment program in Bed-Stuy, would he take another long trip that fall. "I will be walking side by side with you in the ghettos of New York," he told his young colleague.

While Kennedy toured South Africa, James Meredith, the man who'd integrated Ole Miss, had been shot and wounded on the second day of his 220-mile March Against Fear from Memphis to Jackson, Mississippi. Civil rights leaders, King among them, quickly resolved to finish Meredith's journey for him. King thought it would provide a respite from his sputtering Chicago campaign; instead, it only highlighted the fissures in the movement, and his tenuous hold over it. New leaders like Stokely Carmichael of SNCC and Floyd McKissick of CORE considered King and his brand of nonviolence and racial cooperation passé. They championed something different and far more divisive: "We been saying freedom for six years and we ain't got nothing," Carmichael told a crowd the night of June 16. "What we got to start saying now is Black Power! We want Black Power." To King, it smacked of separatism, black nationalism, violence. Just as bad, it put off white supporters.

Unwilling to watch more of his fellow activists be beaten and killed, Stokely Carmichael called for "black power" at the Meredith March Against Fear.

These divisions overshadowed the inherent drama of the resumed march. When the marchers reached the now infamous city of Philadelphia, Mississippi, King confronted officials implicated in the 1964 murders of the three civil rights workers there. "I believe in my heart that the murderers are somewhere around me at this moment," King said at a rally there. "They ought to search their hearts. I want them to know that we are not afraid. If they kill three of us, they will have to kill all of us," he added. "The Negroes applauded," wrote Roy Reed in the *Times*. "The whites hooted." But the march's larger message, said Gene Roberts, also of the *Times*, was that "a new philosophy is sweeping the civil rights movement," one with "Mr. Carmichael as its leader and the late Malcolm X as its prophet."

The change, he went on, put King in a bind, having to mollify his anxious white supporters and donors without antagonizing his youthful support. Meanwhile, King was providing a platform to the very people doing him in: "Reporters and cameramen drawn to a demonstration by the magic of Dr. King's name stay to write about and photograph Mr. Carmichael," Roberts wrote.

Once back in Chicago, King conceded that the movement was "very, very close" to a split. To Pete Hamill of the *New York Post*, King resembled "an aging, just-retired welterweight." "He has caused more controversy in Chicago than anyone since Al Capone, but on this afternoon he just looked very tired," Hamill related. "He knows what is coming up, and none of it will be very pretty. For Martin Luther King it was all a more innocent time when your only goal was to sit in the front of a Montgomery bus."

As if things weren't bad enough for him, King concluded his press conference in Chicago with Vietnam, lamenting how the country seemed more eager to win that war than the War on Poverty. As it sapped away funds that might have been used domestically, Vietnam was also displacing civil rights at the top of the progressive agenda. Meanwhile, more pliable black leaders like Roy Wilkins—"For us, here, Selma is just as important as Saigon," he said—were displacing King as Lyndon Johnson's black interlocutors of choice.

The election was still more than two years away, but already, Arthur Schlesinger had presidential politics in mind. "I am not sure that my notes have adequately recorded one interesting development of recent weeks: that is, serious discussion for the first time of RFK's running for the Presidency in 1968," he wrote in his journal on August 1. "I have not yet broached the topic with him, though I have no doubt that he has it well in mind." State polls in California and Iowa, he noted, were encouraging. "I think that Jimmy Wechsler was the first person to raise with me the notion that we might begin thinking about 1968," Schlesinger continued. "At that point—a month or so ago?—it seemed to me still wholly unlikely."

Like the Kennedys, Johnson was suspicious of MLK, and obsessively combed through recordings and transcripts of FBI surveillance tracking King's every move.

TEN

# A FINE PAIR

By mid-1966, two potentially irreconcilable propositions seemed to be at work. First was Harry Truman's truism, handed down in the Oval Office: "Any shit sitting behind this desk can win his own renomination." The second, apparent to friend and foe alike, was that Robert Kennedy would one day be president. It's interesting that a calamity of the sort that had befallen his brother never seemed to enter into anyone's calculations. That kind of thing occurred once in a century, and already seemed as remote as William McKinley or James Garfield; it could not happen again, let alone to someone in the same family. Everyone assumed that along with all of the other freedoms that luck, both good and bad, had conferred on him—the freedom to buy and have and live and say and do pretty much whatever he wanted—Robert Kennedy enjoyed one more freedom: time, and plenty of it. "Time works for Bobby," Penn Kimball wrote in *Life*. Or, as Andrew Kopkind quaintly put it, "Nothing much is likely to happen to him for five years, maybe more."

The only questions were whether Kennedy would become president while Lyndon Johnson still wanted the job or after—in 1980 he'd still be two years younger than LBJ was when he was elected. Or whether, as much as Johnson hated Kennedy, he might need him more and ask him to be his running mate. And whether, as much as he hated Johnson, Kennedy would agree.

Two years after his landslide victory, Lyndon Johnson was in a shadow war with Robert Kennedy, and both the Gallup and Harris

The off-year elections of 1967 provided Kennedy the opportunity to campaign for other Democrats and hone his oratory. He was starting to look presidential.

Journalist Joseph Alsop called the energy among Kennedy's campaign crowds an "almost terrifying enthusiasm"; cartoonists likened it to that of a rock star.

polls showed Kennedy was winning. "This is a phenomenon that nobody had ever seen before," Adam Walinsky later said. "*He* was the alternative candidate. *He* was the opposition. It wasn't the Republicans, who were then at the nadir of their influence. To the degree there was a genuine debate in the country, it was between him and Johnson." "No American not already nominated or elected in this country has ever been so likely to be President," Kempton wrote.

The upcoming off-year elections let the pundits weigh this bizarre state of affairs and study Kennedy on the stump. For Bobby, it represented a chance to tweak Johnson, hone his campaign skills, polish his message, gauge his appeal, work out his lingering grief, put himself on display—e.g., cover stories in *Newsweek* and *Time*—and earn IOUs. Kennedy was a restless, dissatisfied soul; at some point, his energies, banked by grief, would be fully released. That moment, maybe, was now.

"Have you ever thought about running for president?" a young woman asked him during a stop in October.

"Yes," he replied.

Martin Luther King remained inconspicuous during the election season. According to King's colleague Hosea Williams, Johnson had discreetly asked him to get commitments from all the civil rights leaders to avoid violence — or even demonstrations — until after the vote. King himself was down in the dumps. "Levison advised that King has been very depressed lately over current events, and King told him that he has been talking and making speeches but he really does not know what he is saying," an FBI memo stated.

Kennedy, on the other hand, knew just what he was saying, and said it everywhere, campaigning, by one estimate, for seventy-five candidates in twenty-five states in a couple of months. His entourage grew positively presidential: for a time, even semiofficial presidential chronicler Theodore White came along. Often to their great surprise, reporters accustomed to barely tolerating, if not ridiculing, the candidates they covered *liked* and *admired* Robert Kennedy, and the overflow crowds he generated everywhere displayed what Joseph Alsop called an "almost terrifying enthusiasm" — a joyous juggernaut. The papers were filled with photographs of young women at Kennedy's rallies, and you could swear they were the same young women — with the same faces and old-fashioned eyeglasses and hairdos — as the young women who were photographed in states of shock and grief outside Parkland Memorial Hospital in Dallas almost exactly three years earlier.

There were naysayers — many of them. The John Kennedy references were back, too copious to some. (Because they were thought to be so deeply entrenched, or even genetic, the Massachusetts accent and gestures were OK.) Equally heavy-handed were all those quotations from Frost, Tennyson, Dante, and Churchill still peppering Kennedy's speeches. To James M. Perry of the *National Observer*, so much about Kennedy — his foreign trips, his positions (*slightly* to the left of Johnson), and even his coiffeur—was contrived that the man was surely a contrivance himself. He bestowed upon Kennedy that most stinging of political prefixes: "The New." But Perry had to concede that The New Kennedy *was* an exceptional campaigner; "his enemies can only deeply regret that," he wrote. And one other thing surprised him. "There is this about Mr. Kennedy on a platform: he doesn't *look* ruthless," he said. "His whole manner is somehow tentative."

On the stump, yes. But it's also worth noting that while all this was going on, Robert Kennedy was also busy trying to suppress the publication of *Death of a President*, the book by William Manchester that the Kennedy family had commissioned following the assassination, only to have second thoughts later on. Most of the objections came from Jacqueline Kennedy, though various Kennedys worried that in skewering Lyndon Johnson, Manchester would be perceived as doing Bobby's bidding—an issue, should Bobby elect to run against him. Manchester's experience revived suspicions that lurking beneath the "new" Robert Kennedy was the old and ruthless one, perfectly intact. Manchester ultimately though, even didn't hold it against him. "The only man I have known whom you could love and hate at the same time," was how he later described Kennedy, whom he supported for president in 1968.

Whatever is the opposite of pandering, Kennedy regularly did. Repeatedly, he told college students that he opposed draft deferments (and often, in the end, won applause for that stance). He criticized the Black Power movement to black community leaders in Ohio (they applauded him, too) and told an audience in Berkeley (and everyone else, for that matter) that he was still supporting Lyndon Johnson. In places where firearms were part of the culture, he'd call for gun control. Asked whether he'd run for president in 1972, he'd say something like "six years is so far away; tomorrow is far away. I don't even know if I'll be alive in six years." It was fatalistic, though Kennedy's fatalism and King's were very different.

Befitting someone under constant threat, King talked about death incessantly and matter-of-factly. (The producer Abby Mann, who was to do his life story, asked him in 1966 how the film would end. "It ends with me getting killed," King replied. "He was smiling, but he wasn't joking," Mann recalled.) There was no long run for Martin Luther King; it was all just a matter of time. He discussed the kind of funeral he wanted and the number of eulogies there should be. He seemed to savor and almost embrace the topic, to anticipate and welcome martyrdom. Invoking the William Cullen Bryant poem "Thanatopsis," Grover Hall of the *Montgomery Advertiser* wrote once what many people felt: that King had a morbid fascination with death. (Harry Belafonte took out a life insurance policy for him; it was for $100,000 only because Lloyd's of London wouldn't sell one for a million.)

With Kennedy, the prospect of premature death was equally real; how could it not have been? In October, someone in Sacramento asked him to promise that he would run for president one day and, as Mary McGrory recorded it, his answer was "full of pauses and fatalism." "I don't know where that man way up there is going to take me," he said. But as all the speculation about 1972 and 1976 and 1980 and 1984 proved, people talked about Kennedy's long-term future in a way they did not about King's. The dangers Kennedy faced were not as unrelenting as King's and were generally tossed off rather than wallowed in. So, if such a thing is possible, Kennedy's fatalism was lighthearted, almost flippant, at least in public. Death? Let the advance men worry about it.

And that they did. One of them, Jerry Bruno, was with Kennedy for a rally in Salt Lake City. A crowd awaited the senator in a local armory when police reported a bomb threat in the building. Kennedy nonetheless walked inside, grabbed a microphone, reported the warning, urged everyone to stay calm, and then said he would walk out with them. "These people out there are petrified, and Kennedy didn't show one bit of emotion," Bruno later said. "He stood there until the last one was out, and then he left." In another swing that campaign season, Kennedy was poised to speak on the courthouse steps in Butte, Montana, when the sheriff spotted a rifleman on the roof of a nearby building. His chief of staff, Joe Dolan, and Bruno hovered around the senator. "If someone wants to kill me, there's nothing you can do about it," Kennedy told them. "And furthermore, people that shoot don't talk, [and] people that talk don't shoot. . . . I don't want to live my life in fear. I don't want to be under protection all the time. And so let's stop it, and let's do what we have to do." Sure enough, Kennedy survived. "You know, Bruno, you're really smart," Kennedy said afterward. "You were up front. You're short. The guy's going to miss you. He's going to hit me. You're all heart."

Just what was Kennedy up to, traveling all around instead of tending to his duties in New York and Washington? No one, McGrory wrote, could be exactly sure. Following his brother's footsteps through the Midwest, she equated his campaign with T. S. Eliot's description of April—"mixing memory and desire"—and said that with Kennedy it was hard "to say where one left off and the other began." Later, she added another possible ingredient to the mix. "Sometimes," she said, "he seemed to be campaigning only for his own amusement." At times the trappings—the ecstatic crowds, the legions of reporters—made Kennedy appear all but unstoppable. But many of those cheering the loudest were too young to vote. And the forces arrayed against Kennedy—business, party regulars, organized labor (which had more reliable Democratic friends), southerners, liberals—weren't mainstays at his rallies.

Writers were drawn to write about how Kennedy was drawn to the young, and how the young was drawn to him—he was often described as childlike himself; Gore Vidal once wrote of "Bobby's Holden Caulfield contempt for the grown-ups." Kennedy himself joked that he wanted to lower the voting age to twelve. "I lose them after twenty-five," he explained.

There were lots of stories.

"Hey, mister," a girl shouted to Pete Hamill outside the new Senate Office Building in Washington. "You know where Bobby Kennedy's office is?"

"Why do you want to see him?"

"Who else is there to see here?"

Accompanied by Nora Ephron, then a reporter for the *New York Post*, Kennedy investigated substandard housing conditions of New York's Lower East Side.

Nora Ephron, then a young reporter for the *New York Post* described a tenant on the Lower East Side complaining to Kennedy about her busted bathroom light. "The Senator listened," she wrote, "absently stroking the hair of one of the younger children."

Walking his dog early one Sunday morning near the East River, Truman Capote spotted Kennedy in the distance, shaking two young boys by their arms. "Truman, come over here," he said. Capote had always had some trouble with Kennedy, whom he called "a curious combination of great vanity and shyness," and Kennedy, conventional and prudish, of course had his issues with Capote. "Look at these little punks," he said. "They're twelve or thirteen years old. They're smoking cigarettes." "Honestly, honestly, Mr. Kennedy, I swear we'll never do it again," one of them pleaded. Kennedy let them go, and off they ran. But when they reached the corner, one of them ran all the way back. "Can I have your autograph, Mr. Kennedy?" he asked.

What Jimmy Breslin had happened upon as he followed Kennedy around Queens one afternoon in November 1966 was only a routine football scrimmage, but as the boys from St. Francis Prep went through their paces, Breslin thought he saw the future. "All of it—all the words about whether Bobby Kennedy is a ruthless, mechanical rich guy or a genius mellowed by great tragedy—all of it is superfluous when you see him coming up to a high school football team that is practicing for a game," he wrote, as he watched the awestruck boys watch Kennedy watching them. "Bobby Kennedy can be every inch of the worst SOB we've ever had. Everything he does in public can be a facade. But standing on a football field with kids, nothing matters. There is something between them that is powerful." When St. Francis won that Sunday, the boys saved the game ball for Kennedy, even though he hadn't been able to come back for the game. "The only name they know in politics is Robert Kennedy," Breslin concluded. "Some of them will be 21 in 1968 and all of them will be 21 in 1972 and this is not a story about politics, it is a story about simple arithmetic." Kempton saw a young boy in Harlem approach Kennedy's car at a light to say hello. "I know of no other adult—let alone any other historical object—to whom a 16-year-old talks as though he were talking to a 16-year-old," he wrote. "There is a club of people who think him hard and cold. It has no junior auxiliary."

For months, following embarrassing revelations about improper FBI eavesdropping on a lobbyist named Fred Black—his conviction for tax evasion was overturned on those grounds—Kennedy and Hoover feuded over electronic surveillance. In late 1966 Hoover charged that Kennedy had known of and approved everything the FBI had done; Kennedy insisted he had not. The dispute was largely one of semantics: while the rules for wiretapping and electronic bugs differed, the terms had become interchangeable. Each fashioned a case for himself around this ambiguity. In a sense, both men were right. From this contretemps came word in the

*New York Times* on December 14 that beginning with the Kennedy administration, the government had been listening in on King. It had happened, wrote James Reston, "during the racial disorders, for reasons best known to itself." "Who authorized the taps?" he asked. "We do not know."

That day, King told another *Times* reporter that he'd figured people had been listening to his phone calls (as John Kennedy had told him walking around the White House Rose Garden in June 1963) but that whether local or federal officials were involved, he'd never known. Certainly, nothing he did ever compromised national security, he insisted. Afterward—with the FBI listening, naturally—King attorney and adviser Harry Wachtel complained about how blasé King had been discussing a trespass against him. "When you have a guy doing an illegal act, you should not be so sweet about it," he griped. "Dr. King 'Assumes' Phone Is Tapped" read the headline in the next day's *Times*. What the headline didn't say was that King was about to appear before, and talk with, and be praised by, and be photographed alongside the man who had actually approved that snooping.

It happened on December 15, at the final hearing of Senator Abraham Ribicoff's Subcommittee on Executive Reorganization, known more colloquially as the Senate Cities Committee. In two three-week chunks over the previous four months, the panel had examined the problems of America's ghettos. As Ribicoff surely knew, such hearings would generally have warranted little interest or coverage, but with the junior senator from New York on the panel, it was certain to be followed closely. He appreciated and resented Kennedy both.

And Kennedy hadn't disappointed. Already, he had fenced with several members of Johnson's cabinet, along with assorted big-city mayors, Lindsay of New York and Yorty of Los Angeles among them. (He got along with Yorty no better than King did, faulting him for poor leadership before and during the Watts riots. At one point Kennedy noted that the poor wanted only the same chance in life that he and Yorty had had. "Certainly they won't have the chance *you* had," Yorty replied. "I hope they'll have the chance I've had.") He'd also dueled with prominent blacks, telling Roy Wilkins that given the level of alienation in black neighborhoods, leaders both black and white would have trouble speaking in them, and attacking Floyd McKissick of CORE for preaching black power. The picture he painted of programs for the black poor was bleak. "We talk about poverty and that we are going to do something about it, as long as it is not going to cost too much," he testified. "We talk about giving rights to Negroes as long as it doesn't inconvenience us too much. We talk about doing something about the ghetto . . . as long as we don't have to personally be involved in it."

At one point in the hearings, Kennedy pondered the fate of an entire generation of inner-city black children. His principal interlocutor was Harvard child psychologist Robert Coles, with whom he discussed how failed schools and discredited programs crushed the spirit of black youth. Kennedy said he found himself gravitating to the black neighborhoods he once feared and was especially drawn to the children. He compared the faces of those between, say, six and twelve to their counterparts on Fifth Avenue, and how those ghetto children were "much, much happier than the ones who are being pushed along in their prams."

Coles agreed: adversity had bred in them a certain vitality. And Kennedy then described what he thought happened when these same children became young adults. "Then really sort of a castration begins," he said. "It suddenly dawns on them what is really going on so that they turn, in my judgment much more than before, they turn against society. . . . The family is broken up and the school doesn't mean anything and the educational system is not going to get them anywhere, and they see no way of getting out. . . . I am not so sure that we are not developing a whole class of people, hundreds of thousands within our own society here, who are just going to be completely antisocial and against everything that exists in this country." The implications of that, he said, were "absolutely explosive" for an increasingly urban society. After meeting with Kennedy three years earlier, James Baldwin noted the then-attorney general's failure to understand how "a kid of fifteen's going to be twenty-one day" and what damage is done to him in the interim. Now Kennedy was saying the same thing.

A few days after Coles's appearance, King was called to testify. It was his first appearance on Capitol Hill and, concerned about repeating what the other civil rights leaders had already said, he'd had the Ford Foundation prepare a statement for him. It was longer on descriptions and admonitions than specific policy ideas, with nothing resembling the prescriptions Kennedy had offered in the three speeches on the cities he'd given at the beginning of the year. (In one respect—King's call for a guaranteed annual income—he and King disagreed; to Kennedy, that amounted to a handout.) King's language was sometimes both apocalyptic and wildly inapt. "The affluent Americans will eventually have to face themselves with the question that [Adolf] Eichmann chose to ignore: How responsible am I for the well-being of my fellows?" he asked.

King assailed the stinginess of government efforts to combat poverty, particularly when compared to the lavishness of one of John Kennedy's pet projects: the space program. "Without denying the value of scientific endeavor," he said, "there is a striking absurdity in committing billions to reach the moon where no people live, and from which none presently can benefit, while the densely populated slums are allocated minuscule appropriations." In a few years, he predicted, a man on the moon with a telescope would look down and see slums of "intensified congestion, decay, and turbulence." "On what scale of values is this a program of progress?" he asked.

The greater problem, though, was Vietnam. King had pledged to Levison to bring it up before the committee—"Everything we're talking about really boils down to the fact that we have this war on our hands," he said—and he did. "The security we profess to seek in foreign adventures we will lose in our decaying cities," he said. "The bombs in Vietnam explode at home; they destroy the hopes and possibilities for a decent America." But King broadened his attack to military spending generally. "With the resources accruing from termination of the war, arms race, and excessive space races," King stated, "the elimination of all poverty could become an immediate national reality." King would not only pull out of Vietnam; he would beat swords into plowshares.

In what was surely the most moving moment in his testimony, King described the moment when his older daughter, five years old at the time, first encountered discrimination. She'd pressed to go to Fun Town, a segregated amusement park in Atlanta she'd seen advertised on television. After putting her off for a time, her parents finally had to tell her she *couldn't* go, and why. But by 1966, Fun Town had closed, and, as King acknowledged, the movement had changed, focusing more on intractable economic issues. "It was easier to integrate public facilities, it was easier to gain the right to vote because it didn't cost the nation anything," he said. What was necessary now was "a restructuring of the architecture of American society. It is going to cost the nation something."

Kennedy asked King why nonviolence was so much less accepted in the North than it had been down South. He pressed him on why the ghettos lacked indigenous leadership. He challenged King on the chasm between young blacks and the civil rights establishment. But the tensions between Kennedy and the other black leaders—or, for that matter, between Kennedy and King going back to the New Frontier—were absent. What replaced it was less raw but still real; Kennedy managed to be both fraternal and challenging, polite but provocative. His questions had a bite. It was, in a way, the highest gesture of respect.

King conceded that the movement had been too "middle-class oriented." That was the great challenge, he said—why he was still spending four nights a week in the heart of the ghetto in Chicago. "Would you also agree that the private enterprise system also has a larger role to play in this country?" Kennedy asked. King did, and with that, the hearings were over. "Dr. King, I congratulate you on many of the fine things that you have done for the Negroes and really for the United States and for all of us," Kennedy said.

Chicago, summer 1967: No matter where King traveled, whether in the South or in the North, he was continually under the watchful eye of local law enforcement.

It was their longest public encounter. It was also their last. No one thought to take a decent picture of the two together, at least one that made it into print. In the only photograph that survives, the two men flank Randolph Churchill, Winston's son, who happened to be there that day; King is seen only from behind.

At one point in his testimony, King spoke of the need for far greater federal commitment and funds: "$20 billion," he told Kennedy, "wouldn't be too much. Which, incidentally, would be less than we are spending on the war in Vietnam." But if he had been inviting Kennedy to talk about the war, Kennedy didn't bite. For him, Vietnam was already dicey enough; discussing it publicly with King was worse, and *agreeing* with him about it was political suicide. So it was that when two of the most prominent critics of the war came together, they did not discuss the war. What was arguably most significant about their last public encounter was something that was *not* said.

For Mary McGrory, who attended the hearing, the greatest drama wasn't the unprecedented joint appearance of these two men or even the disclosure that one of them had spied on the other. In fact, Kennedy wasn't even a part of it. It was King she studied. His cause had hit hard times, she wrote, and King himself was now attempting simply to keep up with a movement he had once led. "He still talks with his old splendor," she wrote. "The baroque phrases still roll out in the mellifluous mesmerizing tenor." But King now found himself "harassed by strange gods" preaching anger and separation while the laws he'd helped pass meant little to the millions relegated to urban slums. "The struggle is now economic and political, and Dr. King must prove himself all over again—out of his element, and with no Southern sheriffs for a foil," she wrote. It was a "bad time for a marcher and a preacher," she concluded. Martin Luther King, she suggested, was obsolete.

Maybe, but not to a group calling itself the New Campus Political Action Committee. Around the time the hearings concluded, it announced that were Kennedy to break with Johnson on Vietnam, it would enter him in various presidential primaries in 1968. The group's chairman, Gerald Schaflander of Brooklyn College, also proposed a running mate for Kennedy: Martin Luther King. Kennedy wasn't interested, but word of the fantasy ticket reached the FBI, which passed it around in a memo. That gave Hoover another chance to editorialize. "A fine pair!" he scrawled.

Economic justice was the defining issue of Robert Kennedy's early years in the Senate, but not all communities welcomed his intervention.

# ELEVEN

# CHANGE WOULD COME

Like so many progressives, the political cartoonist Jules Feiffer had long been wary of Robert Kennedy—for his bullying, his foot-dragging on civil rights, his red-baiting. "I was scared shitless of him running for president because I thought he had a very authoritarian nature," he later said. He also hated his equivocations, which is what he spotted during Kennedy's appearance on one of the Sunday morning talk shows in late 1966 or early 1967. His cartoon in the *Village Voice* on January 29, 1967, entitled the "There are the Bobby Twins," was the perfect encapsulation of liberal ambivalence about the man. In each of the six panels, there appeared two Robert Kennedys. "Good Bobby" was a courageous reformer; "Bad Bobby" made deals. "Good Bobby" enforced civil rights; "Bad Bobby" appointed redneck judges. "Good Bobby" favored civil liberties; "Bad Bobby" wiretapped. To Feiffer, Bobby had one thing going for him: he was easier to draw than Jack: movie stars are much harder to caricature. While both of Feiffer's Bobbys, Good and Bad, had their appeal—both were shy and turned inward and almost sweet—they ultimately were dangerous. "This was not an attack on Bobby," he said afterward. "It was a heads up to my liberal, left-wing readers, 'watch out for this guy." The cartoon prompted little reaction when it first appeared, but as Kennedy's ubiquity grew and his public oscillations intensified, it kept reappearing. In fact, "Good Bobby" and "Bad Bobby" entered the language, popping up when people plumbed the paradoxes of the man.

Two weeks after his searing antiwar speech at Manhattan's Riverside Church on April 4, 1967, King addressed a peace demonstration outside the United Nations.

Feiffer passed up another possible panel, or perhaps a whole other set of them: the Good and Bad Bobbys on Vietnam. ("He was moving in a good direction," he later said. "I didn't want to get in the way.") Good Bobby thought the war misbegotten, a colossal mistake; Bad Bobby thought that the idea behind the war remained valid, but that the conflict itself was being mismanaged. Good Bobby wanted to pull back dramatically; Bad Bobby only to fine-tune. Good Bobby considered Lyndon Johnson stubborn, dangerous, and bellicose; Bad Bobby praised him. Good Bobby spoke out ever more frequently and critically about the war (including before the Senate on March 2). Bad Bobby— recognizing that he came to the issue with unclean hands, and that his criticism threatened to split the party and might even prompt a spiteful Johnson to dig in even deeper—steered clear of it. Good Bobby angered Lyndon Johnson; Bad Bobby angered everyone to Johnson's left.

That same month that Feiffer's cartoon appeared, Martin Luther King headed for another vacation in Jamaica, where he'd work on his latest book. (It became *Where Do We Go from Here: Chaos or Community?*) At the airport newsstand, King picked up the latest issue of *Ramparts*. In it, he found a long spread titled "The Children of Vietnam." It consisted principally of horrific pictures of young burn victims, flayed and disfigured by American bombs and napalm. Leafing through it, he lost his appetite and pushed aside the food he had just ordered. "Nothing will ever taste good until I do everything I can to end that war," he told his traveling companion, Bernard Lee.

Over the next several months, King cast aside whatever ambivalence remained and became one of the most visible and vocal opponents of the Vietnam War. It would not be as a presidential candidate, though there were pleas from important people—Allard Lowenstein, Yale chaplain William Sloane Coffin, old socialist Norman Thomas—to enter the race. Rather, it was in his traditional roles as activist and preacher. Fearful that he might antagonize his civil rights constituency and his fund-raising, aides urged caution: it made more sense, Stanley Levison warned, to stick principally with civil rights and work with more mainstream figures, Robert Kennedy among them, to oppose the war, than to associate with those on the radical fringe. But the pictures of those children haunted and emboldened King.

On February 25 in Beverly Hills, in a program he shared with four United States senators (Eugene McCarthy and George McGovern among them), King made his bluntest antiwar statements to date. "We are presently moving down a dead-end road that can lead to national disaster," he said. "Those of us who love peace must organize as effectively as the war hawks." Partly at Levison's urging, his latest statements were more racially tinged: not only was this war wrong per se, he said, but its costs both on the battlefield and at home were falling disproportionately on blacks, who were serving and dying in greater numbers, and would suffer more from the resulting cutbacks back home. They were also the most widely publicized. "Dr. King Advocates Quitting Vietnam" went the headline on the front page of the next day's *New York Times*. King planned additional speeches: one in Chicago in March and another at the massive antiwar protest set for New York in April.

The high stakes for the black community in Vietnam came up as well at a small reception and fund-raiser held for King in New York on March 6. Organizing it was William vanden Heuvel, the lawyer and businessman who'd worked under Robert Kennedy in the Justice Department and had remained close to him. (When Robert and Jacqueline Kennedy tried to halt the serialization of William Manchester's book in Germany, vanden Heuvel handled the negotiations.) But more than anyone else in Kennedy's circle, he was also friendly with King, and, with Belafonte, acted as a back-channel liaison between the two. "There are few men in our time who have acted with greater courage than Dr. King," vanden Heuvel wrote to invitees. "This is the critical moment for those who believe in Dr. King's work and methods to express our support."

Also present that night was Andrew Young, the King aide who became another link in the chain between the two camps. His thank-you note afterward revealed four truths about the King-Kennedy relationship, such as it was: how compatible their worlds were; how fragile and isolated King felt; how marginal, and deferential, and importuning, King and his associates were with the Kennedys; and how negligible the real ties between them were. "Last Monday was quite an encouraging occasion for me," Young began. "It gave me new hope for the country that 'your kind of people' would one day be running things. At times we feel very alone out here in left field with no one in 'the establishment' that really understands or cares."

But together, Young went on, the two camps might mount "a very significant pincer movement against a variety of social problems." "With you working from within the structure of politics and economics and us working on the outside, we can move the country along much more quickly," he wrote. "There are many things that Senator Kennedy cannot say or do that present no problem for Dr. King," he noted. "There should be some established channel for continuing this dialogue." He said he looked forward to what he called "an occasional sharing of ideas." But here, too, the gap was great. As Young's letter suggested, the Kennedy side seemed more resistant, probably because, as the more powerful party, it had less to gain from such an alliance and much more to lose.

As it was, Kennedy was riding high. The *Times* reported that there were a dozen or more Robert Kennedy books in the works, all premised on a presidential bid in the near or not-too-distant future. There were Robert Kennedy biographies, books on Kennedy as attorney general and Kennedy's impact on the young, books of Kennedy quotations and speeches, and a *Ladies Guide to Bobby Kennedy*. Liberals would praise him and conservatives, unmask him. "From what I understand to be the attitude of some of the authors toward me, I hope people will be too bored to read them," Kennedy said.

While his liberal critics said Kennedy was too timid on Vietnam, aides to King worried he was too extreme. King had agreed to participate in the massive antiwar demonstration set for April in New York, even though Levison warned that he'd be surrounding himself with pacifists, socialists, and hippies. To allay such concerns, King agreed to speak beforehand in a less politicized setting, free of Viet Cong flags, "Black Power!" chants, and whiffs of marijuana: the Riverside Church in New York. To him, it was a familiar and politically congenial place, where he'd often spoken before and whose pulpit he thought he might one day assume. Around this time, in fact, he'd weighed accepting a two-year interim appointment there, one which Andrew Young urged him to take because of the platform, and the respite, it would have provided. "I had a talk with him, saying, 'Look, when we started out, none of us thought we'd live to be 40,'" Young later wrote. "'So we didn't concern ourselves about our health, about the long haul. We thought we had a job to do and a few years to do it in. It now looks like we are going to be around for a while and we've got to slow the pace down. We can't take on every fight.'" King ignored him. This address would not be a Sunday sermon but a Tuesday afternoon speech sponsored by a group called Clergy and Laymen Concerned About Vietnam.

His remarks there on April 4, 1967, like Kennedy's most important speeches, would be the work of many hands, some of them even the same: Allard Lowenstein had also helped write Kennedy's Cape Town address. Its principal author was Vincent Harding of Spelman College, who felt he was just putting down thoughts that King was too busy to write for himself. But it would be stitched together too hastily for a speech of such importance. So apprehensive was Levison, whose instincts on such things were flawless, that he was home in bed when it was delivered.

King's tenor that day was atypical: slow, somber, steady, and stately, without the usual flourishes and cadences. It was, in other words, for a white audience. It sounded as if it was being read, which it was, without digressions or improvisation. The speech, he confessed to the overflow crowd, was overdue: for too long he'd listened to those who said "peace and civil rights don't mix." Those folks didn't know him, he said; the path that had begun in Montgomery had led directly to Riverside Church that day.

Never, he said, would America "invest the necessary funds or energies in rehabilitation of its poor so long as adventures like Vietnam continued to draw men and skills and money like some demonic, destructive suction tube." He talked of blacks fighting "to guarantee liberties in Southeast Asia which they had not found in Southwest Georgia and East Harlem." How, he asked, could he tell rioters in Watts that violence couldn't solve their problems when the United States had become "the greatest purveyor of violence in the world today?" Then there was the toll on the Vietnamese. "What do they think as we test out our latest weapons on them, just as the Germans tested out new medicine and new tortures" in the camps?" he asked. "They must see Americans as strange liberators."

Had King stopped there, his speech would have been explosive enough. His program, which included withdrawal and reparations to the Vietnamese, was far more drastic than most critics of the war envisioned. But he went on to say that America had not only been "wrong from the beginning" on Vietnam but malevolent, describing the war as "some horrible, clumsy, and deadly game we have decided to play." At a time when polls showed a majority of Americans still supported the war, King called for the United States to "atone for our sins." Investment, rather than idealism, was what American involvement was all about. As "arch-anti-revolutionaries," the United States and other Western countries were on the wrong side of history; America's values were "thing-oriented" and military-oriented rather than "person-oriented." "A nation that continues year after year to spend more money on military defense than on programs of social uplift is approach-ing spiritual death," he said. "If America's soul becomes totally poisoned, part of the autopsy must read 'Vietnam.'"

Inside Riverside Church, King basked in fellow feeling. And inside his psyche, King, always his own severest critic, felt relieved, even purged: finally, on this toughest of subjects, he had stepped up and acted as a "morally wise man." But outside, the reaction was harsh. To the NAACP, the speech was a "serious tactical mistake." Ralph Bunche, Jackie Robinson, and Thurgood Marshall all slammed him. The black journalist Carl Rowan raised the issue of communist influence on King and traced his evolution from the canny mastermind of Montgomery into egomania and ham-handedness: Vietnam had given blacks a chance to prove their patriotism, and King had sowed doubts about it. Just as bad, he'd burned his bridges to Lyndon Johnson and the Congress. The Jewish War Veterans were put off by King's Holocaust comparisons, something with which he'd been profligate before (for example, comparing whites neglecting the inner cities to Adolf Eichmann). The *Washington Post* and *New York Times* accused King of straying disastrously beyond his bailiwick. Murray Kempton was among the few to push back: "Are Nobel Peace Prize laureates to be instructed by the *New York Times* as to when it is proper or improper for them to state their views on peace?" he asked.

Johnson asked the FBI to get him a copy of the speech. The bureau's campaign against King, which had subsided some, was revived: in a report entitled "Racial Violence Potential in the United States This Summer," the bureau blamed "demagogues like Martin Luther King, Stokely Carmichael, Floyd McKissick, Cassius Clay and Dick Gregory" for incipient riots. King, it said, had embraced "the communist tactic" of linking the antiwar and civil rights movements, and his encouragement to draft resistors "could lead eventually to dangerous displays of civil disobedience and near-seditious activities by Negroes and whites alike."

Even King's allies were uncomfortable with the speech. Levison complained that King's position on Vietnam was marginalizing him much as Soviet sympathies had very nearly destroyed Paul Robeson in the 1950s. King, he felt, "should not have spoken from the point of view of a Viet Cong peasant." Vincent Harding later found himself unhappy for a different reason: he came to think that by stirring up such hatred against King, the speech he

Governor Ronald Reagan and Senator Kennedy defended their continued support
of U.S. involvement in the Vietnam War in a televised town meeting.

had written was in some way responsible for what happened to
him a year to the day after he gave it.

King stood his ground. "I backed up a little when I came
out [against the war] in 1965," he said. "But now I have decided
that I will not be intimidated." But assaulted on all sides—by
militants and moderates and the right wing, by blacks as well as
whites—King grew increasingly tired, discouraged, frustrated, and
strident. Whites—policemen and slumlords—were the ghettos'
real "hardened criminals," he charged. America's commitment to

civil rights was halfhearted. Maybe most whites *really were* racists. Vietnam could lead to World War III with China, he warned, "and whenever China comes in, there's no way to win. They can lose 300 million men and it is just an act of birth control."

One person who never weighed in on the Riverside speech, at least publicly, was Robert Kennedy. King "talked to several of us who were close to Bobby, so that Bobby knew exactly what he was going to do," vanden Heuvel said afterward. (But always, he added, the communications were through intermediaries: "They would never say take the other step of 'You're speaking? I'll be there.'") That Kennedy was warned of what was coming made it no more palatable, however; this time, there was no congratulatory letter or suggestion that they compare notes on the problem. Burke Marshall later surmised that Kennedy considered the speech a mistake. At a televised town meeting a month later, Kennedy's position on the war was closer to Ronald Reagan's than it was to King's. One questioner asserted that the war was "illegal, immoral, politically unjustifiable, and economically motivated" — King's position, essentially. Kennedy said he disagreed. He had "some reservations" about some aspects of the war, he said, but he backed American efforts to let the South Vietnamese "determine their own destiny."

But Kennedy didn't get off altogether. Evidently sensing that King had made an albatross of himself, Kennedy's critics eagerly linked the two. Three weeks after the speech, Drew Pearson, who was close to Johnson, wrote about vanden Heuvel's cocktail party for King in his popular syndicated column. "It wasn't supposed to be mentioned outside civil rights circles, but one of Sen. Robert Kennedy's closest confidants has been raising funds for Rev. Martin Luther King, and the activity is certain to help pose more problems for Bobby when he finally tosses his hat in the presidential ring," Pearson wrote. "LBJ was trying to hurt both of them and if he could put them together and hurt them it was better still," vanden Heuvel later recalled. In letters to his office, several erstwhile supporters asked Kennedy why on earth he was consorting with a communist.

A few days after the Riverside speech, Kennedy headed for Mississippi, where the Senate Labor Committee's Subcommittee on Employment, Manpower, and Poverty was investigating living conditions of the rural poor. It turned out to be one of the seminal journeys of Kennedy's life, as powerful and durable as South Africa. Kennedy had largely lost interest in the South—legal rights for blacks there had now been enacted; it was for others to enforce them—and moved on to the woes of northern ghettos. But a confluence of forces—the mechanization of cotton farming, federal minimum-wage laws and subsidy programs, and the development of chemical weed killer—had thrown thousands of blacks in the Mississippi delta out of work, and, deprived of government support, many were going hungry. Civil rights advocates charged it was all part of a plan by the state of Mississippi to drive such people out.

Kennedy flew to Jackson on April 9. There was a hearing the following day, but, after that, insisting on seeing the poverty firsthand, he led a small entourage to a few of delta hamlets. He talked to the children, asked them whether they had eaten that day—one said he'd not had lunch and had only molasses for breakfast—and walked into their homes. One of the hungry children he visited was Charlie Dillard, ten years old at the time. "He came through the door, and that's when he introduced himself as Senator Kennedy," Dillard remembered. Kennedy's, he said, was the first white hand he had ever shaken. For many there that day, the most memorable moment came in Mrs. Annie White's shack, where Kennedy spotted her twenty-month-old son in a dirty diaper sitting on the dirt floor, picking at and eating grains of rice. Kennedy teared up as he knelt by the little boy for a couple of minutes and stroked his cheek. "Flies were swarming," wrote Curtis Wilkie of the *Clarksdale Press-Register*. "The boy just looked at him with wide eyes." An irate local newspaper editor challenged Kennedy afterward, telling him he should be concentrating on poor people back in New York and insisting no one was starving in Mississippi. "Step over here and I'll show you some," Kennedy replied.

"He went into the dirtiest, filthiest, poorest black homes, places with barely any floor, pot-bellied stoves the only thing; and he would sit with a baby who had open sores and whose belly was bloated from malnutrition, and he'd sit and touch and hold those babies," Marian Wright, the young lawyer for the NAACP who had helped organize the tour, later remembered. "I wouldn't do that! I didn't do that! But he did. And I saw that compassion, and I saw that feeling, and I saw how he was learning." (It was on this trip that she met the Kennedy aide Peter Edelman, whom she subsequently married.)

There was also Hodding Carter III, the scion of a racially progressive Mississippi family who covered Kennedy's visit for his family's newspaper, the *Greenville Delta Democrat-Times*. "I had spent a fair amount of my youth looking at [Kennedy] as being a hit man for Senator McClellan of Arkansas, of being a fan of Joe McCarthy, of being an extremely nasty piece of work," he told the filmmaker Andy Greenspan. "I hated his father. And I could not imagine that I was supposed to see something good in him." But that day, he said, "I saw a human being being visibly affected. I looked at a guy who won't cry or anything, but who was moved in ways that were not the artifice of his PR man."

The expedition made the evening news. "Senator Robert Kennedy, the rich man's son who has specialized so far in the problems of urban slums, has come to Mississippi," reported Daniel Schorr of CBS News. "When a Kennedy travels, he is sometimes more inspected than inspecting, and Greenville was no exception," Schorr said. "Here, even to first-grade children, the name, and the hair, of Bobby Kennedy seem magic."

Standing amid the squalor, Kennedy pointed out to Schorr that the United States spent $70 billion a year on weapons and $3 billion on dogs, but did little for the poor and especially poor children "who have nothing to do with asking to be born into this world but don't have enough to eat." But nothing involving Kennedy was ever entirely free of politics. "He has found that Vietnam as an issue against the Johnson administration doesn't work," said Schorr,

"and that by identifying himself with the poor, he may have found another issue—an issue of a lagging war against poverty, an issue to be used in whatever year he may choose to use it."

When he returned to Hickory Hill that night, Kennedy was still shaken by the experience. "He said, 'I've just come in and seen a family live in a room smaller than our dining room, with their tummies distended and sores all over them because they don't have enough to eat and they don't have healthcare,'" Kennedy's eldest daughter, Kathleen Kennedy Townsend, later recalled. "'Do you know how lucky you are? *Do you know how lucky you are?* Do something for this country.'"

To Belafonte, the trip marked a turning point for Kennedy—"when it became evident to him that our cause was much more righteous than he was prepared to imagine." Martin Luther King was among those commending Kennedy. (His note to Kennedy, if preserved, is not yet available.) "I cannot agree with you more that something must be done," Kennedy wrote him back. "If you have any suggestions, I would appreciate hearing from you." Again, it seems no further correspondence ensued. But expeditions to such pockets of poverty became commonplace for Kennedy, who tried to goose the balky federal bureaucracy to send food to the delta when he returned to Washington. Peter Edelman, who also accompanied Kennedy that day, later said that the trip reflected "that curious way that [Kennedy] had of learning": not from books or testimony, but by *seeing*. And this he did in many other places, visiting Native Americans, coal miners, sharecroppers, and farmworkers.

But Robert Kennedy, like King, was depressed by the state of things, as Arthur Schlesinger discovered at Hickory Hill a few days after the Mississippi trip. Kennedy, he wrote in his journal afterward, "was in good form, but seemed tired, and an indefinable sense of depression hung over him, as if he felt cornered by

Kennedy's 1967 tour of the Mississippi delta deeply broadened his understanding of rural poverty, and fueled his investment in action.

circumstance and did not know how to break out. He said that his speech on Vietnam (delivered before the Senate on March 2) had probably stiffened LBJ's determination to pursue the opposite course. Also, he could not get a hearing for anything he had to say on the merits of his anti-slum initiatives; his every action was always interpreted in terms of political maneuver."

The riots that broke out that summer in Newark and Detroit only heightened the despair of both men. "Most of the times I saw King, he was depressed," said Marian Wright Edelman. "And didn't know where he was going next. He was one of the few adults whom we admired very deeply who could be uncertain, who could share his fears." Coretta King said she had never seen her husband so despondent. For his part, Kennedy was discouraged by Johnson's classic no-response response to the violence: appointing a presidential commission, headed by Governor Otto Kerner, Jr., of Illinois, to investigate them. To Kennedy it certified that Johnson, increasingly preoccupied and hamstrung by the war, had given up on the cities.

Asked what he'd have done, Kennedy said he would have asked the heads of the three television networks to produce a documentary on the hopelessness and degradation of ghetto life, then aired it in prime time. He'd also have held meetings, like those he'd convened before the passage of the Civil Rights Act, to bring together all the interested parties. On *Meet the Press* in early August, he called for a Marshall Plan for American cities. "If we can spend $24 billion for the freedom and the liberty of the people of Vietnam," he said, "certainly we can spend a small percentage of that for the liberty and freedom and the future of our own people in the United States."

The presidential talk persisted. In a cover story, *Esquire* envisioned a Kennedy dynasty running until at least 1988, jumping from John to Robert to Teddy to John, Jr. (The magazine had "R.F.K."—the appellation was still new—reaching the White House in 1973.) The president of CBS News, Richard Salant, acknowledged Kennedy's unique status when he commissioned the correspondent Roger Mudd to do a documentary on the man he called "the only non-nominated, non-elected president we'll ever have." But his prospects for 1968 were fading; his handling of the Manchester book and position on Vietnam had hurt him. A Harris poll that June showed him trailing both Johnson and Humphrey. Without a brother in the White House and with his father out of commission, Gore Vidal wrote, Kennedy had lost his ruthlessness, and become "timid, blundering, and emotional."

King, though, listed Kennedy, along with Senator Charles Percy of Illinois, as the two presidential possibilities with the best civil rights records. Another Harris poll revealed that King could influence as much as a quarter of the black vote were he to pressure Johnson to put Kennedy on the ticket. Meanwhile, Kennedy resisted all the presidential talk and buttered up Johnson ("He has poured out his own strength to renew the strength of the country...") at a dinner for the president in June 1967. Schlesinger neatly described the trade-off. "He avoided charges of ambition and party-splitting by incurring charges of inconsistency and hypocrisy," he wrote. On consecutive days in July the convergence of the two men on urban issues became apparent: first, King announced the expansion of Operation Breadbasket, a plan to promote black employment in the cities, and then, Kennedy introduced tax breaks designed to encourage private investment in the same sorts of neighborhoods.

King often cited the words to the old spiritual "Balm in Gilead" — "Sometimes I feel discouraged/And think my work's in vain/But then the Holy Spirit/Revives my soul again" — to describe his ups and downs. But his revival in early August came from a less celestial source: Robert Kennedy.

The federal bureaucracy still hadn't sent the food it had promised to the delta, and shortly before the SCLC's annual convention later that month, Marian Wright Edelman brought her unhappiness about the logjam to Hickory Hill. Kennedy had a simple suggestion: "Tell Dr. King to bring the poor to Washington," he said. Change would come, Kennedy told her, only when Congress was made to feel more uncomfortable *not* acting. A mass of poor people had to descend on Washington and stay there, he said, until things got sufficiently unpleasant, with widespread civil disobedience and disruption. Only then would remedial action be taken.

The idea was not entirely new. "We ought to come in mule carts, in old trucks, any kind of transportation people can get their hands on," King had told aides the previous fall. "People ought to come to Washington, sit down if necessary in the middle of the street, and say, 'We are here; we are poor; we don't have any money; you have made us this way; you keep us down this way; and we've come to stay until you do something about it.'" But when Wright presented Kennedy's suggestion to King, his "eyes lit up and he called me an angel sent by God." Coretta King, too, recalled the effect Kennedy's idea had on her husband.

At the convention, King talked of plans to "dislocate" northern cities with massive protests, and to "cripple the operations of an oppressive society." It was, he said, an alternative to rioting: still shocking to the system, but without all the destructiveness. It was also, as he saw it, a last resort of sorts. At the same gathering, King pledged to go "all out" to beat Johnson, though he did not see a Democratic alternative: while Kennedy would make a "great president," he'd never be nominated. Instead, King envisioned a return to Daddy King's Republicans: a ticket of Rockefeller and Percy would sweep the country, he predicted.

But more noteworthy to the press was the generally sorry state of the cause, the Southern Christian Leadership Conference, and King. The demoralization was palpable. "The old zeal and spirit of the movement which had logged many miles of marches and brought significant Negro advances now seemed muted," went one report from the gathering. "Even the singing of the familiar 'We Shall Overcome' lacked the ring of faith that had rocked Birmingham, Selma, St. Augustine, Fla., Albany, Ga., and other battlefields of the past."

"The civil rights movement went forward when it had a vision," one speaker said. "To put it bluntly, it is dying because it no longer has a vision to inspire its members, let alone the rest of the country." No one rose to disagree.

Writers of all political hues sensed King's distress. "He has lost much of his following, and increasingly he emerges as the Harold Stassen of the civil rights movement," wrote William F. Buckley. In a piece he called "The Ordeal of Martin Luther King," William Shannon of the *New York Times* described the "pathos" of watching King invoke Gandhi to reckless youth and the rebellious unemployed. He suggested King resume work in the South or, as he put it rather poignantly, to "Look homeward, angel."

To Andrew Kopkind of the *New York Review of Books*, King had become a has-been. Distracted by the wars in Vietnam and on American streets, his white liberal friends had proved fickle. And the riots had produced "a primitive new kind of politics" and "tough black street leaders" who'd made him look outmoded.

Though Kopkind didn't say it and might not even have known it, Robert Kennedy was talking to these new leaders more regularly and easily than he was with King. Far from ducking confrontation, Kennedy sought it out. He was impatient and wanted to make things happen, or at least to mix things up. In May, he'd asked the screenwriter Budd Schulberg, who had set up workshops for writers and poets in Watts following the riots there, to introduce him to some of his young protégés. "And don't stack it with Uncle Toms or middle-of-the-roaders," he told Schulberg. "I'd like to hear from the militants, how they're really thinking." Schulberg obliged, and the black youths he produced "let him have it for an hour and a half," he recalled. They refused even to sit down with Kennedy, whom they saw simply as a member of the white establishment.

Over Labor Day weekend, King got a frosty reception at the largely Jewish beach resort of Seaview, Long Island. Even Stokely Carmichael, who'd visited for a similar program the previous summer, had been more warmly received. "Lifelong friends snub us on the street," the man who lent his house for King's rally complained.

Factionalism and impoverishment continued to plague the SCLC. A series of benefit concerts 'starring Harry Belafonte, whom it called a "well-known Negro vocalist with a subversive background." were marred by bomb threats and poor attendance. (In October, the local black newspaper called King's visit to Houston "an imposition upon this community of the highest order" and accused him of using Aretha Franklin to lure in people to hear his anti-Vietnam diatribe. A few nights earlier, Belafonte, Joan Baez, and Sammy Davis, Jr., played to a half-filled house in Oakland. While others—Andrew Young, Jesse Jackson, Bayard Rustin—opposed the inchoate mass action in Washington, King grew more inflamed about it. (Young, who favored waiting until after the presidential election, saw in King's urgency the conviction that he would not live that long.) He compared it to the famous Bonus March of 1932. He talked of bringing three thousand people to the capital in the spring. Like Kennedy, his concern had become more economic than racial: he would bring poor whites, Native Americans, and Hispanics as well as blacks. They would pitch tents by the White House and sit in by congressional offices. He talked of serious protestors rather than "college kids down for a weekend" and a march on Washington that was more than just "a beautiful day." He foresaw traffic tie-ups, school boycotts, and "waves of sick youngsters" clogging the hospitals. To reporters, he seemed desperate, even despondent. He was, by his own admission, going for broke.

Kennedy, by contrast, was heading up; the only questions were "how" and "when."

# TWELVE

# THE POLITICAL EQUATION

Throughout late 1967 and into the New Year, three constituencies battled over the political future of Robert Kennedy. The more seasoned of the seemingly countless kibitzers hovering around him, grown-ups like Ted Sorensen and Pierre Salinger, urged him to wait. Were he to run for president, he'd surely fail and cloud his future, and maybe even help elect Richard Nixon. Their younger counterparts, notably Adam Walinsky and Peter Edelman, urged him to run: the situation in Vietnam was dire and volatile. Then there was the press, which was divided. "If Kennedy does not run in 1968, the best side of his character will die," Jack Newfield wrote. On the other side, Joseph Alsop was equally adamant. And then there was Kennedy himself, increasingly disgusted by the status quo, but fearing any candidacy would look vengeful and opportunistic and, yes, ruthless. To many, what he really was was exasperating. "Bobby Kennedy: Hawk, Dove or Chicken?" declared a placard greeting him during an appearance at Brooklyn College.

Notwithstanding his disdain for the professional "Bobby-watchers," as he called them, who were forever measuring whether Kennedy measured up, James Wechsler of the *New York Post* was really the greatest Bobby-watcher of them all, though he spent his energies gauging Kennedy's evolution and assessing his political prospects rather than inventorying how often and how far he fell short. And Kennedy's forty-second birthday on November 20, 1967, offered him an excuse for yet more stargazing. The date

It was a foregone conclusion that Robert Kennedy would run for president.
The only question now was, when?

had become doubly significant, of course, thanks to the sadder commemoration two days later. Had John Kennedy served out his second term, Wechsler wrote, Robert Kennedy might well have succeeded him. All those "zealous planners of his life" still envisioned a Robert Kennedy presidency in 1973. Kennedy himself insisted he'd wait, praising Johnson periodically and toning things down on Vietnam. But nothing was certain, especially with Kennedys. "How many strange bounces will the ball of history take in the ensuing four years?" Wechsler asked.

Quietly, Kennedy was letting it be known that he'd back Senator Eugene McCarthy if he ran, but even here, the Bobby-watchers questioned his motives, claiming he was "craftily playing it safe," awaiting the call should McCarthy weaken Johnson. Though people still viewed Kennedy as the "Machiavellian master of events," wrote Wechsler, few people were "so deeply at the mercy of imponderables." "He knows better than most that only a weird combination of accidents can bring him back to the center of the 1968 stage," he concluded. "In this of all weeks he has reason to reflect with a mingled anger and grief on the cruel inscrutable mysteries of history."

McCarthy finally declared his candidacy on November 30 and made the immediate withdrawal of American troops from Vietnam his signature campaign issue. But at the press conference that day, half the questions concerned Kennedy: how McCarthy would react if Kennedy jumped in, whether he'd end up a mere stalking horse for Kennedy, etc. McCarthy wasn't unduly perturbed; he confessed he'd been his own second choice for the post and would gladly have yielded to Kennedy had he opted to run. Even McCarthy supporters conceded what just about everyone knew: that with his name, money, and clout, Kennedy would be the far more formidable antiwar candidate. "A very good middle-inning pitcher" was how one McCarthy supporter characterized his man. Johnson was convinced that McCarthy and Kennedy were in league — an unlikely possibility since they actually disliked one another. Kennedy thought McCarthy lazy and mean, attributing the second quality to the fact that he was half-German. Others thought that McCarthy and Johnson, each of whom despised Kennedy, were in cahoots.

Political junkies studied tea leaves wherever they found them. For Christmas 1967, for instance, the Robert Kennedy family sent out hundreds of what the *New York Times* described as "puckish, garishly colored, psychedelic" cards, showing the ten Kennedy children inside, outside, and atop an antique car. "SANTA in '67," it declared. That was straightforward enough, but on the back was a head shot of an enigmatic Robert Kennedy with his lips "in a Mona Lisa smile" and a cartoon balloon floating out of his head. "Would you believe in Santa in '68, too?" he asked. And just what might *that* mean? The paper reached out to Kennedy, but he was off skiing in Sun Valley. So it turned to his campaign press secretary, Frank Mankiewicz. "Political implications are in the eyes of the beholders," he replied cryptically. Come January, Kennedy remained on the fence. "Robert Kennedy still faces the prospect of becoming, at 42, either an ex-candidate or an ex-hero," Mary McGrory observed. "The stormer of rapids and mountains, the bold invader of hostile states and continents, has been cast in the role of Hamlet, not daring to do what he most wants to do. It is a distasteful and damaging manifestation."

Kennedy still had all those mentors, and he sought out advice from several. Justice William O. Douglas thought he should go for it. So did the hoariest wise man of all, journalist Walter Lippmann. "Well, if you believe that Johnson's reelection would be a catastrophe for the country—and I entirely agree with you on this—then, if this comes about, the question you must live with is whether you did everything you could to avert this catastrophe," Lippmann told him.

One more key person weighed in on Kennedy's decision: his famous sister-in-law. "I hope Bobby never becomes president of the United States," Jacqueline Kennedy told Schlesinger early in 1968. Schlesinger asked her why. "If he becomes president, they'll do to him what they did to Jack," she replied. (When, after

Robert Kennedy's death, Schlesinger reminded her of what she had said that day, she said she remembered, too, and that she'd told Bobby the same thing. Kennedy still kept any such fears to himself, unlike King, who in his famous "Drum Major Instinct" sermon of February 4, 1968, once more spoke about his own death and scripted the eulogies to be given at his funeral. Kennedy and King shared an obsession with death all right. But for Kennedy it was his brother's; for King it was his own.

"If any of you are around when I have to meet my day, I don't want a long funeral," King directed. "And if you get somebody to deliver the eulogy, tell them not to talk too long." They shouldn't speak of his Nobel Peace Prize and various other awards, he advised, but rather of how he'd loved others, tried to be right on the war, tried to feed the hungry and clothe the naked and serve humanity. "Yes, if you want to say that I was a drum major, say that I was a drum major for justice!" he said. "Say that I was a drum major for peace! I was a drum major for righteousness. And all of the other shallow things will not matter."

At an off-the-record breakfast on January 30, Kennedy, in a moment of exquisitely maladroit political timing, stated he wouldn't be a presidential candidate under any "conceivable" circumstances. Before the breakfast ended, word reached Mankiewicz that the North Vietnamese and the Viet Cong had launched comprehensive attacks throughout South Vietnam, including on the American embassy in Saigon. So quickly did the Tet Offensive scramble the political equation that when Kennedy agreed to be quoted on his noncandidacy, Mankiewicz insisted that "conceivable" be softened to "foreseeable."

Kennedy was already losing many of his most fervent and effective potential supporters, as students, especially those from the top schools, volunteered in droves for McCarthy. Kennedy's latest disclaimer prompted rounds of disgust, ridicule, and regret. One came from the writer Pete Hamill, then off working on a novel in

Ireland. Though he wrote in the past tense—Kennedy had made up his mind, after all—Hamill still hoped in the future tense. "I wanted to say that the fight you might make would be the fight of honor," he wrote. "I wanted to say that you should run because if you won, the country might be saved. I wanted to remind you that in Watts I didn't see pictures of Malcolm X or [black activist] Ron Karenga on the walls. I saw pictures of JFK. That is your capital in the most cynical sense; it is your obligation in another." For the next several weeks, Kennedy carried Hamill's letter around with him.

Liberated by his noncandidacy, Kennedy gave his most ringing denunciation of the war on February 8 in Chicago. Tet, he said, had "finally shattered the mask of official illusion" about the war. Military victory was not only not in sight but "probably will never come." By any standard, the United States had honored its commitment to Vietnam and needed to begin to withdraw. The story was big news: even the *New York Times*, despite what Arthur Schlesinger called its "ineradicable anti-RFK prejudice," gave it enormous attention. It also brought charges of treason from erstwhile Kennedy friends like columnist Joseph Alsop.

Thousands of favorable telegrams in response to the speech further convinced Mankiewicz that Kennedy should run—to save not just the republic, but his own sanity. Mentally, physically, and politically, it was now impossible for Kennedy to stay on the sidelines: how, Mankiewicz asked, could he campaign for Johnson without betraying his principles? And how could he *not* campaign for Johnson and preserve his ties to the Democrats and his own political prospects? "I'd keep saying to him, 'What are you going to do all year? Where do you see yourself in May and June and August? Are you skiing?'" Mankiewicz recalled.

There was no escaping the question hanging over him. On February 13, accompanied by thirty carloads of reporters and cameramen, Kennedy held one-man hearings among the Appalachian poor in Kentucky. Before he adjourned, a small girl handed him a note. "Bobby, please run for president," it said. He grinned and stuffed the paper into his pocket.

WHITE WAY
NEWS CENTRAL
CORNER
VETERANS
FOR PEACE
IN VIETNAM
NOW!

men are not
if we kill men, with whom sha
kẻ thù ta đâu có phải là ngườ
giết người đi thì ta ở với ai ?
DOING
WHILE THE

Though Kennedy agonized publicly—"that dark night of the soul about which we have been reading" was how an acidic William F. Buckley described the public hand-wringing—but his friends weren't especially worried. As King canvassed the South for the poor people who'd people the Poor People's Campaign, though, his associates remained alarmed by his demoralized and halting manner. Levison was shocked at his performance during a centennial celebration for W. E. B. Du Bois at Carnegie Hall. His message that night was startling: one of Du Bois's roles, he noted, had been "disconcerting Negro moderates in America," and this he now did himself, praising the role of American Communists in the struggle for civil rights. "It is time to cease muting the fact that Dr. Du Bois was a genius and chose to be a Communist," he said. "Our irrational obsessive anti-communism has led us into too many quagmires." (He then went on to equate American support for the South Vietnamese government to Northern support for Southern "slavemasters" during Reconstruction.) For King to slough off all the usual fears about communism showed anew measure of liberation, or indifference. But while some recall King getting rapturous applause that night, Levison lamented to a friend afterward that he had "never read anything as badly"; it was, he said, as though he didn't understand what he was saying.

Portions of 'King's speech that night could have come from Kennedy. "Let us be dissatisfied until rat-infested, vermin-filled slums will be a thing of a dark past and every family will have a decent sanitary house in which to live," he'd said. "Let us be dissatisfied until the empty stomachs of Mississippi are filled and the idle industries of Appalachia are revitalized." And only a couple weeks earlier, the two men made a joint appearance of sorts on the Tonight Show, where, in an act of extraordinary effrontery, the vacationing Johnny Carson had passed off the program for

On March 25, 1967, King, Dr. Benjamin Spock, and five thousand protesters voiced their opposition to America's course in Vietnam on the streets of Chicago.

a week to Harry Belafonte, knowing that he'd do pretty much what he wanted with it—which would be something politically provocative—and the network suits couldn't do too much to stop it. They were only two of Belafonte's extraordinary roster of guests that week, which included Sidney Poitier, Lena Horne, and Wilt Chamberlain and offered many white viewers their first opportunity to see intelligent, articulate black men and women chatting with one another. (That prospect was too much for some southern stations, which temporarily dropped the show.) The two appeared a few nights apart—Kennedy on February 5, King on February 8. Belafonte, another of the few people close to both men, gave each a half-hour slice of prime time (a far more precious gift in King's case than Kennedy's) with an interlocutor who was both sophisticated and simpatico.

By steering the conversation toward Vietnam, poverty, and politics, Belafonte broached subjects rarely addressed by network television of the time and revealed anew just how much the two men shared; both could toss off the current gross national product ($800 billion) and decry how much of that was earmarked for destructive ends. At the same time, Belafonte flattened their remaining differences. As the Riverside speech made clear, King's views on mainstream American culture had grown quite jaundiced, but having just been admitted for the first time into all those late-night American living rooms, he wasn't about to force people to squirm in their Barcaloungers, and his amiable host wasn't about to make him.

King's appearance was the far more important of the two, and not just because sharing airtime with Ed McMahon and the Jolly Green Giant represented a new level of access and acceptance. Under Belafonte's gentle ministrations—"My task was to make sure that Dr. King was seen in a way that more humanized him than politicized him," he later said—King could let down his guard. His stentorian speech eased into something more casual. For a few minutes at least, he was neither saint nor scold, but a reasonably regular guy among friends. Describing some anxious moments when his plane to New York had "mechanical difficulties," he actually cracked a joke: "I don't want to give you the impression that, as a Baptist preacher, I don't have faith in God in the air," he explained. "It's simply that I've had more experience with him on the ground." For once King could also be something he rarely allowed himself to be: *young*. At thirty-nine, he was the kid on the panel. "You're a young fellow!" joked another of the guests that night, Paul Newman, who was four years King's senior. Some white viewers saw that night was a revelation. No longer would Helen Knapp dismiss him as another "egotistical Baptist minister." "I was so surprised and so pleased to have the opportunity to meet this man as informally as any of Johnny's other guests," she wrote the *Cincinnati Enquirer.* "What a warm, kind human being shown [sic] through!"

There was nervous laughter when Belafonte innocently asked King what he had "in store for us this summer." He'd actually planned events for the spring, King replied, but he gave few specifics about the Poor People's Campaign, which would have thrown a wet blanket over the proceedings. Belafonte then raised the issue of the war in Vietnam—he was surely the first talk-show host to come out against it—asking King whether it was possible to fight abroad and still fulfill domestic needs, as Johnson had said. "Well, Harry, I think that is a major myth," King replied. "When the guns of war become a national obsession, social programs inevitably suffer." Or, as he put it, using a common idiom of the time, one couldn't have guns and butter simultaneously, or even, as King put it, guns and "good oleo." (That was far more mild than what he told a black church in Washington the night before: that the real enemy of the black man wasn't the Viet Cong but some southern Senators and congressmen.)' Belafonte then asked him whether the country would have a real choice at the polls that fall. Not given the current front-runners, he said, but McCarthy offered a channel to those disenchanted with the war. "I'm going for him," Belafonte volunteered. Had Robert Kennedy been watching, he'd have seen two lost Kennedy voters right before his eyes.

Kennedy—interrupted only seconds into his appearance by a few bars of "What the World Needs Now Is Love" as the show broke for a commercial—agreed that the wars in Vietnam and on poverty could not be waged at once. He noted the gap between American rhetoric and reality: starvation amid eighty million television sets. He described a teenager he'd met in Budd Schulberg's Watts writers' workshop, old enough for Vietnam but not to file a complaint about uncollected garbage. When Belafonte asked *him* about the likely presidential choices—he'd hoped Kennedy might announce then and there—Kennedy stammered. His were the minority views on Vietnam, he confessed meekly, and then the interview was over. "Can we end on a happier note?" he pleaded. "How about a commercial or something?" Granting a reprieve, Belafonte mentioned a legend about Kennedy falling into a piranha-infested stream in the Amazon. Voters split fifty-fifty, Kennedy replied, over whether he should have been allowed back on the boat. Belafonte felt lucky to land both men at all, but it was nonetheless a pity he didn't have them at the same time; their convergence would have been startlingly apparent. But Kennedy likely wouldn't have let it happen.

Later that month, the FBI office in San Francisco reported to headquarters about a local man who'd boasted of marking eleven people for "elimination": ten black leaders and Kennedy. But the bureau remained focused on King, and on exposing rather than protecting him.

At the end of February, the panel Lyndon Johnson set up to investigate the race riots of the previous summer, known as the Kerner Commission, issued its report. Its findings—that white racism, rather than a conspiracy of subversives, was responsible for the disturbances; that the United States was "moving toward two societies—one black, one white, separate and unequal"; and that "compassionate, massive and sustained" action was called for— were to King more vindicating than surprising. It was what he'd been saying all along, and only underlined the "absolute necessity" of the Poor People's Campaign. He soon offered an itinerary: on April 22 protesters would stage a "lobby-in" in Congress. The same day, separate caravans of poor people would leave Milwaukee, Boston, and Mississippi for Washington, arriving in early May.

But to Kennedy, the Kerner Commission report, and Johnson's obvious disdain for it, was yet another prod, another reminder that the war had superseded Johnson's domestic agenda. He was ready to jump in; en route to Delano, California, to convince Cesar Chavez to call off a long hunger strike, he'd said so to Peter Edelman. "Now I have to figure out how to get McCarthy out of it," he said. But it wouldn't be easy: the race was already leaving Kennedy behind. With the March 12 New Hampshire primary just a few days off, McCarthy's campaign had picked up a surprising and growing vitality. "What is happening is that violet-eyed damsels from Smith are pinning McCarthy buttons on tattooed mill-workers, and PhDs from Cornell, shaven and shorn for world peace, are deferentially bowing to middle-aged Manchester housewives and importuning them to consider a change in Commander-in-Chief," McGrory wrote the day before the election. "Whatever else happens tomorrow, Sen. McCarthy has taken the place of Robert Kennedy as the symbol of hope and change among America's bright children."

Though technically not a win—Johnson had beaten him by six points—McCarthy's showing in New Hampshire against an incumbent president might as well have been. Kennedy had to move fast, but how fast? "I went home and I wrote a final memo, you know, about 'Listen, buddy, you'd better get off your ass!'" Adam Walinsky later said. When Kennedy called him the next morning, Walinsky repeated himself. "'Look,' I said, 'I think you're bleeding and you've got to staunch the flow. Every hour this guy is picking up more support. You really have to cut it off as fast as you can.... You're just going to have to *move* right now.'"

So Kennedy did. When he landed in Washington on the morning of March 13, he announced that he was "reassessing" his

Kennedy's bond with Cesar Chavez was strong. His trip of support helped convince the United Farm Workers leader to call off his hunger strike.

position, which was tantamount to declaring. Many liberals didn't want to know about it. "When he was needed, he wasn't there," said the playwright Arthur Miller, a state delegate in Connecticut. To James Wechsler, it was already too late; McCarthy had earned the right to go up against Johnson alone. Murray Kempton felt betrayed enough by Kennedy to uncoil, at least temporarily, his famously baroque prose. (It was in the parentheses that he usually told you what he was really thinking," Jules Feiffer later said.) He'd watched Kennedy grow, and coaxed him along, and defended him, and come to admire him. They could take Jack Kennedy's name off the airports and stadiums, he'd written a year earlier; Robert Kennedy "has made himself the only monument his brother needs." But suddenly, to Kempton Kennedy was little more than a coward. And, by jumping into the race, Kennedy had "managed to confirm the worst things his enemies have ever said about him."

Even Kennedy's supporters wondered why, having equivocated so long already, he couldn't have waited a few days and given

McCarthy and his supporters a chance to savor what they'd accomplished. "There is neither moral excuse nor tactical justification for Kennedy's attempt to steal the show," Wechsler wrote. "Like the boy whose baseball idol dumped a World Series, many young Americans are murmuring: 'Say it ain't so, Bobby.'" Fifty students who'd volunteered for McCarthy in New Hampshire picketed Kennedy's office in New York. Bad Bobby was back. On March 16, in the same room in the Senate where his brother had declared eight years earlier, and McCarthy, twelve weeks earlier, Robert Kennedy made it official. When he said, "I do not run for the presidency merely to oppose any man..." a woman was heard to laugh. Even Kennedy did not hold out much hope that he could win.

Others had their own reasons to oppose his candidacy. (At a dinner party at her apartment shortly thereafter, the composer Gian Carlo Menotti asked Jacqueline Kennedy whether she was pleased Bobby was running. "How can I be happy?" she replied. "I know very well that sooner or later they will shoot him as they have already done with my husband." The exchange reportedly cast a pall over the affair, which broke up shortly thereafter.

As the Democratic Party convulsed, Martin Luther King was traveling across the country. In Grosse Pointe, Michigan, on March 14, he experienced what he called "the worst heckling I have ever encountered" when a right-wing group that had protested Kennedy in nearby Detroit a year earlier—urging him to donate *all* of his blood at once to the Viet Cong and supplying a stretcher for his corpse—interrupted King repeatedly with shouts of "Commie!' and "Traitor!" Two days later, King was set to speak to the California Democratic Council. Concerned he might endorse McCarthy (as the California group already had) just as he was about to enter the race, Kennedy tried calling him beforehand. (The FBI told Johnson all about it.) He didn't reach King, but Burke Marshall soon did, and he convinced King to hold off from endorsing any candidate, though in calling McCarthy "one of the truly outstanding, capable, brilliant, dedicated Americans," to the group, he'd come very close.

The war had strengthened reactionary forces in the country and replaced the Great Society with the "Troubled and Confused Society," said King, defended his decision to speak out against the war, regardless of the consequences. "I am not a 'consensus leader,'" he declared. "And I do not determine what is right and wrong by looking at the budget of the Southern Christian Leadership Conference or by taking a Gallup poll. Ultimately [a] genuine leader is not a searcher for consensus but a molder of consensus."

Nothing fundamental had changed about the relationship between Kennedy and King. The two had "great respect" for one another, Marian Wright Edelman said, but that was as far as it went. Shortly after Kennedy declared his candidacy, for instance, syndicated columnists Robert Allen and Paul Scott reported that Kennedy had pledged to support King's Washington protest. It was, of course, ridiculous and clearly a plant designed to embarrass both parties to the purported deal. Kennedy's office moved quickly to squelch the rumors.

But as Young noted, King had come to admire Kennedy more and more. "He was extremely impressed with his capacity to learn, to grow, and to deal creatively in any given situation," he later wrote. "Martin tended to feel overly humble about his own accomplishments and somewhat afraid of 'power'... and saw Bobby as a man of both moral courage and a keen sense of political timing." That quality—the ability to implement—was something King saw in Gandhi, Young wrote, but which, he feared, he lacked in himself. "He admired Bobby's blend of 'crusader' and realistic politician. Closely related to this was the Kennedy 'efficiency mystique.'... Bobby knows how to get a job done as well as talk about it."

There would be no explicit endorsement of Kennedy, but with McCarthy's prospects poor, a way would be found to signal King's support. "They should be realistic enough to see that, if there is any possibility of stopping President Johnson, it will be Kennedy," went an FBI recapitulation of a conversation between King and Levison. Stopping Johnson, Levison stated, could not be done with a "Galahad" like McCarthy, and besides, McCarthy was less progressive on civil rights. King had begun to feel "that if [Kennedy had] come this far, with the greater responsibility he could become one of the outstanding presidents and really be the kind of man the country needed," Levison recalled. "No question: if he had lived, he would have supported Bobby Kennedy."

For the time being, though, King had more pressing concerns. On March 16—the day Kennedy entered the race—his old colleague from the civil rights movement, the Reverend James Lawson, had telephoned from Memphis. Some twelve hundred local sanitation men, nearly all of them black, had been on strike for three weeks. Lawson wondered if King could come and lend his support. Despite the objections of his colleagues, who felt he was already overextended and had too much to do for the upcoming protest in Washington, King agreed. It wasn't so much of a reach, geographically or philosophically; he'd be recruiting volunteers in nearby Mississippi anyway, and the strikers' struggle represented precisely what King saw as the next stage of the civil rights movement: more focused on dollars and cents than on statutes and court cases. But according to Young, that not the only impetus, or the most the chief one. "He went to Memphis because he knew his days were numbered, and he wanted to be seen as giving his life for the poor," he said.

On March 18, just as a newly liberated Robert Kennedy headed to Kansas to deliver the first speeches of his nascent campaign, a depleted, discouraged Martin Luther King headed for Tennessee.

The idea for King to lead the Poor People's Campaign may have come from Kennedy, but it was rooted firmly in Gandhian principles.

# THIRTEEN

# WHAT THEY DID TO JACK

The crowds that greeted Robert Kennedy and Martin Luther King on March 18, 1968, were as different as they could be, but a few things they shared. They were large, they were boisterous, and they brought each man to life, as crowds always did. Both men lived for them. And both men needed them now.

Kennedy's fans were midwestern, white, and green. His first two speeches as a presidential candidate were at Kansas State University in Manhattan and the University of Kansas in Lawrence. He went to them less in search of votes—Kansas had no primary and most of the students couldn't vote—than in search of enthusiasm. He had to show that McCarthy hadn't cornered the market on the young. These Kansas kids may not have been the elite, Ivy League types McCarthy had captured and Kennedy coveted, but for the time being, they would do. Most important, by helping create a populist aura around Kennedy, they would begin to show the party bosses who controlled most of the delegates to the Democratic National Convention that an insurgency built on the fly, and taking on an incumbent president, was nonetheless too mighty to stop. (Stephen Smith, the Kennedy brother-in-law who ran JFK's 1960 operation and was helping with Bobby's now, dug out a handful of leftover "Kennedy" lapel clips early on and declared, "This is it, guys. This is the whole campaign.")

And the Kansans came through, receiving Kennedy ecstatically. "The field house sounded as though it was inside Niagara Falls; it was like a soundtrack gone haywire," Jack Newfield reported in

King saw the next stage of the civil rights movement as focused more on dollars and cents than on statutes and court cases.

the *Village Voice. Look* magazine photographer Stanley Tretick, who was near Kennedy, was caught afterward in the crush. "He's going all the way!" he shouted. "He's going all the fucking way!"

Kennedy's speeches seemed almost secondary, though his address at the University of Kansas (lamenting how the gross national product took in air pollution and cigarette advertising and napalm and nuclear warheads but not poetry or intelligence or integrity) was one of his most moving, and one he would repeat often elsewhere. He had diagnosed the same spiritual malaise King had addressed a year earlier at Riverside Church. Adam Walinsky saw a man restored, ready again to be himself. Peter Edelman compared Kennedy to "a dog finally let off the leash." "Like a volcano erupting," recalled George Stevens, the founding director of the American Film Institute and a close friend of Bobby's. Frank Mankiewicz paraphrased Martin Luther King: Kennedy had "free-at-last syndrome," he said.

His Kansas visits set a pattern. Four years had passed since Kennedy's Senate race, but his crowds, both white and black, remained frenzied, bordering on hysterical. People reached out to touch him and claim a piece of him. He lost so many fancy cuff links that he came to wear plastic ones; he favored clip-on ties lest he be choked as real ones were yanked off. Sometimes he lost shoes. He could have hated, or resented, or feared it all. Instead, he courted it, and it buoyed and sustained him. It helped him forget that the party brass, and liberals, and labor panjandrums, and southerners, and even the trio of Washington Brahmins for whom he'd named three of his latest sons — Maxwell Taylor, Douglas Dillon, and Averell Harriman — all favored other candidates.

"They celebrated his existence, his ties to a slain brother, his own mysterious ability to arouse intense love," wrote Helen Dudar of the *New York Post*. "He knew very well that he stirred extraordinary extremes of reaction — and when I asked him about the depth of hostility he calls up, he nodded and said: 'But also more affection.'" "So many people hate me," Kennedy told the comedian Alan King, "that I've got to give the people that love me a chance to get at me." Always, the question was whether it would help him crack what Newfield called "the totalitarian arithmetic" at the Democratic convention.

As Kennedy returned from Kansas, King arrived in Memphis, where a gathering of fifteen thousand very different people awaited him at the Mason Temple. After checking in at his preferred place, the recently refurbished Lorraine Motel (to meet competition from "newly integrated hotels in the Blues City," *Jet* reported, its owner had added "a modern, luxurious 40-unit extension to his ideally located hostelry"), King rallied the crowd—or, as an FBI's agent put it, "made a demagogic appeal to the baser emotions of [the] predominantly Negro audience." King called for a general strike in four days and said he'd return to Memphis for it.

Fresh from their respective triumphs, the two men set out on their very different itineraries. King's included Batesville, Marks, Clarksdale, Greenwood, Grenada, Laurel, Hattiesburg, McComb, and Jackson, Mississippi, along with Greensboro, Marion, and Bessemer in Alabama and Albany, Macon, and Augusta in Georgia, all to recruit the "beachhead troops" for the Washington protests. It was a backbreaking and demoralizing effort. Volunteers were scarce, and more than once the launch would have to be postponed. So, too, after a freak snowstorm, was the Memphis march. Throughout, colleagues and admirers remained concerned about King's well-being—both short term (given his evident fatigue) and long (given the unending series of threats against him). At a meeting in February, King's SCLC colleagues discussed their fears that King could be assassinated during the upcoming Washington protest, with threats posed by blacks as well as whites. They decided that people armed with guns would be there to protect him and that circles of aides would surround him.

His disdain for security made things worse. "I can't lead that kind of life," he said once. "I'd feel like a bird in a cage." His comments and Robert Kennedy's were generally interchangeable: "There's no way in the world you can keep somebody from killing

you if they really want to kill you" could have come from either. At least one, though, was distinctly King's: "If they couldn't protect [John] Kennedy, how can anything protect me?" he'd ask. He made light of his predicament in Macon when, as usual, he was running behind schedule. "I would much rather be Martin Luther King late than the late Martin Luther King," he quipped.

Robert Kennedy's destinations were larger and more glamorous than King's. Five years after Governor George Wallace attempted to thwart him there, Kennedy got a standing ovation at the University of Alabama. Ten thousand Mexican Americans in Los Angeles practically tore Kennedy from his convertible. "For two days," Farrel Broslawsky wrote in the *Los Angeles Free Press*, Kennedy "bounced around the state like Jesus on a pogo stick, greeted and mobbed by panting, pushing, exultant crowds screaming in orgiastic delight at the thought of all that hair and virility in the White House...cheering and applauding everything that the Senator said, or what they hoped he would say, or wished that someone like him would say."

But reporters like Richard Harwood of the *Washington Post* quickly moved from charmed to alarmed. Kennedy, he wrote in late March, was whipping up crowds with charges concerning Johnson and Vietnam that were "ill-considered" or just plain wrong; his rhetoric—for instance, accusing the president of tapping into the "darker impulses of the American people"—bordered "on the demagogic." The campaign acknowledged as much and vowed to tone things down in more sedate, conservative Indiana, which would hold its crucial primary on May 7. On March 28, the day of King's march in Memphis, Kennedy registered for the primary in Indianapolis, then held a rally there; even the hostile *Indianapolis Star* estimated that ten thousand people came out.

Bobby was now in the race, with two generations of Kennedy advisers backing him. Strategy sessions often took place at Hickory Hill.

King had learned early to devise and control his protest campaigns, so that he could set the agenda, choreograph how events would unfold, and teach what were to some the counter-intuitive principles of non-violence. It was in places where he'd entered late, where the SCLC had not laid the groundwork or trained people properly, that trouble had developed. Memphis was a step backward for him in that regard, and teenagers at the rear of the procession went violent, smashing store windows and looting. A melee with the police — in which four protesters were shot, one killed, and three hundred arrested — quickly followed. King and his aides fled the scene in a car they'd commandeered and, unable to get back to the Lorraine, huddled in another, fancier, predominantly white hotel.

For King, already depressed and exhausted, the disorder was a crushing personal humiliation, and to a movement based on nonviolence, it was a potentially fatal blow. Maybe, he told his colleagues, it was time to let violence run its course. The movement was in "serious trouble," King said to Levison; his rivals in the black community "will now feel that he, King, is finished, that his nonviolence is nothing, that no one is listening to it." Maybe they should call off the Washington campaign. The *New York Times* urged him to do just that. One Memphis paper ridiculed him for fleeing the scene; "Chicken-a-la-King," it called him. The next morning, a despondent King and his entourage left Memphis altogether.

Only over the next couple of days were King's associates able to buck him up. He must not let a few misbehaving kids sully his great movement, they said. They urged him to return to Memphis once more, this time to lead his own, peaceful march. He agreed he would return the following week. By March 31, King was back on his feet, preaching to four thousand people at the National Cathedral in Washington. Robert Kennedy, meanwhile, was flying back from the Southwest, where he'd been meeting with Native Americans. And Lyndon Johnson was about to announce he would not seek, nor would he accept, another term as president, and that he would halt the bombing of North Vietnam and move to begin negotiations. Overnight, the race was transformed. But how?

Recruiting efforts for the Poor People's Campaign took King to cities like Newark, one of many affected by civil unrest in the summer of 1967.

Some Kennedy aides were elated. Even before Johnson had dropped his bombshell, Adam Walinsky, who'd been watching the speech in Kennedy's apartment with Ted Sorensen, had it figured out; it was the logical culmination of the prior two weeks, when the Kennedy campaign had miraculously launched itself, then begun building up a head of steam. "I jumped up and I stopped taking notes," he recalled. "I threw down my pencil and I said, 'He's quitting! No, he's quitting! It's over! It's done! He's out! He's gone! Son of a bitch! We did it!'" He wasn't talking about the election, but the war. One way or another, Kennedy had done the impossible: he'd knocked off an incumbent president. Ethel broke out some champagne.

But Kennedy, still sitting on the plane after landing at LaGuardia Airport, was nonplussed—and quiet. The path to the presidency was clearer. But suddenly he'd been deprived of his two principal targets: the personification of the war and the war itself. Vice President Hubert Humphrey would now become the candidate of the Democratic establishment, and people didn't hate him as they hated Johnson. Kennedy got back to his apartment and promptly cast a pall over the party in progress. "Everybody was euphoric—except Bobby," recalled William vanden Heuvel. "He understood immediately that this made it a much more difficult race for him." A couple of aides stuck with Cokes. "It was not the kind of a night where you go to the whiskey," wrote Jimmy Breslin. "Not when destiny is in the room."

Kennedy moved to mend fences with Johnson, including at an awkward White House meeting on April 3. Then he flew back to Indiana. The primary there promised to be tough. It would be Kennedy's first head-to-head contest against Eugene McCarthy, who'd capture the intelligentsia, and they'd both be taking on the state's popular governor, Roger Branigin, who was running as a favorite son and, now, the Democratic Party's stand-in for Hubert Humphrey. Polls showed him leading. It would be hard for Kennedy to gain ground, for Indiana was a place where several strands of conservatism converged. There was the conservatism of its south, where the Ku Klux Klan once reigned; of its northern ethnic industrial cities, which was the birthplace of the white backlash; of the American Legion, which would view Kennedy as a traitor; and of its Republican core. The state's leading newspaper, the *Indianapolis Star* (owned by the family of a future vice president, Dan Quayle), was a notorious right-wing rag, one that had once opined that "If [Martin Luther] King is not a Communist, he might as well be."

With so much of Indiana arrayed against it, the Kennedy campaign doubled down on its surest constituency: blacks. With the mainstream black organizations allied with the governor, the Kennedy campaign courted the dissidents—the neighborhood leaders and black activists in the inner city of Indianapolis, people like Charles "Snooky" Hendricks and Benjamin Bell of the Radical Action Program. They were rougher-edged, angrier, and grittier than your average NAACP or Urban League officials; Hendricks, for instance, was a convicted drug dealer and user who, by one count, had fathered twenty-six children. For Kennedy aides from Massachusetts, it was, to put it mildly, a clash of cultures. "A lot of guys...shuffling around who had these dashikis on and the little skull caps," was how one Kennedy aide, Gerard Doherty, described them.

The campaign opened storefront offices in every black ward; arranged appearances for Kennedy on black radio stations; scheduled visits by sports icons like Roosevelt Grier, Oscar Robertson (who'd starred at a local high school), and Herb Adderley; worked to increase black registration. (No appeal to the black community was too trivial: when, during one of his typically tumultuous appearances, Kennedy chipped a tooth, staffers searched for a black dentist to fix it.) The campaign's liaison to the black community would be John Lewis, the former head of SNCC, who believed the Kennedys had saved his life during the siege of the Montgomery church in 1961. The moment Robert Kennedy declared, he'd volunteered for his campaign.

Kennedy's first full day in Indianapolis, set for April 4, was to culminate with an evening rally on a basketball court at 17th Street and Broadway, a place in the heart of the ghetto to which few whites ever ventured, least of all at night, and in which the city's newly elected mayor, Richard Lugar, had never set foot at all. After that, the activists would meet Kennedy back at the Marott Hotel, where Kennedy and members of his team were staying. For the black activists, all this was not strictly an altruistic undertaking. "It's a sorry thing to say, but they were looking for money for everything," Doherty remembered. "I finally said to them, 'Look, OK, if the only way Robert Kennedy can get a crowd is to buy them, then it's better we find out now.'" The parties reached some kind of accommodation; the local FBI agent told Hoover of a $650 payment. It was money very well spent. "The mere fact that Kennedy will come into the heart of the ghetto will pull the whole black vote," Hendricks told the *New York Times*. "We hope

Kennedy will be a man the black man can relate to," added Bell. "We dig Kennedy. His brother's image still lingers with us."

Local kids were hired to clean up the littered patch of pavement where the rally would be held. Registration booths were set up. John Lewis spread the word about Kennedy's visit, passing out leaflets, knocking on doors, telling ministers to tell their flocks. Kennedy's advance men went to work, too, arranging for the flatbed truck from which Kennedy would speak, the bunting, and the sound system. One of them, James Tolan, a New York lawyer who'd been volunteering for Kennedy for several years, met with Hendricks and the others. Some of the local Kennedy people "thought that I was absolutely out of my mind because some of these people had records," Tolan later said. But as King had found out, power in the inner cities had devolved to a different group of leaders. To Tolan, it was hard to find leaders *without* records.

On the morning of April 3—around the time Kennedy was at the White House with Johnson—King returned to Memphis. His departure out of Atlanta had been delayed a couple of hours because, the pilot announced, King was aboard and every piece of luggage had had to be inspected. (The plane had been guarded all night.) King begged off delivering another speech at the Mason Temple that night; he was tired, and with the forecast calling for severe storms, the crowd promised to be much smaller than the last time around. Only at the last minute could Ralph Abernathy prevail upon him to come. The stalwarts who *did* show up—around two thousand of them, roughly one-seventh the number who'd come last time—deserved to hear him, he said.

Abernathy gave King a far lengthier introduction than usual, lasting twenty-five minutes. King had earned such a tribute from time to time, he figured, and the longer he spoke, the shorter King would have to. (King hadn't decided whether or not to run for president of the United States, he told the crowd, referring to the ongoing campaign to recruit him for a third-party run, "but he is the one who tells the president what to do.") King's fatigue was noticeable when he began to speak, but he once more drew strength from the crowd. The apocalyptic weather—thunder, lightning, torrential rain, and tornado warnings—lent additional drama to the moment.

King offered a sweeping panorama of human history, explaining why, were God to offer him the chance to live in any era, he'd pass up ancient Egypt, Greece, and Rome, along with the Renaissance, Reformation, Civil War, and the Great Depression, for the here and now. That might seem strange, he confessed, since "the world is all messed up." But whether in Johannesburg or New York, or right here in Memphis, the masses were rising and declaring, "We want to be free!" The audience liked all that—but arguably not as much as when the names of Plato, Aristotle, Socrates, Euripides, and Aristophanes came rolling off his tongue.

The crowd tittered further when King said Bull Connor hadn't understood the laws of physics—that there were certain fires no water could put out. He asked why bricks or bottles or Molotov cocktails were necessary when boycotts—of Coca-Cola or Sealtest milk or other discriminatory companies—were so much more effective. He recounted how, by not sneezing when that letter opener was lodged against his aorta, he'd gotten to experience the sit-ins, and the Freedom Rides, and the Birmingham protests, and the "I Have a Dream" speech, and Selma. Though tempting as cheap props, he ignored the thunderclaps: by this point in his speech, he didn't need them. Finally, he mentioned all the threats he'd been getting "from some of our sick white brothers."

Throughout, the audience had watched him utterly transform himself from the meek soul who'd begun by saying he couldn't recognize the historic figure Ralph Abernathy had just described to something full-throated, defiant, fierce. It was as if three hundred years of humiliation and indignation slowly mounted in the soul of a single man until it could no longer be contained, either in his voice or on his face or in his eyes. King's true radicalism was not in his program, even though it was heading that way, but

Kennedy's overwhelming popular appeal proved invaluable, but he was privately uncertain whether the endorsement was for him or for his late brother.

in his near-universal appeal. The language he spoke, everyone understood. And they knew the soundtrack behind it, with King's half notes and their own sixty-fourth notes interspersed. He was someone that the younger, more radical leaders, whatever their fire-power, never were: one of all of them. It was why, as Bayard Rustin later wrote, "not since the days of Booker T. Washington—when 90 percent of all Negroes lived in the South and were occupationally and socially more homogeneous than today—had any one man come so close to being *the* Negro leader." But not, King hinted, for very much longer. "Well, I don't know what will happen now; we've got some difficult days ahead," he said. "But it really doesn't matter with me now, because I've been to the mountaintop. And I don't mind. Like anybody, I would like to live a long life—longevity has its place. But I'm not concerned about that now. I just want to do God's will. And He's allowed me to go up to the mountain. And I've looked over and I've seen the Promised Land. I may not get there with you. But I want you to know tonight that we, as a people, will get to the Promised Land. And so I'm happy, tonight! I'm not worried about anything! I'm not fearing any man! Mine eyes have seen the glory of the coming of the Lord!"

Each piece in King's peroration he had said many times before—there were limits even to his rhetorical vocabulary—but never with such force, conviction, or urgency. He appeared even to have moved himself; his eyes watered, and as he left the rostrum, he appeared to falter. One of Hoover's many self-appointed vigilantes spotted something sinister in it all—a conspiracy—and wrote the FBI chief afterward about it. "Here was a man that *knew* he was going to die and soon," he said. "I suggest a very careful investigation of those advisers and friends closest to him for hints as to his willingness to die for the cause. The possibility of a planned martyrdom should not be overlooked."

What *was* overlooked was the speech itself, which attracted scant notice in the press; no footage of it in its entirety was preserved. (Later, the *New York Times*' estimable television critic, Jack Gould, did talk about it, deracinating what King said for the benefit of his largely white readers. King "prophetically envisioned the possibility of violence but said that he was at peace with himself and felt sure his people were destined for the Promised Land, even though his own arrival there might not coincide with that of the audience," he wrote.) King left the hall that night refreshed and relaxed. He stayed out late and the next day, April 4, he spent quietly at the hotel. He called the Ebenezer Baptist Church with the title of his sermon for the following Sunday: "Why America May Go to Hell." He looked forward to dinner with friends.

As King lounged at the Lorraine, Robert Kennedy, accompanied by forty-three reporters and twenty staffers, flew into South Bend. At Notre Dame, five thousand students heard him talk about hunger. In Indianapolis, in the meantime, there was great consternation about his rally that evening. Mayor Lugar had repeatedly urged that it be called off. Having hundreds of whites descend on the city's worst ghetto and mixing with many more local residents was just too combustible. It would lead to riots, burning, looting. He threatened to run fire hoses around the square and stop people from crossing them. Half a dozen times, he pleaded with the local Kennedy coordinator, Mike Riley, who'd call Kennedy's campaign manager, Fred Dutton, who'd speak to the candidate, who'd insist on going forward. As the calls continued, Kennedy told Dutton to tell Riley to tell Lugar to go to hell. He would worry about his own safety.

Kennedy staffers made their last-minute preparations. Concerned about low turnout—the forecast called for cold and rain—John Lewis drove through the neighborhood in his green Mustang, loudspeakers blaring and signs declaring "R.F.K. for a New America." Back at the Marott Hotel, Adam Walinsky and Jeff Greenfield, the future political pundit who'd signed on to the Kennedy campaign—Schlesinger described him as "about eleven years old," though, in fact, he was all of twenty-four—worked on the foreign policy speech Kennedy was to deliver the next day in Cleveland. Joining them was John Bartlow Martin, a native Indianan who'd once written speeches for Adlai Stevenson.

April 4, 1968: As King lay dying on the balcony of the Lorraine Motel, several associates pointed in the direction of the sniper, who was fleeing the scene.

From South Bend, Kennedy's entourage flew to Muncie, arriving at 5:45—only half an hour behind schedule. A high school band played "Born Free" as Kennedy stepped off the plane. The visit was an homage to his brother, who'd campaigned there in 1960. Muncie had the image of *the* all-American city; it was the "Middletown" of the famous sociological study. But it had also been a Klan stronghold, with segregated swimming pools, restaurants, and theaters. Eight thousand students and townspeople awaited Kennedy in the men's gym of Ball State University. Spurning the most direct route to the lectern, Kennedy, as he always did, made his way through the throng. "Kennedy talked seriously about international policies, but he probably would have gotten the same response with nursery rhymes," Brian Usher wrote in the *Muncie Star*. The questions, as usual, were livelier.

"How do you feel about laws against cannabis?" he was asked.

"Laws against what? Cannibalcy? Eating your fellow human beings?" Kennedy replied.

"Cannabis!" various voices shouted out.

"What? You've got me. I don't know. You're right, that's one I haven't got an answer on," Kennedy finally said.

"Mr. Kennedy, I agree with the programs and proposals that you are making..." shouted out a black student in the rafters.

"Thank you..." Kennedy interjected.

"And I congratulate you on..."

"Can you stop just there?" said Kennedy. Laughter burst out in the cavernous hall.

"But in order for them to work, you're placing a great deal of faith in white America. My question is: is this faith justified?"

The question was followed by applause and cheers.

"Yes," Kennedy replied, as the place broke out into applause again. There were white people who believed blacks were inferior, he conceded, but they were "a small minority." "I think the vast majority of American people want to do the decent and the right thing," he said. That got the biggest applause of the evening.

As Kennedy was speaking, James Earl Ray crouched by the window of a flophouse at 422½ South Main Street, 205 feet and 3 inches away from the Lorraine Motel. Savoring the soul food he'd soon be served at the home of a local clergyman, waiting for Abernathy to finish dressing, King sauntered onto the balcony outside his room. He asked a local musician to sing "Precious Lord, Take My Hand" for him at the rally to be held later that night—to "play it real pretty," he said. Then he directed his driver to start up the white Cadillac the local funeral home lent him whenever he was in town: they were about to head out. "It's cold, Dr. King," the driver replied. "Put your topcoat on."

"OK, I will," he replied.

Gunshots always sound like firecrackers; but when Abernathy looked outside, he saw only King's feet. He rushed to King's side and lifted his head. "He seemed to be trying to communicate to me with his eyes," he later said. "His eyes seemed to say to me, 'Ralph, I told you so: I told you this would happen, and now it has happened. But, for God's sake, Ralph, don't let me down.'"

At the *New York Times*, Murray Schumach, who'd written King's obituary a year and a half earlier, was about to head home when the city editor, Arthur Gelb, asked him to stick around.

Outside the gymnasium in Muncie, a young mother suffered a bruised leg and sprained wrist trying to protect her two children from the crush of people surrounding Kennedy's car. The vehicle soon joined the motorcade back to the airport, where the candidate rushed out to greet one last batch of well-wishers behind a fence. Then he headed back to the plane. By this point, the local lawyer escorting Kennedy, Marshall Hanley, had heard the news about King and told Kennedy about it as he approached the ramp. "He seemed stunned and dropped his head. 'Is he dead?' he asked. I said I didn't know and then he went up on the ramp to the plane," Hanley recalled.

Soon, Kennedy was huddling with Frank Mankiewicz, discussing what to do once they reached Indianapolis. Nothing should be decided, Mankiewicz urged, until King's condition was known. But Kennedy had already passed that point, Mankiewicz later said, offering a photograph of the two taken aboard the flight as evidence. "Robert Kennedy knew he was dead somehow," he said, pointing to the look—weary, wary, angry, as if he could see that fate was up to its old tricks—in Kennedy's eyes. Remarks had been prepared for Kennedy that evening, and had even mentioned King, connecting his dream to the Founders'. Now that would have to be changed, and he asked Mankiewicz what he should say. Something very short, Mankiewicz replied—something almost like a prayer. Kennedy asked him to write down a few sentences, and quickly: there wouldn't be much time. He could hone it on the car ride there.

Kennedy sat down next to John Lindsay of *Newsweek*, one of the many reporters covering the campaign to whom he'd grown close. That black student who'd just asked about white tolerance was on Kennedy's mind. "You know, it grieves me a little bit that

Inside room 306 of the Lorraine Motel the day after King's death.
The physical man was gone but his spirit remained.

I just told that kid this and then walk out and find that some white man has just shot their sort of spiritual leader," he said.

Kennedy's far-flung brain trust also pondered what to do that night. His chief of staff, Joe Dolan, in Denver for a political event, called Burke Marshall in Washington. They agreed that Kennedy should cancel his speech — stressing that it was out of respect for King and not for fear for his own safety — and call Mrs. King. Another key aide in Washington, John Nolan, concurred. So did Pierre Salinger, who was back at the Marott Hotel. But left to his own devices, Dolan figured, Kennedy would give the speech; he'd insisted on doing so two years earlier after learning that his best friend, Dean Markham, had been killed (along with Ethel Kennedy's brother) in a plane crash. They passed along their recommendation to James Tolan, who was at the airport, awaiting Kennedy's plane. (That the matter would bounce between Tolan, Dolan, and Nolan said something about the ethnic composition of Kennedy's staff.)

By 8:40, when the plane landed in Indianapolis, King's death had been announced. (When ABC cut away from *Bewitched* for the bulletin, a hundred people in New York called in to complain.) Both Tolan and Leroy Aarons of the *Washington Post* rushed onto the plane with the news. Kennedy recoiled. He "just put his hands up to his face...and said, 'Oh, God. When is this violence going to stop?'" Lindsay recalled. "He was trying to put his arms around Ethel," Joseph Mohbat of the Associated Press remembered. "I couldn't see his face, but he was terribly, terribly shaken up." Tolan told Kennedy the consensus was to cancel his appearances, but Kennedy brushed that aside. "I'm going to 17th and Broadway," he declared. "I'm going to go there, and that's it."

Walter Sheridan, another advance man (he went back with Kennedy to the Hoffa investigation), agreed: from the site of the speech, he reported that all was calm and that the militant leaders had assured him they could maintain order. They said nothing to the crowd about King; they'd leave that to Kennedy when he arrived. Dolan agreed with Kennedy's decision; King's death had changed the calculations. If he canceled, there might be riots. Also agreeing, also from 17th and Broadway, was John Lewis. "You can't have a crowd like this come, and something like this happen, and send them home without anything at all," he said. "Kennedy has to speak, for his own sake and for the sake of these people."

Kennedy got up from his seat, kissed Ethel on the cheek, and walked off the plane. Then—"his face drawn and his eyes downcast," as R. W. Apple, Jr., described it in the *New York Times*—he made a short statement to the press. City officials, including the chief of police, still urged Kennedy to call off the event. They could not ensure his safety, they said. But Kennedy was adamant—and confident. Perhaps he remembered how enthusiastically black Indianapolis had greeted his brother during the 1960 campaign: the reception that time had been icy until they reached the slums.

"Thousands of Negroes cheered from the sidewalks," Simeon Booker later wrote. "Black people have a good memory, and they could be a politician's best friend."

The motorcade assembled. Kennedy insisted it be kept small and quiet—no sirens—and that the police peel off when they approached the black section of town; he did not want to be seen entering a black neighborhood under the police's auspices. En route, Kennedy asked Dutton, too, what he thought he should say; Dutton suggested something about nonviolence and racial reconciliation. As he remembered it, Kennedy ruminated along the way: "he sat in the back there, and he didn't have a piece of paper and a pencil or anything. He was just thinking about it." At some point, though, he appears to have written something down (either on yellow paper or the back of an envelope) and stuffed it into his suit pocket. Mankiewicz followed in the press bus, assuring some nervous reporters they'd survive this visit to the inner city. At Kennedy's instructions, a young campaign worker named Bill Gigerich took Ethel Kennedy (pregnant with her eleventh child) back to the hotel. On previous rides, she had spoken animatedly with Gigerich; this time she sat silently, her head down, in the back. He assumed she was praying.

At the Marott for another function—celebrating his high school's basketball team, which had made the state finals—Mayor Lugar improvised a command post, deploying policemen to the surrounding neighborhoods. "I really was very, very fearful about the life of Robert Kennedy and the lives of everybody else who was going to be involved in this," he later said. It was bad judgment to locate the speech there in the first place, he felt, and "to continue to pursue this was really to court potential disaster." Walinsky, who was having dinner at the hotel when he learned of the shooting, rushed with John Bartlow Martin to the speech site; Kennedy would need something to say. (Martin asked a policeman parked outside the hotel whether he thought Kennedy should go ahead as planned. "I sure hope he does," the officer replied. "If he doesn't, there'll be hell to pay.")

On the paved basketball court outside the Broadway Christian Center three camera crews set up equipment. A black band played. The crowd appeared festive—most of them near the center of things had yet to hear about King—but already there were undercurrents. There were really two crowds there that night. By far the smaller one was white, primarily Kennedy fans and Democratic party activists. They'd come early (who among them would have shown up in a black neighborhood after a black icon had been assassinated, and by a white man at that?) and clustered around the truck and had yet to hear the news.

Then there were the locals, who'd ambled over more gradually. Their ranks continued to swell. Some who hadn't heard soon did: it was the era of transistor radios. The farther from the epicenter you stood, the likelier you were to know. Tensions between blacks and whites mounted: "What are you doing here, whitey?" "Get out of here, you white son of a bitch." "Dr. King is dead and a white man did it!" a black woman cried. "Why does he have to come?" "He" was Robert Kennedy.

The organizers asserted their authority—telling the black band to keep playing, sending their younger and more nimble members up in the trees to guard against possible snipers leaning out of windows. The same sorts of young men who had ignited Memphis, leading Martin Luther King to return—and, ultimately, to die, there—were now protecting Indianapolis. Militants Snooky Hendricks and Benjamin Bell walked through the crowd murmuring, "Not now. Not now. This is not the time, not the time." At the same moment, members of a gang calling itself the "Ten Percenters" were trying to blow everything up. "Man, there was going to be trouble," one member recalled. "They kill Martin Luther and we was ready to move." All the while, it was getting darker and colder and rainier. And more and more people *knew*.

Darlene Howard, nineteen and from the neighborhood, hadn't wanted to come; she'd just been carried along by the mob. "We got into the park and they were talking about killing all the white people in the world and burning and doing this and doing that," she later said. "I just remember being swept along in the crowd and people talking about they were going to burn it out and kill the honky: 'They killed Martin and nothing was left.' 'We don't have anybody.' . . . You could smell gas. . . . People had guns and chains and knives and all this stuff, and I'm thinking, 'Where are they going?' It was crazy. I was so terrified."

Kennedy's entourage pulled up around twenty-five minutes past nine. His advance men and a couple of security guards formed a phalanx around him and escorted him from the car toward the rickety steps that led up to the back of the small truck. Lots of people were up there already, jockeying for space.

Adam Walinsky arrived with his draft speech just as Kennedy did. "It was just a phantasmagoric scene," he said. "It was dark. There was almost no lighting, just a couple of floodlights on the platform." He rushed up to Kennedy, who had an "an absolutely blank look" on his face, and offered him what he'd written. "He just gave a little gesture with his left hand that said, 'I don't need it. I know what I'm going to say. I don't need your fine sentences,'" Walinsky recalled. By the time Mankiewicz ran up with his own offering, Kennedy, wearing his brother's old overcoat, was already on the stage. The cheers and whistles for him were loud and enthusiastic. Only the applause was muted, perhaps because many people were wearing gloves.

Another local resident named JoMarva Bell struggled to describe the man now standing behind the microphone:

> He was very pale. I mean, it looked like he wasn't there. I mean, it was like he was spaced out. It's almost like, I don't know, he didn't look like a person that was . . . He looked like a very, very pale and scary lookin' . . . He looked like someone who had a heavy burden on him. He had what the old folks used to call that sad look on his face — that real concerned look on his face. It wasn't a smiley look like the Kennedy family men usually smile. He didn't have none of that on his face at all. He just didn't look right.

"This little guy, this little bitty, small white man started talking," said Darlene Howard, "and you realized and you could see it was Robert Kennedy and I thought, 'Oh, my God, they're going to kill him. He's white.'" One of the few photographs from that night shows one of Kennedy's veteran advance men, Jerry Bruno, standing to Kennedy's left and looking out at the crowd apprehensively. But that made sense: Bruno, after all, had been in Dallas. But as Jesse Jackson later saw it, the crowd posed no risk to Kennedy that night because it sensed—and appreciated—that Kennedy felt no fear himself. It respected his respect. "At a time when there was such absolute, abject rejection, you didn't have to do much to be a liberal," he recalled—"just be relatively decent. I'd have been surprised if he *had missed* the opportunity, if he had stepped away," he said.

Kennedy prepared to speak. Only one microphone, the one in front of him, projected the sound that evening, making everything seem even quieter than it already was. "Do you want me to go ahead?" he asked. "I have already introduced you, Senator," the man next to him, a short fellow with glasses, maybe a local minister, replied. "You can go right ahead," a second man added. "Do they know about Martin Luther King?" Kennedy then asked. "To some extent," the first man replied. "We have left it up to your own volition to be handling this," he added. Kennedy reached into his coat pocket, and took out his own piece of paper, though more to fidget with than to read. He held up the palms of his hands and then began to speak. Kennedy had improved, but he still wasn't a great orator. He'd given many fine speeches, but only because he'd been given many fine speeches to give. His voice was all treble, no bass. There was something almost effeminate about it. It sounded like, and was, a poor imitation of another voice everyone still remembered—and missed. The accent

After hearing King had been shot, RFK en route to Indianapolis conferred with Frank Mankiewicz and other aides as to whether to cancel his campaign appearance, but Kennedy disagreed. "I'm going to 17th and Broadway," he declared. "I'm going to go there, and that's it."

340

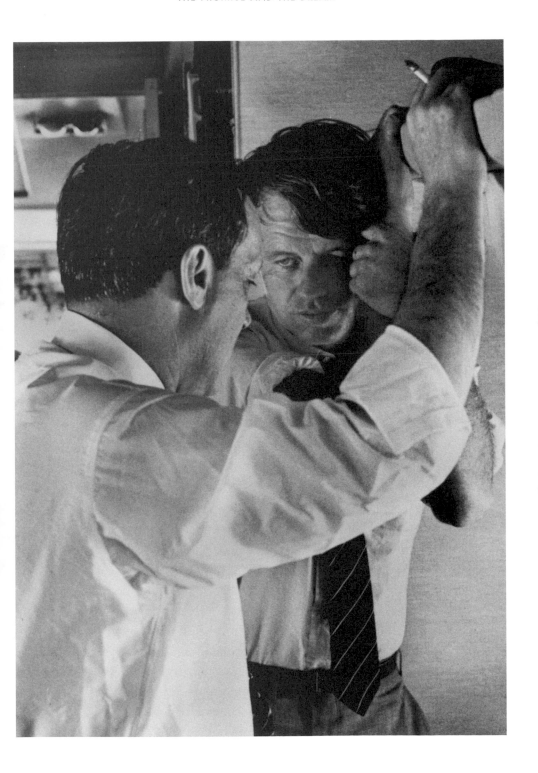

that was once such fun—that everyone loved imitating—was now tinctured with sadness.

"Ladies and gentlemen," Kennedy began, looking down at the paper, pausing, clearing his throat, "I'm only going to talk to you just for a minute or so this evening, because I have some very sad news for all of you." He stopped, but only momentarily; he was not going to draw this out. "Could you lower those signs, please?" he asked, referring to the placards—"Bobby for Prexy," "RFK in '68"—waving in front of him. "I have some very sad news for all of you—and, I think, sad news for all of our fellow citizens, and people who love peace all over the world. And that is that Martin Luther King was shot and was killed tonight in Memphis, Tennessee." A collective sound—an amalgam of groans, screams, and gasps—went up from those who either still hadn't heard or else hadn't yet come to grips. It was the sound, a reporter for the *Indianapolis Star* wrote, of "a wounded animal." Officer Tim Martin could hear it six and a half blocks away.

On the fringes, there were shouts of "Black Power!" that the microphone, and probably the crowd, didn't pick up. Kennedy let everyone absorb what he had just said, patting down his hair as he so often did. (Years later, people remembered the quiet Kennedy generated almost as much as anything he had to say. "You could hear him," said Darlene Howard. "You could *hear* him.") "This unbelievable stillness, this complete silence, came over the crowd," John Lewis recalled. "I've never been in a situation where the collective mood of a group of people changed so quickly," recalled Kevin Chavous, whose mother had brought him, then eleven years old, and his three younger siblings there that night, told them "to see the next president of the United States." "Everyone was so upbeat and then all of a sudden it was like the end of the world," he said. "As sad as I instantly felt, I was determined not to cry. I wanted to be strong. I do remember thinking, however, as the light drizzle fell on my face, that it would help to camouflage my tears."

"Martin Luther King dedicated his life to love and to justice between fellow human beings," Kennedy continued. "He died in the cause of that effort. In this difficult day, in this difficult time for the United States, it's perhaps well to ask what kind of a nation we are, and what direction we want to move in. For those of you who are black—considering the evidence evidently is that there were white people who were responsible—you can be filled with bitterness, and with hatred, and a desire for *revenge*..." he said, leaving it dangling for a moment. "We can move in that direction as a country, in greater polarization—black people amongst blacks, and white amongst whites, filled with hatred toward one another. Or we can make an effort, as Martin Luther King did, to understand and to comprehend and replace that violence, that stain of bloodshed that has spread across our land, with an effort to understand, with compassion and love."

In a way, Kennedy himself constituted a start: even when he mentioned white culpability, there were no catcalls, at least audible enough to have been preserved. He picked up from there. "For those of you who are black and are tempted to be filled with hatred and mistrust of the injustice of such an act against all white people, I would only say that I can also f-feel in my own heart the same kind of feeling," he went on. "I had a member of my own family killed, but *he* was killed by a white man."

It was one of the most remarkable of Kennedy's lines that night or any other night, and like so much that he said, how you felt about it depended on how you felt about him. If you didn't like him, it was almost coy; who didn't know that? And why would he phrase it so evasively? But if you knew and loved him, it was extraordinary, for as profligately as he talked about President Kennedy, he had never, ever mentioned his murder, at least publicly. There were only circumlocutions: "the events of November 1963." Whenever it came up—like when sadistic students asked him for his views of the Warren Report—he changed the subject. But if he had held it in reserve until the occasion warranted, that time had now come. More than anything else he said that night, it leached out any remaining venom in the crowd. "It changed everything," said Chavous. "It quelled that anger that was bubbling up." The interviews that two researchers from Purdue, Karl Anatol and John Bittner, conducted a month later with people who had been there that night, including several gang members, confirmed as much. "After he spoke we couldn't get nowhere," one of them said.

"My favorite poet was Aeschylus, and he once wrote," Kennedy continued, pausing before reciting his words, " 'Even in our sleep, pain which cannot forget falls drop by drop upon the heart until, in our own despair, against our will, comes wisdom through the awful grace of God.' " Whether it was tone-deaf or flattering to use such material in such a place really didn't matter. Words like "pain," "heart," "despair," "awful," "grace," and "God," said solemnly, were the building blocks of black urban life. The grouting didn't matter.

What was needed in the United States, Kennedy went on, wasn't division or hatred or violence or lawlessness, but love and wisdom and compassion toward one another, "and a feeling of justice toward those who still suffer within our country." The line, delivered as his voice cracked a bit, prompted whoops and cheers, reminding Kennedy aide Fred Dutton of the character of crowds. "Despite the first audible gasp and the beauty and moving quality of Bob's speech, the audience was not able to turn around emotionally," he later said. "They had come for a political rally. They were festive. A crowd has a whole life and vitality and mood of its own. It cannot turn around as fast as an individual can. As a crowd, it still needed to cheer."

"So I ask you tonight to return home, to say a prayer for the family of Martin Luther King—yeah, it's true—but more importantly to say a prayer for our own country, which all of us love," Kennedy continued. The blacks listened to him, said another neighborhood resident, Vechel Rhodes, Sr., because of the way Kennedy spoke to them—honest, respectful, blunt—and because he had the courage to come to speak to them at all.

"Naturally, when something like that happens, certain people in the crowd, you're gonna hear them say, 'Let's go burn that city up.' 'Do this, and do that'—I mean, that's just normal anywhere," Rhodes said. "It's the nature of us." On that night people "just wanted to go out and destroy the white man." But "when they started talking like that, he started talking another way. Calm and peace, what Martin Luther King and he wouldn't want you to do this and that." Had Kennedy not been there, "there is no telling what might have happened in Indianapolis." It was easy to imagine, since it happened in more than a hundred other American cities that night. And in Indianapolis, unlike the other places, the white targets were readily at hand. One of them was a McCarthy volunteer named Joel Connelly, then an undergraduate at Notre Dame, who found himself re-evaluating someone who in his camp was derided as an opportunist with second-rate supporters – as McCarthy's daughter put it, the "leapers and the shouters" rather than "the thinkers and the doers" behind her father.

Kennedy had said he was only going to speak for a minute. He'd now gone on for six. One minute wasn't long enough to engage, comfort, calm, and instruct as he had, but seven or eight of them would have diluted what he had just said. He had to end it. Like King twenty-four hours earlier, Kennedy said he saw difficult days ahead. "It is not the end of violence, it is not the end of lawlessness, and it is not the end of disorder," he said. But he stood by what he'd just told that student in Muncie: the vast majority of white people in the country wanted justice for all. So did the vast majority of blacks. He then turned to another of his pet phrases — the one he'd once inscribed on a photo to Burke Marshall and he'd said when he left the Justice Department. "Let us dedicate ourselves to what the Greeks wrote so many years ago: to tame the savageness of man and make gentle the life of this world," he said. "Let us dedicate ourselves to that, and say a prayer for our country and our people. Thank you very much."

Kennedy's fans reached for him as they always did, though now it reflected not just his magnetism but their neediness. A torch had passed, and not only at 17th and Broadway. Raymond Coffee of the *Chicago Daily News* surveyed some black marines stationed at the embattled garrison at Khe Sanh in Vietnam. "I guess I'd have to sit with Kennedy when it comes to hope for the future," Naval Corpsman Horace Ragin of Washington told him. Marine PFC Jeffrey Cherry of Columbus, Ohio, agreed. "About the best man I can think of now is Kennedy," he said. "When Dr. King was shot, I sort of had what I call an executive session with myself," John Lewis was to write. "I said something like, 'Well, we still have Bobby Kennedy.'" To Belafonte too, Kennedy was the real heir apparent, "the next person to fill that space." "I told him that, I told Bobby, 'There's a lot of space here for you to fill.' And he understood it." "You couldn't get someone who at times was more cynical about Robert Kennedy than me," said Clarence Jones, King's longtime lawyer. "My cynicism began to diminish substantially when I heard that speech. As Richard Pryor says, 'You can't make that shit up.'"

The crowd *did* disperse; Kennedy and his aides went back to the hotel, where police officers were on the roof and in the lobby. Mayor Lugar greeted Kennedy and his aides. "They looked, to say the least, pretty ashen and worn by the experience," he said.

There was much for Kennedy to do. He was to meet with the black militants. He had to decide whether and when and for how long to suspend his campaign. On that as on so many questions, there was a general divide. Dutton, who was roughly Kennedy's age, was reluctant to cancel anything. "He thought this would blow over, it wasn't all that big, people forget, life goes on, let's not get excited and cancel everything," John Bartlow Martin later wrote. "Bobby said, 'There are a lot of people who just don't care.' He said it flatly, without emotion.... The kids [Walinsky and Greenfield] thought King's murder would tear the country apart. It turned out they were closer to right than the rest of us." Ultimately, the decision was for Kennedy to give the speech scheduled for the next day in Cleveland—it would be a chance to speak about King's assassination—then cease campaigning until after King's funeral.

Kennedy also needed to unwind. At one point, Lewis recalled, he invited several people into his bedroom, and they all cried together. At another point, he stopped by to see Joan Braden, an old friend who'd come to Indiana to work on the campaign. "I remember him loosening his tie and sitting back and saying, 'My God. It might have been me,'" she recalled. Then they, too, cried.

The first order of business was calling Coretta King. "What do I say to her?" Kennedy asked yet again. "Just tell her how you feel," John Bartlow Martin advised. "It has to come from you." Mankiewicz overheard Kennedy's end of the conversation. He offered the usual condolences, then asked if there was anything he could do, then listened. "Oh, yes, of course, we'll do that," Kennedy then said. "That" was to help get King's body back to Atlanta. That meant chartering a plane and calling the police, the coroner, the funeral home. Kennedy made clear that he wanted no publicity about anything he was doing.

"Calls came in one after the other," Coretta King's assistant, Xernona Clayton, later wrote. "Everybody had the same script. 'This is Senator So and So. This is Mr. So and So. I'm just calling to say we've heard the news, we're so sorry, let us know if there's anything we can do to help.' Now, Robert Kennedy, his call was different. His call was like this: 'This is Robert Kennedy. It's obvious you need more phone lines; we've been trying to call you since six o'clock. So Mr. John Jones of AT&T is en route. He'll be there at 1:30 this morning.... I heard on the news you'd like to go to Memphis. So we've arranged for a private jet. It will be at Hangar 2, the tail number is 123, the pilot's name is...' And so on." Kennedy thought of all sorts of things no one else did, like calling the managers at the leading hotels to lock down all of the rooms for the funeral. "We wouldn't have thought of that," Clayton recalled.

On both ends, people worried a bit about propriety. "It just came up spontaneously and a little bit awkwardly," Dutton later said. "He couldn't tell the woman, 'no.'" Some people, black and white, viewed Kennedy's offer to King's widow as a campaign stunt, the 1968 version of the 1960 phone calls to Mrs. King and the Georgia judge. "I heard some of that, and I knocked it down," Clarence Jones recalled. "My attitude was: he had experienced grief in his own life, and he probably better than anyone could understand that moment. I consider that an act of graciousness." Coretta King decided not to worry about accepting Kennedy's help. "Although they were political figures...they were human beings first, and their humaneness reached out to the needs of other people," she wrote.

Kennedy's speech that night had left the activists from the Radical Action Program unmoved, and when, with everything he had to do, he kept them waiting for the meeting with him, they grew even more irritated. Snooky Hendricks, for one, wanted to bolt. Kennedy finally arrived, but the day had left him shrunken, dwarfed by his cigar and the enormous chair he sat in. "He looked like he was caving in on himself," said Tolan. "He sat with his feet up like an orphan...with his hands around him." What ensued was another, coarser version of the 1963 Baldwin meeting, without even its pretense of politeness. And yet here Kennedy was again, listening. "We had an interesting diatribe that went on for about twenty-five minutes," said Kennedy aide Gerard Doherty. "They accused him of taking advantage of them and who the hell did he think he was and they weren't going to do anything for him."

Here, too, Kennedy played the aggrieved benefactor: I don't need all this aggravation. I could sit next to my swimming pool. God's been good to me, and I really don't need anything. But I just feel I should try to put something back in. And you all call yourself leaders and you've been around here moaning and groaning about all personal things and you haven't once talked about your own people. And I'm just telling you, with or without you I'm going to win this thing. I'd like your help. It seemed to work. They agreed to help get out his votes.

Rafer Johnson, the black Olympic gold medalist who had become close to Kennedy and campaigned for him, observed that Kennedy realized quickly how King's death, coupled with the growing militancy in the black community, made fast action imperative. "Bob Kennedy knew better than anyone else, better even than Martin Luther King, that if something wasn't done... to somehow solve the racial strife, then we're in deep trouble," he later said. No black man could have brought black militants and moderates together as Kennedy could have, Johnson continued, and no American could have spoken to both races as he did. "Senator Kennedy proved that color doesn't make any difference," he said. "He was—in terms of the Negro—as much a Negro as Adam Clayton Powell.... As Ralph Bunche or Senator [Edward] Brooke. He was as much Negro as Jesse Owens or Joe Louis because he did right by people."

The revisionist mythology about the bond between King and Kennedy was born that night. In the *New York Times*, R. W. Apple described King as Kennedy's "close friend." The *Washington Post* said something similar. In fact, when he wasn't crying that night, Kennedy, in fact, seemed oddly detached. "You know, Martin Luther King was not that close a friend of mine," he told George Stevens. Donald Wilson, a *Time* executive and family confidant who worked for both John and Robert Kennedy observed that "he clearly felt it was a dreadful thing... but in terms of real sorrow over a human being who he loved and cared about, I didn't get that at all." Which was not to say that any part of Kennedy's remarks was insincere. "I heard him talk about Dr. King from time to time," Ramsey Clark later remembered. "What he said in Indiana... tells what he thought; maybe it's because that's what I thought. That's what I hoped he thought; that's what everything I ever saw him say or do made me think he thought."

Unable to sleep that night, Kennedy wandered the halls. "He was troubled, restless, thinking, thinking, thinking," Tolan recalled. Kennedy did something he'd never done before, dropping in on Walinsky and Greenfield as they labored over the next day's speech in Cleveland. "He came in and just sort of sat down and didn't say much," Greenfield recalled. "And he said, 'You know, that fellow Harvey Lee Oswald, whatever his name is, set something loose in this country.'" "Harvey Lee Oswald": it was how Kennedy's assassin had first been identified on November 22, and apparently how Robert Kennedy had remembered it, because he hadn't dealt with it since.

As for King's demise, "he seemed remarkably unaffected by it," Greenfield remembered. "He said, 'You know, the death of Martin Luther King isn't the worst thing that ever happened in the world.' And I was really struck, I mean, I was genuinely startled in a very negative way to hear Kennedy say that. It sounded like a very cold thing." Perhaps, as Greenfield surmised, Kennedy had meant King no disrespect and had only been thinking of his brother. Or perhaps he cared more about King than he was letting on, but it was embarrassing, even unmanly, to admit it: His self-image as a tough guy had suffered that night, and, needing to reestablish his credentials, he offered up an unconvincing display of indifference. Or perhaps that was how he really felt. "A little later, a friend remarked that this new act of violence must have brought back intolerable memories," wrote R. W. Apple (who was surely the "friend" in question). Kennedy "looked away for two, perhaps three minutes. Then he replied, very softly, 'Well, that's part of it, but it makes me wonder what they might do to me, too.'"

Around two thirty that morning, Kennedy checked in again on his pair of young speechwriters. He found Walinsky asleep, typewriter still in his lap, and Greenfield passed out on his bed. Greenfield awoke to find Kennedy tucking him in.

"You aren't so ruthless after all," Greenfield told him.

"Don't tell anybody," Kennedy replied.

Not only did King's death open old wounds for Bobby; it made real for him the possibility that he could be a target as well.

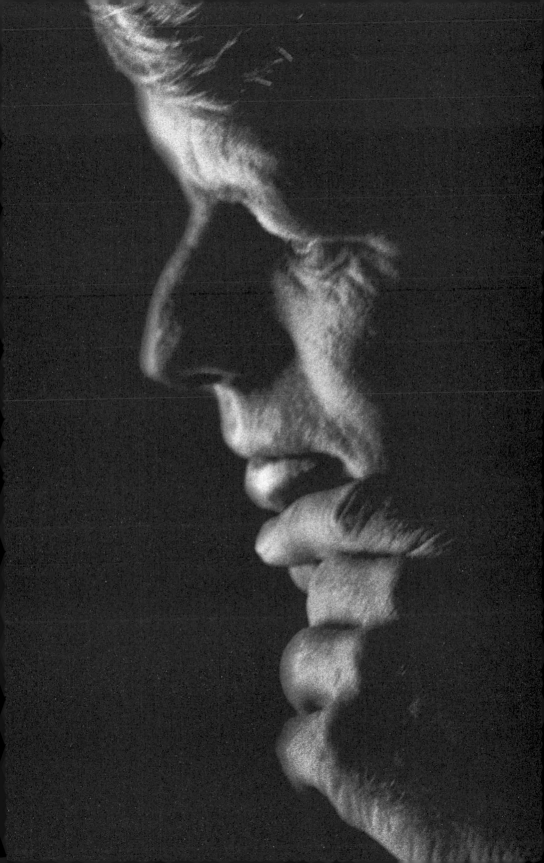

# FOURTEEN

# THERE WERE NO WORDS

The American Electra jet that Robert Kennedy arranged for Coretta Scott King lifted off in Atlanta at 9:15 on the morning of April 5. It would land in Memphis a little more than an hour later. She did not get off the aircraft. She kept her composure as the casket carrying her husband was removed from the hearse but collapsed on the shoulder of a companion as it was lifted up for Martin Luther King's final journey home. An unidentified SCLC official in Atlanta was asked who King's pallbearers would be. "Every black man in this country," he replied.

While Coretta King made her way to Tennessee, Kennedy sat down with his old friend Jack Paar in a television studio in Indianapolis. Back when the wall between television personalities and politics was a bit lower, Paar was available for partisan purposes — in this instance, for the kind of question-and-answer session in which, Kennedy's admen still believed, the candidate was most appealing. They would edit the conversation into small bits and use them in commercials. Calibrating his message to conservative Indiana, Kennedy talked more with Paar about law and order than civil rights, and more about national security than either. Asked to identify his greatest single accomplishment as attorney general, Kennedy veered off into the Cuba Missile Crisis and how he'd helped save the planet. Whenever Paar tried to get him to talk about King, Kennedy put him off. Even with King gone, Kennedy was keeping his distance.

Bobby and Ethel toured the wreckage along 14th Street in Washington, one of more than one hundred cities that smoldered in the wake of King's murder.

Kennedy then headed to Cleveland for his previously scheduled lunchtime speech to the Cleveland City Club. Both en route and afterward, he avoided any appearance of politicking: the hundreds of people chanting "We want Kennedy!" outside the hotel where he was to speak had to content themselves with a wave from an upstairs window.

Kennedy's speechwriters must have understood that no one would want anything long-winded; he spoke only a couple of minutes longer than he just had in Indianapolis. In the aftermath of both the shooting and the violence that followed, he made another plea for brotherhood and a denunciation of violence, which he defined far more broadly than usual. Brutality, he said, came not just from snipers, mobs, and gangs, but from lawless law enforcement, Hollywood, armies killing innocent civilians in far-off lands, and apathetic and indifferent bureaucracies.

> There is another kind of violence, slower but just as deadly, destructive as the shot or the bomb in the night. This is the violence of institutions, indifference and inaction and slow decay. This is the violence that afflicts the poor, that poisons relations between men because their skin has different colors. This is a slow destruction of a child by hunger, and schools without books and homes without heat in the winter. This is the breaking of a man's spirit by denying him the chance to stand as a father and as a man among other men. And this, too, afflicts us all.

Three times, Kennedy remarked on how short life was, a theme he had never dwelt on before. He also made the appealing but ridiculous claim that assassinations were futile. "No martyr's cause has ever been stilled by his assassin's bullet," he said. Walinsky later called it more "Sunday school sermon" than an appraisal of human history. And William F. Buckley later described it as a plea from Kennedy to his own assassin, "whose name neither he nor anyone else knew, but whose existence he had frequently conjectured."

At a time when the name of Martin Luther King was on everyone's lips, Kennedy never mentioned it that day. It's no doubt true that, as the *Village Voice*'s Jack Newfield was to write, King's death gave Kennedy the purpose his candidacy had lost with Lyndon Johnson's withdrawal. His would be a broadened version of King's own fight for the disenfranchised. But King's name would rarely be invoked in the process, beginning, strangely, even before he'd been buried.

Thus, the students in Mrs. Zelda Garfinkel's American history class at Julia Richman High School in Manhattan, who'd reminded Kennedy that laws helping the poor and oppressed would be a fitting memorial to King, heard more from him on the subject than voters over the next couple of months. "Martin Luther King Jr. represented the best in our nation," he wrote them back. "Dr. King lived and died not only for the Negro but for all Americans—and, in particular, for the youth of our nation." The few comments Kennedy did make on King were private and were more about the FBI. "It's very interesting that they can't find the killer of Martin Luther King, but they can track down some 22-year-old who might have burned his draft card," he told Pete Hamill at one point.

Others, though, connected the two men in ways that weren't always apparent. It was on a Wednesday—trash collection day in Pasadena—shortly after King was killed that a sanitation man named Alvin Clark encountered Sirhan Bishara Sirhan, a young Palestinian-born man whose house was on Clark's route. Over the past three years, the pair had become friendly; Sirhan would sometimes bring Clark coffee or a soft drink and something to eat during pickups. "He was upset about the death of Martin Luther King," Clark later testified. "He says, 'What do you think the Negro people are going to do about it?' and I says, 'What *can* we do about it? There wasn't but one person involved.'" Sirhan then asked him about the California primary, now only a couple of months away. "I told him I was going to vote for Kennedy," Clark recalled, "and Sirhan said, 'What are you going to vote for that son of a bitch for? Because I'm planning on shooting him.'"

The Kennedys visited Coretta Scott King at her home before the funeral. "Although they were political figures . . . they were human beings first," she wrote.

"You'd be killing one of the best men in the country," Clark replied, noting how Kennedy had arranged to have King's body brought back to Atlanta. He'd just done that for "publicity," Sirhan replied. He did not say why it was he hated Kennedy enough to want to kill him.

Kennedy returned to Washington right after his Cleveland speech. The view from the air as they approached National Airport was cataclysmic; smoke was billowing out of the black neighborhoods. Kennedy wanted to go directly to where the rioting was taking place to try and stop it. "I think I can do something with these people," he kept saying as his aides tried to dissuade him. "He finally went home. Very reluctantly," the speechwriter John Bartlow Martin, who was with Kennedy, recalled.

But the next day, Palm Sunday, Kennedy spoke briefly from the pulpit of Washington's New Bethel Baptist Church, in the midst of where the turmoil had taken place. Then, with Ethel but without bodyguards, he walked twenty-two blocks through the area, where the rubble smoldered and the scent of tear gas still hung heavy in the air. (He'd campaigned here only five days earlier—he and Rosey Grier had sung "Spanish Harlem" together.) Marion Barry, then a local activist and later mayor of Washington, viewed Kennedy as an invader. "What in hell is *he* doing here?" he asked. But neighborhood residents, especially children, fell in line behind him. For part of the walk, he held a small girl's hand.

"There was none of the grabbing, pushing and mauling that has become a part of the Senator's campaign tours," wrote R. W. Apple in the *New York Times*. "Both he and the onlookers were subdued as he greeted weary policemen, shook hands with soldiers, and poked his head into burned-out shops." Few residents there that day would have endorsed Stokely Carmichael's charge that by dragging his feet on civil rights, Bobby Kennedy had "pulled that trigger just as well as anybody else."

The next day, Robert and Ethel Kennedy flew to Atlanta for King's funeral. They visited Coretta King at her home, sitting down for a time with her in her bedroom. He told her that if it meant something to her, he would encourage Jacqueline Kennedy to attend the funeral, and he did, and she did. And, as various SCLC officials—Andrew Young, James Bevel, and Hosea Williams among them—and members of the King family sat on the bed or the floor, he stopped by to see Daddy King in his room at the Hyatt Hotel, where the family later received people.

"Robert Kennedy came in by himself," Andrew Young recalled. "And he really just poured his heart out about his brother and our brother. He even mentioned that he lost his first brother. It was not like he knew what he was saying, he just started kind of like he wasn't even talking to us, knowing what we were going through, and remembering what he went through. It wasn't *what* he said; it was the fact that he was there, saying *anything*, and his being there, and his *total* identification. And it made us identify with him."

Young recalled Daddy King, is his robe and pajamas, sitting up in bed and declaring again and again, "Hate is too great a burden to bear. I will not let anybody make me hate." At another point that evening, John Lewis accompanied Robert and Ethel Kennedy to see the body of Martin Luther King, lying in an open casket by the pulpit of Ebenezer Baptist Church. Kennedy crossed himself, and said nothing.

Well into the night, Kennedy held a series of meetings with black activists, politicians, and celebrities in the suite next door to his hotel room, attempting to tamp things down and divine what should come next. The sessions degenerated at times into internecine posturing and one-upmanship—"This is a lot of shit!" Bill Cosby said at one point—and anger at Kennedy himself, either for being too political (why was he there?) or, because he insisted he'd come principally to listen (for not being political enough). Robert Kennedy was once again the attorney general, or perhaps he was already the president of the United States. Young later said he seemed more sensitive to the situation than the black leaders themselves. "I guess the thing that kept us going was that maybe Bobby Kennedy would come up with some ideas for the country," Hosea Williams later said. "I remember telling him he had a chance to be a prophet. But prophets get shot." A couple of times, Ethel came in to fetch her husband. "Is he ever going to get to bed?" she asked. Eventually, he did. "At the end, and it was getting very late, he said, 'We've got to get up and go bury our leader,' " John Lewis recalled.

The next day at Ebenezer Baptist Church, an usher—self-appointed, it turned out, an encyclopedia salesman by trade—escorted Kennedy to his pew with the words "Come right this way, Robert. We have security here." Kennedy later changed seats to comfort a weeping Charles Evers. James Baldwin was also there, wearing the new dark suit he'd bought for King's appearance at the W. E. B. Du Bois centennial commemoration only a couple of weeks earlier. He spotted Kennedy—"one of the most headlined mourners

Mrs. King and the couple's young children led a crowd of forty thousand in a silent
march through Memphis before returning to Atlanta for Dr. King's funeral.

at King's funeral," the FBI called him in an internal memo—but
didn't speak with him. "He was surrounded by millions and millions of people," Baldwin remembered. "He didn't see me." For
much of the service, Kennedy's head was down—because, people
speculated, he did not want the cameras focusing on him, and
because he was remembering. Outside the church afterward, he
told Allard Lowenstein he was sorry he'd never really known King,
and expressed his surprise that King had had a sense of humor.

Later, behind the mule cart carrying King, Kennedy joined
the procession on the three-and-a-half mile trek from the church
to Morehouse College and the cemetery. He and Sammy Davis,
Jr., seemed to elicit the most attention and cheers from the people
lining the streets. When Jimmy Breslin, who walked alongside
Kennedy, remarked on how few white faces there were along the
route and predicted that nothing would change as a result of King's
death, Kennedy agreed, as did Evers. "Didn't mean nothing when

my brother was killed," Evers said. "I know," Kennedy replied. ("Of course people feel guilty for a moment, but they hate feeling guilty," Jacqueline Kennedy later told Arthur Schlesinger. "They can't stand it for very long.")

Even here, Kennedy was criticized: with his suit jacket slung over his left shoulder and his shirtsleeves rolled up in the eighty-degree heat, some deemed him insufficiently respectful. Roger Wilkins, for one, thought the way Kennedy smiled and waved at the crowd unseemly. "Well, what's he supposed to do when people wave at him? Should he not wave back?" he was asked. "Well, maybe he waves, but he sure as hell doesn't have to smile!" Wilkins replied.

On the graph of public acceptance and promise, King and Kennedy had for the past couple of years been criss-crossing lines: King heading downward, Kennedy shooting up. With his martyrdom, King began reversing course, and gradually became fit once more for the American mainstream. From the standpoint of historic acceptability, his death was, as Gore Vidal famously said of Truman Capote (and several others), "a good career move." And Kennedy, now holding issues like racial harmony and economic fairness almost entirely to himself, began a still steeper climb.

The presidential campaign was transformed — and sobered up — by King's death and the ensuing violence. This was especially true in conservative Indiana, which would vote in a month's time, and where Kennedy following advice, soon toned things down. "The ordinary Hoosier at home watching TV was sick of scenes of violence in Vietnam, of rioting in the cities after King was killed, and of kids pulling Kennedy's clothes off," John Bartlow Martin later wrote. "Kennedy was too exciting. The people, I thought, did not want to be excited."

And, Martin believed, Kennedy was devoting too much of his energy to blacks. ("Kennedy has a ghetto hang-up," Richard Harwood of the *Washington Post* once wrote.) While his heart may have been with them, they did not provide enough votes to win.

For that, Martin advised, he needed to go into "redneck backlash factory cities" like Hammond, Whiting, Kokomo, and Marion, which were filled with ethnic whites and former Appalachians, many of them bigoted. Kennedy proposed bringing Rafer Johnson along on one trip. "I exploded and told Kennedy if he took a Negro into southern Indiana, including Vincennes and Evansville, or into the northern backlash factory towns like Kokomo, he could kiss them goodbye," Martin wrote. "He took this advice."

In hardscrabble Indiana, Eugene McCarthy, cerebral, cynical, patronizing, detached, was really a fringe candidate, his appeal confined largely to college towns, and, to the national press at least, Governor Branigin was little more than a local sideshow. Most of the interest, and almost all of the action, centered on Kennedy. "It's clear that the real rival of Robert F. Kennedy, the glamorous restorer of Camelot, is Robert F. Kennedy, the brash opportunist trying to seize the White House on the strength of his slain brother's name," Arlen Large wrote in the *Wall Street Journal*.

The smallest details about him—like the ebb and flow of his hair (in Indiana, it ebbed noticeably) and the cut of his clothes (his suits looked more off-the-rack)—were matters of intense curiosity. So, too, was his effectiveness as a campaigner: how his initial jitters had gradually eased, his voice stabilized, his confidence increased. He was learning on the fly, as was his operation. "Whenever anybody talks about that 'well-oiled Kennedy machine,' I just have to remember that campaign and shake my head," Jeff Greenfield later said.

Saul Pett of the Associated Press, who'd covered John Kennedy eight years earlier, described a man at once more haunted, less poised, more intense, less disciplined, more liked, and more disliked than his older brother. "Now, after midnight, he moves through the last crowd with his glazed crowd-look, seeing no one, his hands dipping into the pleading hands of strangers, his body grabbed and tugged and beseeched by strangers, a small set smile protecting the private little island no one reaches, hiding his distaste for the scenes he invites, the motion and the frenzy that look like votes on TV." At the end of a long day, he went on, "there comes then into those blue eyes, like a shadow over a turquoise sea, a look of such infinite sadness, of such terrible hurt one feels compelled to look away." Those who studied Kennedy up close saw someone older, grayer, more deeply lined than they'd imagined, certainly for a man of forty-two. Following Kennedy in Oregon, the reporter Gail Sheehy noticed "an old man's hands on a young man." He was becoming something no one had ever seen: an aged, or at least aging, son of Joe and Rose.

Kennedy honed a finely calibrated stump speech, talking about law and order *and* justice, switching the arrangement and proportions depending on his audiences. He'd get lusty applause for denouncing violence, and by the time he denounced injustice, Martin wrote, "they didn't applaud but they didn't mind." Speaking to Rotarians, he'd talk about the role of private enterprise in his Bedford-Stuyvesant program. Knocking government, calling for local autonomy, deriding the dole, he'd sound at times like Barry Goldwater. It frustrated Walinsky and Greenfield, who wrote sardonic limericks (strictly for internal consumption) about Kennedy joining the Ku Klux Klan. (Or at least Martin so remembered. Greenfield did not.) At times even Kennedy chafed: he asked Martin once when he could have a "liberal day." But he was a pragmatist. "I'm the Negro candidate in the race," he explained to his aides. "Gene McCarthy doesn't have to prove that he cares about white people. He's never done anything about civil rights. I'm the Negro candidate. I have to tell white people I care about what they care about."

But Kennedy's idealism and fatalism and fame and poor prospects, at least this time around, continued to free him, more than most politicians, to say what he really thought. He spoke of the poor with an explicitness and frequency and intensity and bluntness that had always been, and would soon become again, quite unimaginable from a mainstream candidate in American politics. Sometimes, he just didn't give a damn what people thought. Other times, he set out to provoke them, particularly when he felt those people thought only of themselves.

A prime example came in late April during an appearance at the Indiana University Medical School. One of several hostile questioners that day asked Kennedy where the money for the enhanced health care for the poor he envisioned would come from. "From you," he replied. He then noted the scarcity of black faces in the room at a time when blacks were serving—and dying—disproportionately in Vietnam. "Would you end medical school draft deferments?" someone shouted. "The way things are going here today, probably yes," he joked. When he was done, he got a standing ovation.

Lots of people didn't want to hear his descriptions of life in the Appalachian coal towns or the suicide rate on Indian reservations or starvation in the Mississippi delta or rats biting sleeping black children in the inner cities—but, as John Bartlow later recalled, "he plodded ahead stubbornly, making them listen, maybe even making some of them care, by the sheer power of his own caring." "You sure you want to talk about hunger?" Greenfield asked him before another campus appearance. "I don't think they care." "If they don't care, the hell with them," Kennedy replied. "I have always thought that Bobby's views in his last years were penitential," Daniel Patrick Moynihan once told Arthur Schlesinger. "Pat's theory," Schlesinger wrote in his journals, "is that Bobby felt guilty about his early conservative views and therefore compensated by moving too far to the left."

At times, Kennedy would stop where there were no votes to be had, like at the Beatrice State Home for the Mentally Retarded in Nebraska. "The superintendent twittered: 'Would you like to see the wards?'" wrote Helen Dudar of the *New York Post*. "Kennedy, in the flat, imperious voice he uses for people who fawn, replied, 'I would like to see the children.'"

> We went to the nursery floor—the superintendent, Kennedy, his dog, Freckles, a line of men and women busy scribbling in notebooks—and found the little ones. These were not children likely to coo over the candidate nor

good prospects for tomorrow's morning edition showing his magical contact with the young.

Lying inert in a playpen was a hydrocephalic, a child with a head the size of a basketball. Kennedy leaned in and scratched its stomach for a while. I cannot tell what its response was because I found I could not look at that child.

Then he patted a vacant-eyed little girl, who grabbed his hand and began chewing his fingers. He let her gnaw for a while. Finally he picked her up and carried the slobbering child as he walked about touching other children—a vegetabloid creature slumped unseeing in a chair, a baby with a grapefruit-sized lump on its head that made it look two-headed, all those pathetic grotesques hidden away from the world, suddenly and impulsively objects of Kennedy's charity and compassion.

On the sidewalk outside, as Kennedy prepared to leave, a girl gave him a note. "We vote for you, Kennedy," it said.

One day, Kennedy whistle-stopped from Peru to Wabash to Huntington to Fort Wayne aboard the Wabash Cannonball. Lots of people despised Bobby Kennedy, and lots of reporters remarked upon it at the time—an untidy fact all but airbrushed out of his biography later on. America was in a mood to hate, wrote Russell Baker of the *Times*, and when Lyndon Johnson quit the race, Kennedy inherited his portion of it. (Kennedy called Baker after the story appeared, and told him he had it "exactly right.") "Almost chemical" was how James Reston described this animus. The image of the "ruthless opportunist" proved every bit as durable as "Tricky Dick," he wrote.

But behind him, always, stood the same firewall, now enhanced by two assassinations. "Bobby benefits from the merging of two strong emotional currents: that of expiation for the death of John Kennedy, and that of the redemptive death of Martin Luther King,"

With victories in Indiana and Nebraska under his belt, Kennedy found catnaps
were important as he faced the all-important California primary on June 4.

Max Lerner observed. "Kennedy manages to cement them by a
fiery emphasis on the wrongs done by whites to the Negro and the
need to right them." And, as things progressed, Kennedy sensed
anecdotally what the polls showed statistically: that enough white
voters liked him enough to forgive him for his stances on race and
Vietnam for him to win.

On election eve, Kennedy rode triumphantly through the
industrial towns — Hammond and Michigan City and Mishawaka
and Gary — of Northwest Indiana. Black to white to mixed to
black to white to mixed: the colors of the faces of the people
cheering him on kept switching. Kennedy felt that the people of
Indiana — in contrast to the movers and shakers of Manhattan,
for whom he retained an astonishing degree of disdain, the
contempt of a perpetual outsider — had given him a fair chance:
"When they hated me here, at least it was in the open," he said.
"It wasn't hypocritical, like in Washington or New York." He
preferred the meat-and-potatoes Poles in Gary to the fancy New

York reformers, who were "so filled up with hate and envy" and worried more "about not being invited to the important parties, or seeing psychiatrists" than more serious things, or about what to do with all their affluence. Even the Indianapolis papers—which depicted him and Ethel as Bonnie and Clyde, roaring through "Indianer" tossing out his daddy's money—were preferable to the *New York Times*: they, too, were honest about their biases.

Kennedy spent Election Day playing touch football. "You're a dirty player, and a lousy one, too," Richard Harwood of the *Washington Post* declared after Kennedy committed pass interference on him to break up a touchdown. With a few words, he'd hit Kennedy on the two spots that hurt most: competence and, even more important, character, a.k.a. ruthlessness; and Harwood's incisiveness and candor surely impressed Kennedy, and brought the two men closer together. (The unending accusations of ruthlessness amused Rose Kennedy, who campaigned for him in the state; when Bobby was a little boy, she said, "I was warned that I was making a sissy of him.")

He won the Indiana primary with 42 percent of the vote to Branigin's 31 and McCarthy's 27. There was little doubt who made the difference. "Don't you just wish that everyone was black?" an ingenuous Ethel Kennedy asked. But plenty of whites had come along for the exhilarating ride. "Simply stated, Kennedy is gambling that the average white American is at heart willing to see the average black American take his place in society, as long as the Negro conforms to the same laws by which the white man is bound," wrote Joe Mohbat of the Associated Press. Maybe, but in all likelihood, something far less elevating was at work: he was a Kennedy. That was enough.

In fact, the race was closer than Kennedy would have liked. "He made the painful discovery in Indiana that it is dangerous for him to do what he does best—that is, commiserating with the blacks and the poor and lashing out against injustice," McGrory wrote. Newfield thought he remained a man in search of himself, and he was not alone. "Sometimes I think the best thing we could do for him would be to let him alone and let him go out and find himself," one aide told McGrory. "Bobby's therapy is going to cost the family $8 million," Ted Kennedy once said.

Only after midnight did Kennedy finally get around to eating, and then, at the only restaurant in Indianapolis that was still open, at the airport. There, with several reporters in tow, he ran into two sleep-deprived and disappointed McCarthy volunteers, a young man and woman, both undergraduates, still sporting their campaign regalia. Beyond having to watch their hero lose to a Johnny-come-lately, they'd missed their flights out. Kennedy invited them to join him in the terminal's coffee shop, and for the next couple of hours he questioned them: about McCarthy, the campaign, their futures. They highlighted his deepest wound: he may have beaten McCarthy, but he still hadn't won over his bright, idealistic young supporters. Once, he'd wondered why such people would ever have supported him. "Why do those on the left like me?" he asked Arthur Schlesinger's son, Stephen. "I don't like beards. If they talked to me for five minutes, they would dislike me." Now he craved their acceptance. It wasn't only ego; such people could cleanse him of his "ruthless" rap. That they despised him only made him admire—and desire—them more. "You have to hate in order to run a good campaign," he once said.

"He kind of neutralized me," one of them, Taylor Branch, then a student at the University of North Carolina and, later, one of Martin Luther King's principal biographers, told the journalist Richard Stout. "I still worked for McCarthy, but I was drawn to Kennedy because of his flair and passion for black people." So drawn, in fact, that after Kennedy left them that night, Branch and his fellow volunteer, a woman named Pat Sylvester, wrote him a note, expressing how much they admired his candor and commitment. They then slipped it under his motel room door. "For days afterward, he talked about that boy and girl in the airport coffee shop—how great they were, in their idealism and determination," Fred Dutton later said.

Given Kennedy's reputation for seductiveness, political reporters approached him with more than their customary wariness. Covering him in the 1960 campaign, John Lindsay of *Newsweek* thought him "wooden as a stick," and rude to boot. But sitting alongside Kennedy, who'd ease into his floppy old slippers and a sweater with its sleeves rolled up and nurse a weak drink between campaign stops, he'd realize the man was open, endearing, and incredibly funny. And his experience was typical. Even Richard Harwood of the *Washington Post*, a hard-boiled former Marine with scars from Iwo Jima, eventually succumbed. Kennedy wasn't pompous, took himself less seriously than his enemies took him, and "was full of whatever human quality it is that makes one man say to another, 'You're all right,'" he later wrote. To him, the danger lay instead in getting *too* close—cheerleading. Harwood eventually vowed to take himself off the story for that reason.

Early on in the campaign, a group of reporters sat together. "Do you think this guy has the stuff to go all the way?" Breslin asked. Of course he did, Lindsay replied, but it would never come to that: somebody was going to shoot him. "I know it and you know it just as sure as we are sitting here," he said. "He's out there waiting for him." There was "sort of a stunned silence around the table," Lindsay recalled. Then, one by one, everyone agreed. They would not let him out of their sight, lest they not be around when "it" happened. So tenaciously did Joe Mohbat of the Associated Press stick to Kennedy that some people mistook him for a Secret Service agent.

Kennedy's sole bodyguard, a former FBI agent named Bill Barry—"a security man without a gun," Harwood called him—cut the odds however he could. "We have the cars hidden at night so they can't put a bomb in them," he told Breslin, "and the locals wherever we are watch the room at night." But Kennedy had tied his hands. He was defiantly reckless, wading into crowds, riding in

Bobby's children rarely joined him on the campaign trail, but his springer spaniel, Freckles, was always in tow—and a favorite of press photographers.

convertibles precisely because his brother had been killed in one. "I'm not afraid of anybody," he might say, sounding like Martin Luther King on his last night in Memphis. "If things happen, they're going to happen." It was very different from King, whom photographers like Harry Benson and Steve Schapiro also covered. King never stayed out or marched any longer than he had to. And he scanned crowds continuously, forever looking for anything amiss.

Barry was never working entirely by himself. Plenty of people— Guthman, Dutton, Mankiewicz, advance men like Tony Bruno and Jim Tolan—would have taken a bullet for Kennedy. Maybe some of the reporters and photographers, who sometimes formed an informal cordon around him, would have, too. Others were his eyes and ears. "I never rode in a motorcade or went into a crowd with him that I did not watch the windows of surrounding buildings and watch people in the crowds," John Bartlow Martin recalled. There'd been a man at one stop who'd questioned Kennedy "with a look of sheer hatred on his face." "If he had made any move like reaching in his pocket I would have knocked Kennedy down," he wrote. Often there were false alarms: a popped balloon in Eugene, Oregon, firecrackers in San Francisco's Chinatown.

John Herbers of the *New York Times* later recalled a campaign motorcade heading back one evening to Indianapolis. "There was no news," he wrote. "There had been none all day. It could reasonably have been predicted there would be none that night. Robert Kennedy's campaign was then essentially the same as it had been at the beginning—the same speeches with the same jokes and the same George Bernard Shaw ending, the same crowds and the same anarchy and adulation around the candidate."

"I knew why I was there late at night when there had been an opportunity to leave the motorcade for a few hours," Herbers continued. "I had thought of it often, but I had never put it into words or heard it spoken. In the darkness of rural Indiana, someone blurted it out: 'It's the death watch.'"

Mohbat knew that Kennedy didn't like "introspective, personal-type questions," but on a late flight from Omaha to

Washington—Nebraska had a primary a week after Indiana—he asked him whether he ever worried about his safety. "There's nothing I can do about it," Kennedy replied. "I've got to present myself to the people as intimately as possible and get rid of some of these old bugaboos about me—let them know that I'm a human being." But what would it do to the country, he asked, to lose another person of his stature? "That wouldn't be good, but I can't help that," Kennedy replied. "If they want to get me, they're going to get me—whether it's in a crowd or whether I'm alone. I play Russian roulette every morning when I get up."

Some thought that if anything, King's murder made Kennedy even more reckless. "I'll tell you one thing," he continued, with a vehemence that stuck with Mohbat. "If I'm elected president, I'm not going to ride around in any of those trucks," he said, referring to those bubble-top limousines that had become commonplace after Dallas. "I'm going to be in an open car where the people can see me. I think that's important.... Anyway, this really isn't such a happy existence, is it?" he added, ending his brief, uncharacteristic foray into introspection. "I'm going to take a leak. Do you think America would believe that?"

Reporters weren't the only ones having premonitions. "The Negroes would say, 'I'm for that cat, but he's going to get shot,'" Newfield once wrote.

On May 14, two days after Ethel Kennedy had joined with Coretta King to mark the opening of the Poor People's Campaign on the National Mall in Washington, her husband won in Nebraska, proving his appeal to what Jeff Greenfield called "Grant Wood kind of characters"—as well as to blacks and hyphenated whites. ("Help!" he cried once after a gust of wind scattered his prepared remarks. "There goes my entire farm program!") A few days later, he was once again on the cover of *Time* magazine, as one of Roy Lichtenstein's superheroes, one of the few actual people he'd ever portrayed. What he most liked about Bobby, Lichtenstein explained, was his "lively, upstart quality and pop-heroic proportions." But Oregon, a state without ghettos or fissures, in which ex-Canadians constituted the largest immigrant group, proved more problematic. Kennedy courted the reliable Democratic base, including Jews—appearing, for instance, at Temple Neve Shalom in Portland on May 26, two days before the primary. There, once he managed to get a yarmulke to stay on his head, he voiced his support for Israel "against outside aggression." Assertions like these—Kennedy had pledged to send Israel fifty Phantom jets—inflamed Sirhan Sirhan, the Palestinian-American who'd told his trash collector friend six weeks earlier of his plans to kill Robert Kennedy. "My determination to eliminate R.F.K. is becoming more and more of an unshakable obsession," he'd written in a notebook a week before that synagogue appearance. "R.F.K. just die...R.F.K. must be killed...Robert F. Kennedy must be assassinated before 5 June 1968." That was the eve of the first anniversary of the Six-Day War.

Eugene McCarthy's victory in Oregon marked the first electoral loss ever for a Kennedy. "I died in Oregon, but I hope California will be 'Resurrection City,'" he joked, referring to the shantytown built by participants in Martin Luther King's Poor People's Campaign.

And so it proved to be, though it wasn't easy. First, McCarthy claimed—falsely—that Martin Luther King had endorsed him. (Coretta King promptly issued both a statement saying it wasn't so, which was released, and her own endorsement of Kennedy, which was not.) Then Drew Pearson's Washington Merry-Go-Round column detailed how Kennedy had approved the King wiretap. Pearson's sidekick, Jack Anderson, called DeLoach to alert him to the story, and to say how he and Pearson "felt that Kennedy should receive a death blow prior to the Oregon primary." Kennedy couldn't deny it; instead, he said simply that he'd authorized taps when national security required them, and of course could not by law discuss such things now. In case it came up during a debate with McCarthy, he would use the question as an excuse to praise King. "I felt he was one of our great Americans," went one possible answer. "He will be remembered as one of the great contributors to American history." In the actual debate, he offered something blander, calling King "a loyal, dedicated American who in my judgment made a distinct contribution to this country."

Frank Mankiewicz asked Charles Evers to gauge reactions to the disclosure in the barbershops, bars, and restaurants in black Los Angeles. "Well, you know, it's like if somebody comes up to you and tells you that your wife is sleeping with somebody: you know it's probably true, but you love her so much it just doesn't matter,'" one black man told Evers. It brought to mind Adam Walinsky's point that at on some level, King may have viewed Kennedy as a rival within his own constituency. Black Californians undoubtedly revered King, but they *adored* Kennedy. And they forgave him his trespasses.

There were rallies in Watts and then a meeting with black militants in Oakland, put together in part by a young Willie Brown, later the mayor of San Francisco. Kennedy told aides why he met with black radicals: "After all the abuse the blacks have taken through the centuries, whites are just going to have to let them get some of these feelings out." "What do you think about black people?" a woman asked near the end of that raucous, often vitriolic meeting. Coming at the end of a long day on the trail, he could have been annoyed, or flip, or patronizing. "I like some. Some I don't like," he replied. On the Sunday before the vote, he kept rich supporters including Shelley Winters and Shirley MacLaine waiting downstairs at the Ambassador Hotel to meet with black power advocates. "He's into this and not leaving until he understands these guys," one of Kennedy's advance men, Murray Richtel, was told when he came up to fetch the candidate.

On election night, journalistic loyalists, campaign aides, and favored writers watched returns in Kennedy's private quarters in the Ambassador Hotel. To Jack Newfield, the candidate was the most serene he'd been since Johnson withdrew, the most liberated from gloom, fatalism, and guilt. And also, the most optimistic: "It was only in the last two hours of his life that he finally saw a way he could actually be nominated," Newfield later remembered.

Kennedy had outpolled his brother in California, he told one interviewer, which represented two firsts: the first time he had topped Jack, and the first time he'd said so.

But the way forward would be hard, especially in his non-native New York. "He knew that New York was going to be a bloodbath," Hamill later said. "He couldn't quite understand what it was all about in a way...that there was so much anti-Bobby hatred, really. And we were trying to figure out ways to get out of it. Breslin was saying, 'It's the God-damned Jews! Ya gotta get to the Jews!' And Bobby was laughing at him, you know. He said 'I'd like to get to the *New York Times* first.'"

With the encouragement of Cesar Chavez, Hispanics had voted for Kennedy even more overwhelmingly than had blacks, whose pro-Kennedy vote was overwhelming enough. Together they had put him over the top. "Well, of course, you know who won this election for you," Schulberg told him.

Around midnight, Kennedy and his entourage headed to the ballroom downstairs. To some, the electrified scene there was almost frightening—as if the crowd had been waiting since November 22, 1963, for something like it. Walking toward the podium, Kennedy flashed several peace signs tentatively, almost flaccidly, as if embarrassed by the gesture. He fiddled for a time with the lifeless microphones. At Mankiewicz's suggestion (but awkwardly, without the awe any true baseball fan would feel), he expressed his "high regard" for Don Drysdale of the Dodgers, who'd just pitched his record-setting sixth straight shutout. He thanked his brother-in-law, Stephen Smith, and "all of those other Kennedys" who'd worked on his campaign, and then Freckles and then Ethel—"I'm not doing this in order of importance," he conceded—and then Chavez, and then Rafer Johnson and Rosey Grier, "who said that he'd take care of anybody who didn't vote for me." Then he talked about unifying the nation.

With his remarks in Indianapolis yet to enter the annals, some thought it his best speech of the campaign. But it was less the lofty rhetoric than Kennedy's entirely ordinary closing line, to be replayed in the endless postmortems and reprises to come, that stuck: "So it's on to Chicago and let's win there." With that, he reached up, flashed another peace sign, patted down his hair, and prepared to step off the platform.

It happened in a nearby pantry, en route to a press conference. This time the crowded path to anywhere that Kennedy generally favored was just too clotted. And this time Mankiewicz and Barry, who generally formed a protective circle around Kennedy, stayed behind to help the pregnant Ethel Kennedy climb down from the stage. "He was smiling and shaking hands with a waiter, then a chef in a high white hat," the British journalist and broadcaster Alistair Cooke later wrote. "Lots of Negroes, naturally, and they were glowing with pride, for he was their man." Nearby was Sirhan, who'd test-fired his .22 revolver at a local shooting range earlier in the day, then replenished his supply. "I want the best box of shells you have...some that will not misfire," he told the range master. An ad he'd read over dinner that night for a "miracle mile march" for Israel had rekindled in him a fury he later said he'd felt since he was four years old. In the pantry, he blended in nicely with the Mexican workers. Someone later testified that he was "smirking" as he shot Kennedy—arm straight out, like a pro, from an inch and a half away, or less. To Richard Harwood, the shots sounded exactly like those firecrackers in Chinatown, "but somehow we knew...I mean, I knew it wasn't."

Perhaps one sees in the face of a dying man whatever one wants. In Martin Luther King's, Ralph Abernathy had seen both vindication—he'd always *said* this would happen—and a plea to carry on. In Robert Kennedy's, Jimmy Breslin saw sadness and knowledge—he, after all, knew all about assassinations, while Pete Hamill saw "a strange look of almost sweet acceptance on his face. The eyes seemed to know that it had come to him at last, the way

After a victory speech at the Ambassador Hotel in Los Angeles, an unplanned shortcut through the kitchen put Kennedy within close range of his assassin.

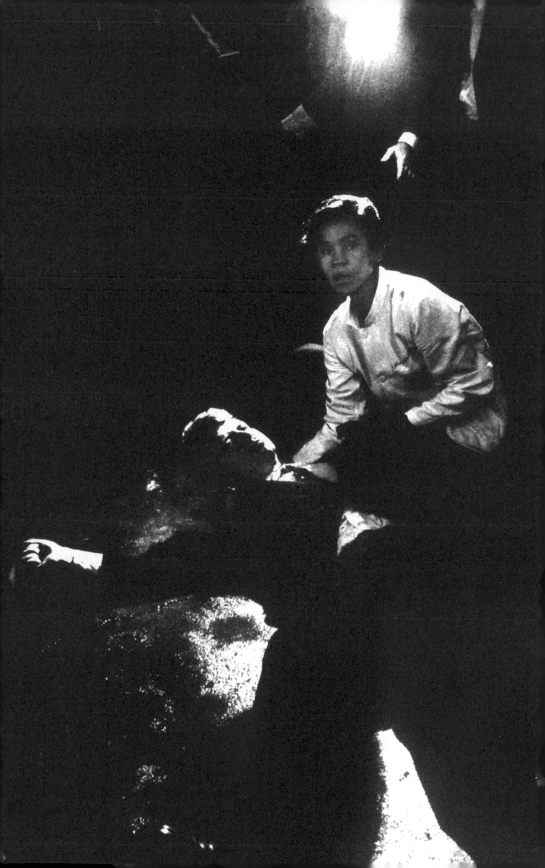

it had come to his brother, the way it had come only a few weeks before to the Rev. Martin Luther King." To Harwood, Kennedy simply looked dead, though another day would pass until he officially was. Looking at him on the floor, Kennedy aide Earl Graves expected Kennedy to stand up at any moment and shake it off. "He was such a strong individual that I just didn't think he could die like that," he said. In fact, he clung to life by a thread.

Sirhan was quickly subdued, and spared. "We're getting better at these things," Dutton told Breslin afterward. "We learn. Now we know it's important to keep the assassin alive. A couple of more things like this, and this country will have the whole business of assassination down pat." Kennedy had come to oppose capital punishment after reading Albert Camus's essay, "Reflections on a Guillotine," the previous year, and though Arthur Schlesinger opposed it as well, he later told Kennedy's longtime secretary, Angie Novello, that he saw no point in keeping Sirhan alive. "Oh, no, Bob would not have liked that," she remonstrated. "If by any chance Bob had lived, no one would have been more forgiving." That the whole thing had happened before—that people woke up the next morning thinking it was *Jack* Kennedy they were talking about on television—colored the way everyone viewed it now. In place of shock, there was weariness and resignation and rage and impatience with all of the pious platitudes. The new reality promised to be cumbersome: from now on, when talking about a Kennedy assassination, or a grieving Mrs. Kennedy, you'd have to specify which. Over the next few days, the press attaché at the American Embassy in London recorded fewer mourners for Robert Kennedy than for John Kennedy or Martin Luther King. "He said he thought people were becoming inured to political assassination," one story noted.

To whites, there'd now been two assassinations, and two points made a line. In his own misanthropic way—which shocked even his own campaign manager—Eugene McCarthy saw a direct connection between them: both men, he said, had brought assassination upon themselves, King by immersing himself in a violent strike,

Kennedy by stirring up frenzied crowds. To blacks, there'd now been three, or four (with Medgar Evers), or five (with Malcolm X), and they could argue, far more plausibly, that these deaths were the products of an elaborate political and social machine designed to keep them down. "It's like they're saying, no matter how many friends the black community makes, no matter how many good people are on our side, somebody always takes them away from us," said a community leader in Watts. On television, a man on the street was more blunt. "Every time we get someone who's going to do something for all of us, some crazy, stupid nut—I don't know where they get them—conks him out."

Coretta King, in Washington to spend a few days with the women of "Resurrection City," had just gone to bed at the Willard Hotel when she was awakened with the news. She'd thought Kennedy had only been shot in the leg, and went back to sleep. In the morning, Stanley Levison, who'd been staying down the hall, visited her in her room. "Mrs. King was sitting before the television set, weeping copiously," Levison recalled. "She said, 'You know, I have almost never been able to cry about Martin because I couldn't permit myself to. Before the children, everyone else...I have had to restrain myself. But now, I don't have to restrain myself, and I can't control my feelings.'"

She telegrammed Ethel. "You, your husband, and your entire family have been most comforting to my family in our times of grief and difficulty, and I am prepared to do anything which may be of some service or consolation to you now," she wrote. Within a few hours, she was en route to Los Angeles, and shortly after 6 p.m., she was at the hospital. Robert Kennedy's condition was still critical. While she was airborne, so were Robert Kennedy's three eldest children. And so, too, was Jacqueline Kennedy, on a private plane from New York. She arrived at the hospital an hour and a half after King, "wearing dark brown, or black—no one could tell for sure because she rushed by so quickly."

"The Church is a marvelous thing at a time like this," she told Frank Mankiewicz in the corridor. "The rest of the time it's often rather silly—little men running around in their black suits. But the Catholic Church understands death." She paused. "I'll tell you who else understands death are the black churches." "I remember at the funeral of Martin Luther King, I was looking at those faces and I realized that they know death. They see it all the time and they're ready for it. They're prepared for it in the way in which a good Catholic is." "And then she said a thing which just absolutely chilled me," Mankiewicz later recalled. "She said, 'Well, now we know death, don't we, you and I? As a matter of fact, if it weren't for the children, we'd welcome it.'"

Early that morning, residents of Resurrection City were awakened by an announcement on the public address system. "We began to cry, like another chunk of our heart had been taken from our bodies," Jesse Jackson, who was there, recalled. Later that day, on a spot of the muddy encampment called "Martin Luther King Plaza," a prayer service was held. Protestors then marched on the headquarters of the National Rifle Association. A few days later, the reporter Jack Nelson described what Resurrection City had become: fetid, disorganized, off-putting. "The [Poor People's] campaign sorely misses King," he wrote. "Not that he necessarily could have successfully pulled it off. In fact, had he not been assassinated, the campaign may well have been his Waterloo." It was a reminder of just how uncertain King's path forward would have been.

At 1:44 on the morning of Thursday, June 6, Robert Kennedy died. Returning his corpse for the funeral, which was to be at St. Patrick's Cathedral in New York on Saturday, was a simpler but grander proposition than it had been for King's: this time, Lyndon Johnson supplied the jet for the family. But that triggered a different concern: Jacqueline Kennedy would board it only after being assured it wasn't the one that had carried her and her late husband back from Dallas. Robert Kennedy's old friend Dave Hackett asked that on the way to the airport, the procession drive through Watts, then through Harlem once it landed; the FBI nixed the idea.

The flight east, delayed by Kennedy's autopsy, took off early that afternoon. Aboard was one of the most extraordinary trios in American history—Coretta King had joined the two Kennedy women. "There they go...three widows of men murdered by political assassinations," David Brinkley remarked on national television, with what one viewer called "concealed anger." "The truest symbol of America," Newfield called this triumvirate of bereavement. Normally so conscientious about documenting everything—Robert Kennedy would soon have an oral history collection of his own— the Kennedys had no photographer present to record the scene. While they talked to one another in pairs, it's unclear whether, as they crossed a troubled land, the three women actually conversed, and compared notes. The three journalists aboard—Joseph Kraft, Rowland Evans, and Sander Vanocur—were officially off duty that day, there strictly as friends of the family.

But appearing on NBC after they'd landed, Vanocur described what he had seen. Buoyed by her faith (after all, Jack and Robert Kennedy were now together again), Ethel Kennedy was said to have been in good spirits. For half an hour or so, she spoke to Jacqueline Kennedy. "And then after that was over, Mrs. Robert F. Kennedy walked down the aisle, stopping with various people along the way, just talking with them, sitting with them," Vanocur related. "I used the word 'joking' with them, because that's what she did." "She was the one who was trying to psych people out of their gloom," he recalled on another occasion. As for the others, "nobody was in much of a mood to talk about the future because it didn't seem like there *was* any future. It was just kind of, 'What's the use?' Everyone was too exhausted to...it was kind of a mixture of rage and anger and exhaustion." It reminded him of a Eugene O'Neill play.

Rowland Evans, who spent most of the flight speaking with Ethel and the youngest Kennedy sister, Jean Kennedy Smith, was struck by their strength and resilience. "I remember Jack Kennedy telling me once that he never worried about a situation over which he had absolutely no control," he said. "This is a philosophy that really, I think, goes to all of them. Bobby was shot. Bobby was dead. Nothing could possibly change that fact, and it immediately became an accepted fact and they dealt with it." Others were expected to follow suit. A Kennedy family friend spotted an unidentified person crying by the coffin, which was at the front of the aircraft, wrapped in a maroon cloth. "Listen," he told the person, "if the family can take it and the kids can take it, then *you* shape up."

Ethel Kennedy "seemed very strong and really bearing up very well, I thought," Coretta King remembered. "I hope that I was able to give, in part, some strength to her because I was far enough removed from my own situation that I felt that I could be, in that situation, stronger." But to her the mood was grim: "the same kind of feeling that people around my husband had at the time of his death. The kind of feeling of, 'What do we do now? We've lost our leader.'"

For a while, Jacqueline Kennedy talked with Mankiewicz. One topic was the Mass card to be used at the funeral; Ethel wanted it to include the quote from Aeschylus, which someone now needed to find. Ted Kennedy spent much of the flight alongside Robert Kennedy's casket. Shortly before landing, Ethel, too, lay down by it and fell asleep. Friends brought her a pillow and rosaries.

The next day, an ever-changing honor guard flanked Kennedy's casket at St. Patrick's. And the day after that, June 8, came the funeral. Ted Kennedy gave a much-praised eulogy. But it's tempting to speculate how, had he been around and been asked to speak on Kennedy's behalf as Kennedy had for him, Martin Luther King might have handled things. His speech would not have been as dramatic, for the circumstances were so different from that night in Indianapolis. It would not have been as personally risky, for he'd have delivered it from a much safer spot. It would not have been as significant or as heeded, for no black man's pronouncements about a white leader would have mattered as much to most people. Nor would it have been as terse, because King's speeches never were; nor as raw, for King was a more practiced orator; nor as blunt, because King was more guarded; nor as emotional, for King hadn't lost a brother to assassination; nor as contrite, for King's

Even after his death, King's Poor People's Campaign lived on: Activists erected a shanty town on the National Mall on May 12, where they lived for some six weeks.

community had nothing for which to apologize. But his remarks would surely have been as generous, and his message—of peace and brotherhood—would have been very much the same.

Coretta King reflected on the two assassinations and talked about conspiracies. Lots of people thought about them then, and continued to do so for many years afterward. "A conspiracy is not always three guys sitting in a room plotting," Belafonte later said. "Sometimes, conspiracy comes out of a cultural reality." On the way out of the cathedral that day, word reached her that a man named James Earl Ray had been arrested in London for killing her husband. Some thought the timing of the announcement constituted J. Edgar Hoover's final dig at Robert Kennedy: an attempt to steal his thunder on what should have been *his* day. If that were so, it worked; Ray's arrest shared a banner headline with the Kennedy story in the next morning's *New York Times*.

The most select of the parishioners at St. Patrick's were soon passengers on Robert Kennedy's funeral train, heading from Penn

Station to Washington with connections to Arlington National Cemetery. It was an homage to Kennedy's favorite moments on the campaign trail: his whistle-stops through Indiana, Nebraska, and, only a week or so earlier, California. Even the configuration of the train cars was the same, with the candidate and his family at the rear.

With its collection of Kennedys, Kennedy friends, Kennedy staffers, and Kennedy chroniclers—"all of Kennedyism," as Russell Baker later put it—the train ride was, among other things, a celebrity spectacular, comparable, as one observer put it, to Truman Capote's famous Black and White Ball a year and a half earlier. (Capote had attended the funeral but begged off the train ride with a cold.) The variety of those on board attested to Kennedy's extraordinary reach. "The mood in every car was different," Newfield recalled. "In one car you would find political people; in another car you would find athletes; in another car you would find the intellectuals." Even he was struck by the diversity. "I could walk through the train," he wrote, "and see people like John McCone and McGeorge Bundy, who I considered to be war criminals, and they were equally as grieved as I." Also on board were token McCarthy supporters who, through some strange masochist twist, somehow felt responsible for Kennedy's death.

Mankiewicz studied the passengers, divining their backgrounds with anthropological exactitude. "The Catholics, the Irish, were sort of having a wake, drinking a little too much, telling great stories about Robert," he said. And that was fine: they were grieving as much as, or more than, everyone else. The Protestants "weren't quite sure, I think, how to act," he went on, remaining "all buttoned up and looking straight ahead, not revealing any grief." And then there were the Jews: they wore the grief everyone felt. "The Jews were crying for the most part," he said. "I think they would have torn at their clothes if they'd have thought about it." Reminded that he'd overlooked the blacks, he noted there hadn't been many on the train. But according to Budd Schulberg, they most closely resembled the Jews. "All these strong men like Rosey Grier were messes," he said.

Kennedy and King might be gone, but the tendrils between those they had left behind remained entwined, and even strengthened, as the train headed south. Early on, near Newark, Ralph Abernathy walked to the rear car to express his condolences, and ran into Jacqueline Kennedy. "Oh, Reverend," she said, "you'll be able to lift this." "This" was the casket, which, resting only a few inches off the floor, wasn't visible, she feared, to those standing along the tracks. So Abernathy and some others lifted it onto some chairs. To him, pallbearers had a far loftier status at funerals than preachers—it was an honor one bestowed only on one's closest friends—and he felt privileged to have raised Robert Kennedy high enough heavenward for everyone outside to see.

Ted Kennedy later said that Bobby's death was the only time he'd ever seen his mother's faith falter. But when Coretta King spoke to Rose Kennedy, she was worried about Bobby's children but seemed otherwise at peace. "You know, we wonder why these things happen," she said, "but we accept it because it's God's will. We go on and make the most of it." Later, in the alcove of the last car, King told Schlesinger how amazed she was by Ethel Kennedy's composure—"I don't see how she has been able to go through this awful experience with such dignity and strength"—though, of course, she'd just done just that herself.

For a long time, Schlesinger had viewed Robert Kennedy as an imperfect version of his older brother. But by now, he'd concluded that RFK would have made the greater president. He was more radical than JFK; he better understood the problems of the marginalized; he'd come along at a time more propitious for radical action. "JFK had much better manners," he wrote in a long list of comparisons he drew in his diary between the two brothers. "RFK was often diffident and had no small talk. He would do much better at Resurrection City than at the Metropolitan Club." To Schlesinger, Robert Kennedy's death marked what he called "the progressive decomposition" of the system: "We have now murdered the three men who more than any other incarnated the idealism of America in our time," he wrote. Like many who'd grown close to Kennedy, he vowed to steer clear of any more such relationships: they were simply too heartbreaking.

Ethel Kennedy walked up and down the train as she'd walked up and down the plane back from California, greeting, thanking, comforting. At one point, she spotted and embraced Joe Mohbat, the Associated Press reporter who'd dogged Kennedy—so much so that before returning belatedly to the press bus from Kennedy's burial, other reporters speculated that perhaps he'd jumped in with him. "We loved having you along so much," she told him. "You were closer to him most of the time than anybody else." "I didn't know what to say," Mohbat recalled. "All I could say was, 'It's the best thing I've ever done in my life, and I'll always be grateful for it.'"

Some important figures from Kennedy's story weren't aboard that day. But perhaps it didn't matter, because they'd already shared their own journeys with him. One was Roger Wilkins, who had joined the Justice Department as an assistant attorney general shortly after Kennedy had left it. He retained a host of grievances against Kennedy—for dillydallying on civil rights, for tapping King's telephone, for showboating at King's funeral. In the Washington, D.C., primary two months earlier, he'd voted for Hubert Humphrey. But he could have sworn he'd seen Kennedy grow before his eyes. Had he been nominated, he knew he'd have campaigned for him furiously. James Baldwin, too, had come to respect him: there was a kind of hopefulness, he said, when the Kennedys were around. So had another participant in that stormy session five years earlier, Kenneth Clark, to whom Kennedy had recently said he was willing to put his entire political future on the line to improve public education. So had Jerome Smith, the Freedom Rider who'd confronted him that day in the meeting with Baldwin. He'd followed Kennedy, and come to believe that, touched and humbled by his own catastrophe—"He would not know my emotion until tragedy had knocked at *his* door"—he'd have made a great president. Kennedy since that time had come to remind him, he said, of the tough old Irish priest at the school for white boys in New Orleans that he'd pass every day en route to his own segregated school,who'd always greet the black boys as they walked by, imparting lessons and encouragement. "Kennedy's mission was about service, not power or money," he said. "He would have been about doing decent things." So had Jules Feiffer. To him, it wasn't so much that by the time Kennedy was killed, 'Good Bobby' had prevailed, but that both Bobbys, Good and Bad, were so much better than anyone who'd come along ever since.

Something epochal, something atavistic, was in the air. Stanley Levison—who himself had supported Kennedy's candidacy—had tuned in to follow the train's progress on television. "At one point," he recalled, "I only heard the commentator saying, 'The people are lined up along the tracks...particularly black people. They built bonfires for miles, and the train is proceeding within the parallel lines of bonfires.' I called to my wife and said, 'This is extraordinary. I expected something, but I didn't expect this!' Then, as she came in to listen, the commentator concluded, saying, 'And so, the train bearing the body of Abraham Lincoln reached Washington.'"

In a way, Kennedy's procession was just as remarkable. Lining the tracks were an estimated two million people of every background, description, and class, all there to pay their respects. Here, far more than for King himself, was that broad swath of humanity—"all of God's children, black men and white men, Jews and Gentiles, Protestants and Catholics"—whom King had described in the "I Have a Dream" speech. Anyone doubting the range and depth of Kennedy's appeal need only have looked out the window. "Some stood at rigid attention, hand over heart," Schlesinger wrote. "Some waved. Some buried their faces in their hands. Some knelt. Some held up hand-printed signs—'Rest in Peace, Robert,' or ominously, 'Who Will Be The Next One?' or, desperately, 'We Have Lost Our Last Hope,' or, more starkly, 'Pray For Us, Bobby.' Many cried. Some threw roses at the last car." It was all in marked contrast to the almost monochromatically black crowd that had lined the streets of Atlanta for Martin Luther King, though surely many, many of those along the tracks, having had no such chance before, were mourning publicly for him as well. "God Bless Bobby, King," one sign read. "We must wave at them," Rose Kennedy admonished those around her. "They've come out for Bobby."

Undeterred by the train's slow progress—two spectators were killed in accidents along the way—the crowd thickened, and its racial composition changed just as it had that last day in Indiana. Newfield saw only black faces on one side of the train all the way from Wilmington to Washington, and especially in Baltimore. "Those are the only votes they're going to have for President this year, to see that train go by," he wrote. "They were casting their vote for President for a coffin." Kenneth O'Donnell, the Kennedys' hardheaded political pragmatist, was equally bitter. "Marvelous crowds," Schlesinger remarked to him as he gazed out the window. "Yes," O'Donnell replied. "But what are they good for now?"

As endless as the ride turned out to be—eight hours, door to door, ensuring that Kennedy would be buried in the dark—many must have agreed with John Lewis when he said he didn't want that train ride to end, for only then could the final reckoning begin. Buses would take most of the passengers from Union Station to Arlington. For the family, there would be a cortege. Inserted among all the black limousines, there would be a single bus carrying the journalists who'd covered the campaign. Until the Secret Service, accompanying Lyndon Johnson to the burial, stopped them by force, the reporters pressed for the spot they had always held: right behind the car carrying Robert Kennedy.

The motorcade stopped ceremonially outside Kennedy's Senate office, then made its way down Pennsylvania Avenue to the Justice Department, where Attorney General Ramsey Clark and other officials lined up along the street in tribute. "Finally, we saw the stream of lights coming down the Hill," Wilkins recalled. "It slowed. It stopped. In the front seat of the hearse, you could see the pale, white face of Senator Edward Kennedy. And then it moved on, out to the cemetery." But there were at least two more stops, by the Lincoln Memorial, and by the entrance to Resurrection City, whose residents, holding candles, sang "The Battle Hymn of the Republic." Only then did it proceed to the gravesite. The more elaborate memorial dedicated nearby three years later would include a reflecting pool and engraved excerpts from two of Kennedy's speeches: the "ripple of hope" address from South Africa, and excerpts from his remarks from Indianapolis. The second selection, Frank Mankiewicz later theorized, became probably the only extemporaneous words ever carved into the stones of Arlington.

A year after Robert Kennedy's death, Andrew Young captured the complex relationship between him and Martin Luther King, which he called a "distant camaraderie." Theirs was, he said, a "genuine spiritual brotherhood," one requiring "no formal tie or physical link," that "leaped across the widest chasms of our time—a bridge across lines of race, class and geography which nevertheless led them to a common, tragic destiny."

"If there is an afterlife," he wrote, "and I have no doubt there is, I am sure they are together—finally able to share the much-denied love that could never be fulfilled in a world such as ours."

" 'In psychic communication' would be the right way to put it," said Adam Walinsky. "They were each clearly conscious of what the other was saying and doing. You couldn't *not* be conscious of the other one. There were all sorts of people in common and the audiences were often in common. They didn't have to sit down and strategize. They couldn't have been more directly going down the same path if they'd spent an hour on the telephone every day. They each knew what the other was doing and they were each going in the same direction, each in his own way. It's the same struggle, it's the same fight, it's the same adversaries, it's the same dialogue."

That two men whose interests and passions so overlapped interacted so little is but another illustration of the enduring chasm between the races, one which, for reasons of sentimentality, practicality, and shame, our culture has had every reason to minimize. As additional papers pertaining to both men are opened or become more widely accessible, we'll understand this divide more fully and may even learn of the additional, carefully concealed connections between them.

It's hard not to ponder what would have become of King and Kennedy, separately and together, had fate not intervened. Would a second President Kennedy have reached out to King, or kept keeping his distance? Would he have considered King too radical, or too diminished, and sought out other black leaders? Would Kennedy, presiding over a perpetually divided country, have maintained his commitment to civil rights, or bowed to reality? Would he have finally written off the powerful Democratic Senators who'd hamstrung his brother and him for so long, or still attempted to accommodate them? Would King, conversely, have let down his guard and reached out to Kennedy? Would he, with a friendly figure back in the White House, have felt rejuvenated enough either to take still bolder steps or to reenter the mainstream? Would he have had renewed authority in the black community, or would he have continued to be marginalized?

By any historical measure, King will always be the more significant of the two men, though by the time of his death, Kennedy was just coming into his own; ultimately, their accomplishments might have been more nearly equal. But to borrow a phrase from King, it doesn't really matter to us now. Thanks to their common goals and trajectories and calendars, how they came to belong to the ages in tandem, they are linked as no other black man and white man in the history of civil rights have ever been. In the popular mind, whatever kept them apart has evaporated. They have become a team. It isn't only in the afterlife that they are together. So, too, are they in the here and now — inspiring us still.

In an homage to Kennedy's whistle-stop tours during the campaign, a twenty-one-car train carried his casket — and his mourners — from New York to Washington.

Nearly two million people lined the tracks — black and white, many crying, praying, or saluting as the final car carrying the coffin passed. (overleaf)

# BIBLIOGRAPHY

Arsenault, Ray. *Freedom Riders: 1961 and the Struggle for Racial Justice.* New York: Oxford University Press, 2007.

Belafonte, Harry, and Michael Shnayerson. *My Song: A Memoir.* New York: Alfred A. Knopf, 2011.

Bohrer, John R. *The Revolution of Robert Kennedy: From Power to Protest After JFK.* New York: Bloomsbury Press, 2017.

Boomhower, Ray E. *Robert F. Kennedy and the 1968 Indiana Primary.* Bloomington, Ind.: Indiana University Press, 2008.

Branch, Taylor. *At Canaan's Edge: America in the King Years, 1965–68.* New York: Simon and Schuster, 2006.

——. *Parting the Waters: America in the King Years, 1954–63.* New York: Simon and Schuster, 1988.

——. *Pillar of Fire: America in the King Years 1963–65.* New York: Simon and Schuster, 1999.

Bruno, Jerry, and Jeff Greenfield. *The Advance Man.* New York: William Morrow, 1971.

Clarke, Thurston. *The Last Campaign: Robert F. Kennedy and 82 Days That Inspired America.* New York: Henry Holt and Company, 2008.

DeLoach, Cartha. *Hoover's FBI: The Inside Story by Hoover's Trusted Lieutenant.* Washington, D.C.: Regnery Publishing, 1995.

Edelman, Marian W. *Lanterns: A Memoir of Mentors.* Boston: Beacon Press, 1999.

Garrow, David J. *Bearing the Cross: Martin Luther King, Jr., and the Southern Christian Leadership Conference.* New York: Perennial Classics, 1986.

——. *Protest at Selma: Martin Luther King, Jr., and the Voting Rights Act of 1965.* New Haven, Conn.: Yale University Press, 1978.

A funeral Mass at the Dixie Grove Baptist Church, Catherine, Alabama, 1970. While the Kennedys and King often clashed in life, in death and in the public imagination they lived on as collaborators—icons of the civil rights movement, unified in a common goal.

——. *The FBI and Martin Luther King, Jr.: From "Solo" to Memphis.* New Haven, Conn.: Yale University Press, 2001.

Guthman, Edwin O. *We Band of Brothers.* New York: Harper & Row, 1971.

Halberstam, David. *The Unfinished Odyssey of Robert Kennedy.* New York: Random House, 1969.

Kennedy, Robert F., Edwin O. Guthman, and Jeffrey Shulman. *Robert Kennedy, in His Own Words: The Unpublished Recollections of the Kennedy Years.* New York: Bantam Books, 1989.

King, Coretta S., and Barbara A. Reynolds. *My Life, My Love, My Legacy.* New York: Henry Holt and Company, 2017.

King, Jr., Martin L., Clayborne Carson, Peter Holloran, Ralph Luker, and Penny A. Russell. *The Papers of Martin Luther King, Jr.*, vol. 1, *Called to Serve, January 1929–June 1951.* Berkeley, Calif.: University of California Press, 1992.

King, Jr., Martin L., and Clayborne Carson. *The Papers of Martin Luther King, Jr.*, vol. 2, *Rediscovering Precious Values, July 1951–November 1955.* Berkeley, Calif.: University of California Press, 1994.

——. *The Papers of Martin Luther King, Jr.*, vol. 3, *Birth of a New Age, December 1955–December 1956.* Berkeley, Calif.: University of California Press, 1997.

——. *The Papers of Martin Luther King, Jr.*, vol. 4, *Symbol of the Movement, January 1957–December 1958.* Berkeley, Calif.: University of California Press, 2000.

King, Jr., Martin L., and Tenisha Armstrong. *The Papers of Martin Luther King, Jr.*, vol. 5, *Threshold of a New Decade, January 1959–December 1960.* Berkeley, Calif.: University of California Press, 2005.

King, Jr., Martin L., Clayborne Carson, Susan Carson, Susan Englander, Troy Jackson, and Gerald L. Smith. *The Papers of Martin Luther King, Jr.*, vol. 6, *Advocate of the Social Gospel, September 1948–March 1963.* Berkeley, Calif.: University of California Press, 2007.

——. *The Papers of Martin Luther King, Jr.*, vol. 7, *To Save the Soul of America, January 1961–August 1962.* Berkeley, Calif.: University of California Press, 2014.

King, Jr., Martin L., Clayborne Carson, and Kris Shepard. *A Call to Conscience: The Landmark Speeches of Dr. Martin Luther King, Jr.* London: Little, Brown, and Company, 2001.

Lasky, Victor. *Robert F. Kennedy: The Myth and the Man.* New York: Trident Press, 1968.

Levingston, Steven. *Kennedy and King: The President, the Pastor, and the Battle over Civil Rights.* New York: Hachette, 2017.

Lewis, John, and Michael D'Orso. *Walking with the Wind: A Memoir of the Movement.* New York: Simon and Schuster, 1998.

Mankiewicz, Frank, and Joel L. Swerdlow. *So As I Was Saying . . . : My Somewhat Eventful Life.* New York: Thomas Dunne Books, 2016.

Matthews, Chris. *Bobby Kennedy: A Raging Spirit.* New York: Simon & Schuster, 2017.

Navasky, Victor S. *Kennedy Justice.* New York: Atheneum, 1971.

Newfield, Jack. *RFK: A Memoir.* New York: Thunder's Mouth Press/Nation Books, 2003.

Schlesinger, Arthur M. *Robert Kennedy and His Times.* Boston: Houghton Mifflin, 1978.

Shannon, William V. *The Heir Apparent; Robert Kennedy and the Struggle for Power.* New York: Macmillan, 1967.

Stein, Jean, and George Plimpton. *American Journey: The Times of Robert Kennedy.* New York: Harcourt Brace Jovanovich, Inc., 1970.

Thomas, Evan. *Robert Kennedy: His Life.* New York: Simon and Schuster, 2000.

Tye, Larry. *Bobby Kennedy: The Making of a Liberal Icon.* New York: Random House, 2016.

vanden Heuvel, William J., and Milton Gwirtzman. *On His Own: Robert F. Kennedy, 1964–1968.* Garden City, N.Y.: Doubleday, 1970.

Witcover, Jules. *85 Days: The Last Campaign of Robert Kennedy.* New York: William Morrow, 2016.

Wofford, Harris. *Of Kennedys and Kings: Making Sense of the Sixties.* New York: Farrar, Straus and Giroux, 1980.

Young, Andrew. *An Easy Burden: The Civil Rights Movement and the Transformation of America.* New York: HarperCollins, 1996.

Posters pay tribute ten years later: the Piazza Della Repubblica in Florence, Italy, 1978.

## CREDITS

## ENDPAPERS

The flight manifest for the White House jet leaving Los Angeles on June 6, 1968 omitted its most important cargo: the remains of Robert F. Kennedy, shot a day and a half earlier. But listed as numbers 4, 5 and 56 of those aboard were the widows of the three most infamous assassinations of 20th century America: Ethel Kennedy, Jacqueline Kennedy, and Coretta Scott King. Courtesy of Murray Richtel.

## PAGE 1

February 26, 1962: Attorney General Robert Kennedy at a press conference in France (L); February 22, 1956: Martin Luther King, Jr., arrested for violating Alabama's antiboycott law. (R)

## PAGE 2–3

Voting rights activists marched a fifty-four-mile route from Selma to Montgomery, March 1965.

## PAGE 4–5

King delivered his first national address from the steps of the Lincoln Memorial at the Prayer Pilgrimage for Freedom, May 17, 1957.

THE PROMISE AND THE DREAM

For information, please contact RosettaBooks at production@rosettabooks.com, or by mail at 125 Park Ave., 25th Floor, New York, NY 10017.

This book has been made possible with the generous cooperation of Getty Images, Contact Press, Magnum Photos, Steve Schapiro, the Jacques Lowe Estate, and the photographers and archives on the credits page.

Produced by WS Productions, Inc.
Lawrence Schiller, Principal
J.M. Rappaport, Editor
Henry Sanders, Art Direction and Design
Matt Maranian, Photo Editor
Amy Morris, Head of Research

First edition published 2018 by
RosettaBooks

www.RosettaBooks.com
Printed in the United States of America

Library of Congress Control Number:
2018933667
ISBN: 978-1-9481-2226-9

TRAVEL PARTY

Wednesday, June 6, 1968

9:30 am    West Imperial Terminal (707 White House Jet)

4  Ethel Kennedy & 3 children
5  Jacqueline Kennedy   S.S.
6  Edward M. Kennedy
8  Steve and Jean Smith
10 Stash and Lee Radziwill
11 Kay Evans
12 Louella Hennessey
14 Jim and Blanche Whitaker
16 Ed Guthman and wife
17 John Seigenthaler
18 Burke Marshall
19 Jack Walsh
20 Dave Burke
21 Dun Gifford
22 Frank Mankiewicz
23 Richard Goodwin
24 Fred Dutton
25 Bill Barry
26 Rafer Johnson
27 Roosevelt Greer
28 Jerry Bruno

Secret Service
68. John Wilson
69. Dennis Prouty
70. Carl Hardy
71. Paul Sweeney
72. William Williams